NEVER BUY
ANYTHING NEW

Other Local Guidebooks by Heyday Books

Berkeley Inside/Out

The East Bay Out:
A Personal Guide to the East Bay Regional Parks

Let's Park in San Francisco

Roads to Ride:
*A Bicyclist's Topographic Guide to
Alameda, Contra Costa and Marin Counties*

Roads to Ride South:
*A Bicyclist's Topographic Guide to
San Mateo, Santa Clara and Santa Cruz Counties*

NEVER BUY ANYTHING NEW

A GUIDE TO 400 SECONDHAND,
THRIFT, AND CONSIGNMENT
STORES IN THE BAY AREA

~~~~~~~~~~~~~~~~~~~~

Charlene Akers

Photos by Nate Levine

~~~~~~~~~~~~~~~~~~~~

Heyday Books, Berkeley

Cover design and maps by Jeannine Gendar.
Editing and interior design by Tracey Broderick.
All photographs by Nate Levine.
Cover photograph of Charlene Akers taken in Pierre's Once Upon a Time, Oakland.
Back cover photograph of the Three Stooges taken at Harrington Bros. Moving & Storage, San Francisco.

Published by Heyday Books, P.O. Box 9145, Berkeley, CA 94709, (510) 549-3564, FAX: (510) 549-1889.
ISBN: 0-930588-59-2
Printed in the United States of America.
10 9 8 7 6 5 4 3 2 1

Acknowledgments

This book could never have been written without the help of my sister, Jobyna Dellar, who not only accompanied me to each and every store, but also mapped out every day's itinerary and drove every mile. Her unflagging spirits kept me on schedule—sometimes at a grueling pace. We saw quantities of junk, passed up a lot of great buys, met a host of fascinating friendly folks, and had at least a million laughs. Thanks for the good times, Sis.

Thanks are also due to my loving husband Nate Levine who, although he had never set foot inside a secondhand store before, generously supported me in this quixotic effort. And, of course, to our son Ryan.

Dedication

To my parents, Victor and Jeanne Akers.

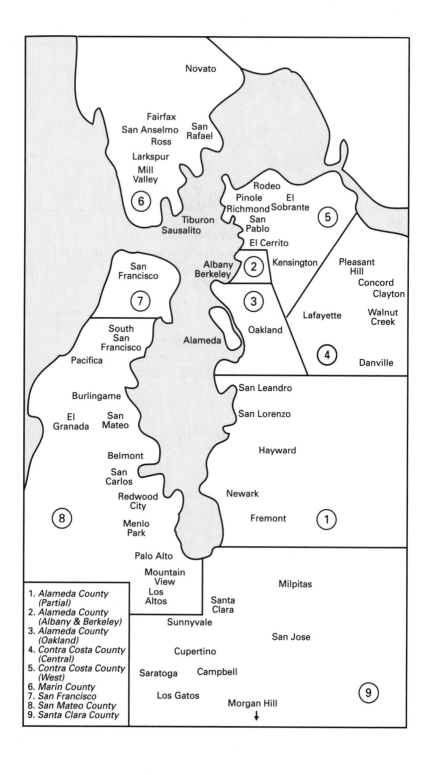

Novato

Fairfax
San Anselmo
Ross
Larkspur
Mill
Valley

⑥

Tiburon
Sausalito

San
Francisco

⑦

South
San
Francisco

Pacifica

Burlingame

El
Granada

San
Mateo

Belmont

San
Carlos

Redwood
City

⑧

Menlo
Park

Palo Alto

Mountain
View
Los
Altos

Santa
Clara

Sunnyvale

Cupertino

Saratoga   Campbell

Los Gatos

Morgan Hill
↓

San
Rafael

Rodeo
Pinole   El
Richmond Sobrante
San
Pablo

El Cerrito

Albany   ②   Kensington
Berkeley

③

Oakland

Alameda

San Leandro

San Lorenzo

Hayward

Newark

Fremont   ①

Milpitas

San Jose

⑨

⑤

Pleasant
Hill
Concord
Clayton

Lafayette   Walnut
Creek

④   Danville

1. *Alameda County
   (Partial)*
2. *Alameda County
   (Albany & Berkeley)*
3. *Alameda County
   (Oakland)*
4. *Contra Costa County
   (Central)*
5. *Contra Costa County
   (West)*
6. *Marin County*
7. *San Francisco*
8. *San Mateo County*
9. *Santa Clara County*

TABLE OF CONTENTS

(continued)

TABLE OF CONTENTS

INTRODUCTION

Secondhand shopping is nothing new; thrift shops and junk dealers have been peddling previously owned merchandise for hundreds of years. What is new is the growing crowds of wise, fun-loving, and conscientious shoppers who are embracing secondhand shopping as a sensible economic strategy that fits into the 1990's notion of smart spending and planet-friendly consumerism. Once the refuge of dirt-poor college students, older people on fixed incomes, a few funky hippie types and eccentric artsy folk, second-hand shopping is now entering the economic mainstream. Anyone—you, me, your neighbor, well-dressed women, businessmen on their lunch hour, antique dealers, decorators, collectors, young couples setting up housekeeping, college kids, working parents, artists—we can all be found snapping up the good buys in the Bay Area's secondhand stores. Whether you're an old hand at sleuthing out one-of-a-kind trea-sures at dusty thrift shops, an experienced outlet shopper seeking to stretch your dollars even farther, or a curious newcomer to the adventure of secondhand shopping, I hope you will find this book to be a useful guide to the hundreds of thrift shops, consignment stores, children's resale outlets, and vintage clothing emporiums in the Bay Area.

In these store you will find a vast array of quality merchandise, from designer clothing to housewares and furniture. If it's clothing you crave, secondhand fashion can be a blessing for the budget conscious and a bonanza for the economy-minded clothes horse. Devotees of high fashion have been known to faint at the sight of the price tag on a new designer gown, but when you buy secondhand you can afford to fill your closet with the designer labels of your dreams. Go ahead, indulge yourself in an outrageous outfit you may only wear once, or keep up with the latest trends without fearing the styles will change and catch you with your knees bare when skirts go back down to the ankles. If you make a mistake, it's no big deal—just gather up the unworn garments hanging in your closet and donate them to your favorite thrift shop or drop them off at a consignment store for resale.

If you're setting up a house, you've probably been staggered by the cost of new furniture. But when you buy secondhand you can afford the best that someone else's money paid for. Discards can be the basis for an interesting home furnished in your own unique and individual style. When you have the eye for seeing beauty in other people's rejects you can surround yourself with 1940's Woolworth, kooky 1950's kitsch, or classy contemporary. Emulate trendy interior designers by recreating your grandparents' home or evoking a past you never had, and do it for next to nothing.

Whatever it is you buy, this is your chance to be a friend of the earth and still consume to your heart's content. Secondhand shopping means saying good-bye to the throw-away society. It's guilt-free environmentally sound consumerism; you don't need to worry about exhausting the planet's natural resources when 100% of the merchandise is recycled. Reusing objects in their original form is even better than recycling them—it conserves energy and materials required to break down and reconfigure them into new products.

Products are often better in the old form anyway. You'll be amazed by the quality of objects others give away and find yourself muttering under your breath, "They just don't make stuff like this anymore." So many of the treasures you will find in secondhand stores are painstakingly hand-crafted products of a bygone era. Instead of cheaply made, mass-produced new schlock that doesn't survive long enough to make it to secondhand shops, you may find yourself paying less for better made goods.

If you frequent nonprofit stores, you can also take satisfaction in the knowledge that your shopping dollar is contributing to a good cause. Isn't it nice to know that you are doing good while doing well?

Basically, for cheap thrills and adventure you just can't beat secondhand shopping. You never know what you're going to discover when searching for treasures among the trash; every moment holds possibility when serendipitous discovery is just around the corner. Where else will you find rare, unique, one-of-a-kind items? Not cruising the malls. You can bet your last dollar that department store aisles will never yield the emotional satisfaction you will get from buying a bit of history that evokes your grandmother, even if you do end up covered with dust.

Of course, secondhand shopping is not for everybody. But you'd be surprised at the number of recent converts. Take my friend Niki, who smiled with amused tolerance at the tales of secondhand shopping adventures. Niki replenishes her stylish wardrobe every season with a ritual trip to I Magnin. She's not a shopper; she's never seen the inside of a Kmart or a Sears, let alone a secondhand shop. Just to please us, she agreed to pay a visit to Circles, an upscale consignment shop in Menlo Park. Afterwards, she left this brief message on the answering machine: "I'm converted." We raced over to view her purchases. She proudly displayed a St. John knit, three pairs of Ferragamos, an Escada sweater, a silk blouse, a fabulous Byblos cocktail dress, and a Hermes scarf, all purchased for the cost of two new pairs of Ferragamos. Even my sister Jobyna (exquisitely dressed Pacific Heights matron that she is) once left a particularly elegant consignment shop, leaned over the hood of her Volvo, looked me straight in the eye, and declared, "Cut off my hands if I every buy anything new again."

The moral of the story is that there is a secondhand store right for every shopper. Whatever your shopping style in the big world of retail, you will find a corresponding secondhand shop. In the midst of getting this book ready for press I received this note from my editor, Tracey Broderick.

Yesterday morning I walked through what has been a rather empty living room in my house, got in my car, and drove to the St. Vincent de Paul in East Oakland. I was nervous, worried about getting lost and mugged, and then there it was—that huge, huge place, and a crowd of people standing outside. As I walked up to the door, a whistle blew and the crowd of people rushed into a shed. My God, I've found it! The St. Vincent de Paul "As-Is!" I followed the crowd, and the chaos and scuffle was one of the funniest and most enjoyable things I have ever seen in any type of store. I bought a lamp shade for 50¢,

and then proceeded into the store itself to buy a lamp, a television stand, a desk, and a sofabed, all for $70. And I absolutely loved it. I emerged from the depths of unknown neighborhoods with things that I like, a full pocketbook, and a sense of cunning and ingenuity. If I hadn't already been converted, this would have done it.

Like their retail counterparts, secondhand stores come in all sizes and descriptions. You will find grand emporiums stocking everything from major appliances to golf clubs and exclusive salons handling high-end clothing and jewelry. Stores vary from one another in quality of merchandise and ambiance as much as Saks Fifth Avenue varies from Sears. The trick is to know which is which and where to go to find what you're looking for.

HOW TO SHOP SECONDHAND

For the novice and the veteran secondhand shopper here are a few words of advice:

1. Check the hours of operation found in the heading of each listing. Hours change, shops come and go, and stores staffed solely by volunteers have been known to close when no one shows up.

2. Bring cash. While most privately owned secondhand stores

accept personal checks and credit cards, many nonprofit thrift shops operate on a cash-only basis. Check the heading of each listing.

3. If you see something you like, buy it! It may not be there another day...or even in the next 10 minutes.

4. Shop often. Stores receive new merchandise regularly, and you never know when something magnificent will turn up.

5. Only buy things you can use. It's not a bargain if it sits in your closet, no matter how cheap it was. Remember, most sales are final—very few secondhand stores make exchanges or give refunds.

6. Poke around. The best items are often hidden away in drawers, suitcases, barrels, or dusty corners.

7. Expect the unexpected. Serendipitous finds are the greatest thrill of secondhand shopping. Be flexible! The Salvation Army is not Sears; you can't march in and ask them to show you a powder-blue wing chair to go with your sofa. On the other hand, when you need a chair, your favorite secondhand store may be the best place to start looking.

8. When you're shopping for clothing, go with an open mind. Some garments may look awful on the hanger but great on you.

9. Try everything on if at all possible. Remember, most stores have a no-returns policy, and you have to be careful. Sizes in vintage clothing are different (usually smaller) than contemporary sizes. A size 10 may fit, even though you're

a size 8. In contemporary fashions, expensive clothing is usually cut larger than moderately priced garments. (Hadn't you ever wondered why most socialites wear a size 4?)

10. Check garments carefully for water spots, scorch marks, pills, snags, underarm stains, and odors that probably won't come out. Stay away from garments you can't alter yourself.

11. Spread the word. Take a friend with you on your next expedition. No need to hem and haw when people ask you where you got that great suit. It's stylish to be frugal. In case you hadn't noticed, some of the most popular American designers are copying the thrift-shop look, France's hottest young couturier unveiled his fall collection in a Salvation Army store on the outskirts of Paris, and even Macy's is selling men's vintage vests and jackets.

12. Never throw anything usable away. Why contribute to the landfill problem when your discards may be someone else's heart's desire? Recoup a little of your loss by selling your castoffs at a consignment shop or donating them to your favorite charity's thrift shop.

HOW TO USE THIS BOOK

Chapters

Never Buy Anything New is organized by geographic area.

Chapters are usually defined by counties. In each chapter cities are listed alphabetically, and stores are listed alphabetically within each city. Contra Costa County has been divided into a western section and an eastern section, and Alameda County has been divided into three chapters—Alameda County (partial), Alameda County (Albany and Berkeley), and Alameda County (Oakland). San Francisco also has its own chapter, and Oakland and San Francisco are each divided into neighborhoods.

Charts

At the end of each chapter you will find a chart indicating the type of merchandise you are likely to encounter in each store. Out of the millions of possibilities I have selected the thirteen categories I hope will be most useful. An "X" indicates that the store specializes in or regularly stocks items in this category. Given the nature of secondhand shopping, nothing is absolutely guaranteed. A shop that usually carries large appliances, for example, may be fresh out of refrigerators on a particular day. On the other hand, you may find a dozen maternity outfits in a store bearing no "X" in that column. Please use the chart as a guide and not a guarantee; if you are looking for a particular item call before you go to be sure it's in stock. A bold "**X**" tells you that the supply is

exceptional, possibly the best we found in our adventures through the area.

Listings

After the name of each store you will find the address, telephone number, hours of business, and the acceptable purchase methods— cash, checks, layaway, or credit cards. At the end of each listing I have identified all nonprofit thrift stores and the charity they support. For consignment stores or privately owned resale shops I have indicated the hours goods will be accepted, and the consignment or purchase policy. I've also given a general idea of what you can expect to find in each store.

Terms

Appliances/large refers to stoves, refrigerators, washers, dryers, and the like.

Bridal. Although you may find lovely dresses suitable for a wedding ceremony in almost any store specializing in women's clothing, I have used the term "bridal" in the charts and the listings to mean those long white formal confections you see in the pages of *Bride Magazine*. Smaller thrift stores often have one or two beautiful wedding gowns on hand—usually at bargain prices. A phone call to your favorite store will tell you.

Much to our surprise, in thrift store after thrift store Jobyna and I encountered gorgeous, spanking-new Jessica McClintock wedding gowns. The dresses were so beautiful and so numerous that we were prompted to ask where they came from. We received so many different answers to our inquiries that I finally called Jessica McClintock's San Francisco headquarters to get the straight scoop. Was it true, I asked, that Jessica McClintock had donated 10,000 new gowns to Bay Area thrift stores? Although they couldn't confirm the exact number, it was true that somewhere in the neighborhood of 10,000 new gowns (all 1991 styles) had been given away in 1992. Although such generosity could not be guaranteed on an annual basis, it is entirely possible that such largess could again befall lucky Bay Area stores. If I were planning a wedding, I certainly would jump at the chance to walk down the aisle wearing one of these confections, especially at one-tenth the regular price.

Children's furnishings includes cribs, strollers, car seats, playpens, high chairs, and all other equipment (except clothing and toys) necessary for rearing children.

Collectibles. If an object exists, there exists someone who collects it. From linens to lunch boxes, porcelain to political paraphernalia, the variety of objects is overwhelming. One of the great joys of secondhand shopping is finding the coveted object you need to round out your collection sitting on some thrift store shelf at a ridiculously low price (although many savvy secondhand store owners have taken to labeling anything more than 30 years old a collectible and charging accordingly). Although I don't pretend to be an expert on collectibles, I've used the word as a blanket term to cover a variety of delightful old, amusing, or oddball items that are more special than ordinary secondhand merchandise.

Everything can mean just that. Stores marked with this designation could, with the exceptions of edibles and living creatures, carry almost anything you could purchase new, including clothing, furniture, large and small appliances, books and records, small appliances, tools, and electronics. However, just because a store bears this designation doesn't mean that you can expect to find items in every category at every given moment. If you are looking for a specific item, it's wise to call first and ask. Most stores will be more than happy to tell you what they have on hand.

Maternity. With contemporary one-size-fits-all fashions, expectant mothers can often walk into any store that carries women's clothing and find wonderful roomy garments to take them right up to their delivery date. But I have marked as "maternity" only the stores which carry items made specifically for pregnant women.

Tools, etc. For the purpose of this book, "tools" has been defined rather loosely to include hand tools like hammers, saws, screwdrivers, wrenches, power tools, garden tools, and other manly implements. The "etc." is meant to cover a variety of useful objects that do not fit into the housewares category—sinks, for instance.

Vintage means any article of clothing dating from the 1970's or earlier. While it is possible to find wonderful old clothes with a good bit of history to them in almost any thrift store, only those stores specializing in vintage clothing have been given this designation.

TYPES OF SECONDHAND STORES

The secondhand stores in this book can be classified into four major categories: children's resale shops, consignment stores, non-profit thrift stores, and vintage clothing boutiques.

Children's Resale Shops

Of all the secondhand shopping options, none makes more sense than children's resale. More and more smart parents are turning to these shops (which are sprouting up everywhere like mushrooms) for everything from strollers to sleepers. They sell name-brand clothing and equipment at 50%–80% less than the retail price, and most are so fussy about what they accept that you can't tell the garments have ever been worn or the toys have ever been played with.

Some of the shops listed here accept kids" items on consignment, and others pay cash for everything from overalls to fancy party dresses. All of the stores want clothes and equipment that are in good condition. Because children's resale shops differ from one another so slightly in terms of price and quality, I recommend you try the ones in your own neighborhood first.

Consignment Stores

With approximately 15,000 in the United States and new ones opening every day, it's not surprising that consignment shops comprise over 25% of the listings in this book. Consignment stores have nothing of the thrift store look about them. The majority are chic secondhand boutiques selling slightly used clothing and furniture at bargain prices. You're likely to find an elegant salon-like atmosphere complete with wall to wall carpeting, trendy pastel decor, and luxurious dressing rooms.

Consignment stores usually have high standards and accept only items no more than three years old in perfect condition. Goods sell for 30%–50% of their original cost; the consignor receives 40%–60% of the selling price after the item is sold and the store keeps the rest. Items are usually reduced after 30 days, kept on the floor for another month, and then returned to the consignor or donated to charity. This speedy turnover keeps the merchandise fresh and interesting to regular customers. If you are a newcomer to secondhand shopping, you might want to start with one of the upscale consignment stores mentioned in this book. If you are already a dedicated bargain shopper in funkier secondhand stores, don't be put off by the sleek organized atmosphere. Good buys can be found in these stores, too.

〰 NonProfit Stores 〰

Nonprofit thrift stores run the gamut from tiny upscale boutiques specializing in women's clothing to giant department stores stocking everything up to and including the kitchen sink. Roughly half the stores listed in this book are nonprofit thrift stores supporting charitable organizations, including religious institutions, schools, health organizations, and senior citizen projects. Some are staffed entirely by volunteers, others are run by paid staff, and some are a combination of both. All merchandise is donated by individuals, local retail stores, and manufacturers. Your shopping dollars help support these worthwhile organizations.

The four best-known nonprofit secondhand chains—American Cancer Society Discovery Shops, Goodwill, St. Vincent de Paul, and Salvation Army—are well represented in the Bay Area, with more than 60 stores. With slight variations on the norm, each chain has a consistently recognizable style, image, and business philosophy that lets you know what to expect.

American Cancer Society Discovery Shops. The most upscale and certainly the most expensive, American Cancer Society Discovery Shops are immediately identifiable by the royal blue awnings and stylish window displays outside and the blue carpeting and elegant floor displays inside. Discovery Shops are very selective about the quality of merchandise they sell in the store. If they can't put a $5 price tag on a blouse, it's not worth keeping. Their philosophy is strictly business, and their business is raising money to fight cancer. If you prefer to do your shopping in a clean, well-lighted, gracious atmosphere and don't mind paying a little more for high-quality clothing and housewares, check out their ten Bay Area locations.

Goodwill. Well-known among the thrift store giants, Goodwill has been collecting used goods for resale since 1902. As their old slogan, "Turning Waste Into Wages," suggests, Goodwill originally trained the disabled and disadvantaged to repair goods which were then sold in the thrift stores. Keeping in step with changing times, they eventually made the shift from a used goods repair shop to a vocational training and contract production center with a new slogan, "To Give Not Charity But a Chance." The stores, too, have been revamped to resemble better department stores. All 23 Goodwill stores we visited were clean, well-lighted, and organized into departments, with each department further organized by color. Dressing rooms for men and women, attractive floor displays, and a truly astonishing quantity of clothing make shopping at Goodwill a pleasure. With regular reductions on already low prices you can dress the whole family for practically nothing.

If you choose to donate your discards to Goodwill, you can rest assured that nothing will go to waste. Items that don't sell in the stores are sent to the As Is stores. From there, unsold textiles are sold to rag dealers or distribution centers, where woolens are sent to reclaiming mills to be rewoven into new garments, cottons are sent to the wiping rag market, and wearable items are shipped off to Third World countries.

Salvation Army. The best-known of the thrift store giants, the Salvation Army was founded in 1865 and operates 823 thrift stores across the nation (16 in the Bay Area) to support Salvation Army Adult Rehabilitation Centers, which help many men and women win their personal wars on drugs and alcohol. The Sears of non-profit department store, most Salvation Army shops do, indeeed, have everything (except dressing rooms). Furniture, appliances, housewares, books, clothing...you can find it all—good, bad, ugly, beautiful—in stores that range from organized and immaculate to disordered and dingy. Many of the bigger stores have established in-store boutiques which sell better merchandise at higher prices. But for ordinary housewares and clothing, you can't beat the Salvation Army.

St. Vincent de Paul. The oldest and my personal favorite of the big four, the Society of St. Vincent de Paul was founded in Paris in 1833 and has been operating in the United States since 1845. Their fourteen Bay Area stores range in atmosphere: some are among the funkiest we've seen, and some are neat as a pin. Although I cannot recommend St. Vincent de Paul stores to the fastidious (they can get downright dingy and odorous), I like the sense of adventure that their very chaos inspires. "Your purchase and donation help the needy" read the signs, and the needy are often clearly in evidence.

Donated articles are repaired in rehabilitation workshops and sold at very attractive prices in the thrift stores, which are often located next to the service agencies. In the Bay Area the society operates a transitional housing program for homeless parents, a shelter for battered women, a multifaceted resource center, a free dining facility which serves over 2000 meals per day, and many other programs.

For-Profit Chains. If you like one-stop shopping at big stores you should investigate the for-profit chains—Thrift Center, Thrift Town, Thrift City, and Savers—that together have 15 branches in the Bay Area. Although they are privately owned, these giants work with local charitable institutions by either buying merchandise from them or turning over a percentage of the profits to them. They are usually chock-full of merchandise for the whole family at very fair prices, but they tend to be more expensive when it comes to housewares, furniture, and collectibles.

⌇⌇⌇ Vintage Clothing ⌇⌇⌇

If your secondhand shopping has been confined to thrift shops, consignment stores, and children's resale, I suggest you investigate another fascinating area of second-hand adventure. You will be surprised by the variety of vintage stores in the Bay Area; they range from exclusive boutiques selling antique designer gowns for $1000 to sizeable warehouses offering 1950's funk by the pound. In addition to fragile Victorian dresses and slinky Jean Harlow gowns, vintage clothing includes smart suits from the 1940's, poodle skirts from the 1950's, minis from the 1960's, and even hippie finery from the 1970's!

"Who buys these clothes?" I asked vintage store proprietors. "All kinds of people," they answered. Customers are high school and college students, members of the Art Deco Society and classic car clubs, and of course guests at mystery parties, theme weddings, and costume balls, as well as men and women of all ages and levels of wealth who want to make a fashion statement. Snappy dressers buy vintage suits to wear to the office and vintage tuxedos and gowns to wear out—they know they'll never see the same outfit at work or at a party. Anyone who appreciates quality fabrics, exquisite handwork, and superbly made clothes with details rarely seen today can find a unique look for a bargain price in one of the Bay Area's many vintage shops. Vintage enthusiasts can wallow to their heart's content in a full range of vintage fashions at Vintage Fashion Expo, co-sponsored by the Federation of Vintage Fashion. Shows featuring the wares of a hundred vintage dealers from the Western United States are held at the Oakland Convention Center at Broadway and 10th the last weekend in September and the second weekend in January and at the San Francisco Concourse at 8th and Brannon the last weekend in March.

Between January and June of 1992 Jobyna and I personally visited each and every store listed in this book. Whenever possible I interviewed the owner or a volunteer to get information about sales, markdown policy, and the history of the store. No one paid to be listed in this book, and no one had an opportunity to read, approve, or make changes in their listing. I have tried to give you some indication of atmosphere, available merchandise, and price range in the hopes that you will find the shops that best suit your own personal shopping style and budget. I often describe items we saw and their costs. Needless to say, you cannot expect to find the same items at the same price when you visit, but you may find something twice as wonderful at half the price.

Even though we made a conscientious effort to visit every secondhand store in the Bay Area, undoubtedly some stores offering equally good values have inevitably been left out, for a variety of reasons. I would love to hear comments from you about places we missed or your favorite secondhand stores. Please write to me in care of my publisher, Heyday Books, P.O. Box 9145, Berkeley CA 94709.

ALAMEDA COUNTY (Partial)

~~~ City of Alameda ~~~

ALAMEDA PENNY MARKET
Island Auto Movie, 791 Atlantic Way, Alameda 94501, (510) 522-7206. Sat–Sun 7 am–4:30 pm. Purchase method varies by dealer.

If you want to shop at this popular flea market, it will cost you 50¢. If you want to sell there, it will cost you $10 for Saturday, $12 for Sunday, or $20 for both days.
Everything

CLOTHES ENCOUNTERS OF THE SECOND TIME
1707 Lincoln Ave., Alameda 94501, (510) 521-4006. Wed–Sat 11 am–4 pm. Cash, checks.

It takes a while for a consignment store to develop a personal style. *Clothes Encounters* was a mere six weeks old when we encountered it, and it had yet to define its image. Marge Hayden, owner of this big and well stocked store, looks for garments a woman can wear to work. She carries everything from sportswear to formal dresses, in all sizes from Tinkerbell on up, marked at 1/4–1/3 of new prices. Hayden also sells new jewelry she assembles herself from gemstones acquired in the Orient.
Consignment: By appointment, 50/50 split, 60-day contract
Women's clothing

THE GARMENT BAG
1415 Park St. (between Central and Santa Clara), Alameda 94501, (510) 522-1548. Tues–Wed 10 am–5:30 pm, Thurs 10 am–7 pm, Fri and Sat 10 am–5:30 pm. Cash, checks, MC/VISA/DISCOVER.

The Garment Bag was so crowded the Saturday we visited that women were waiting in line to use the dressing rooms. Consistently low prices and high volume make this store a favorite with a broad spectrum of Alameda residents, from high-school students to great-grandmothers. There is a lot to choose from on the crowded racks, everything from casual everyday wear to holiday dress-up. Quality varies; merchandise from high-class designers, Nordstrom, and Mervyns hang side by side.
Consignment: Tues–Sat 11 am–3 pm, 50/50 split, 60-day contract
Women's clothing

THE GASLIGHT EMPORIUM
1708 Lincoln Ave., Alameda 94501, (510) 522-1900. Tues–Sat 11 am–6:30 pm, Sun 11 am–5 pm. Cash, checks, MC/VISA.

You cannot go to Alameda without paying a visit to *The Gaslight Emporium*. A journey to another age, this dreamlike shop is pure indulgence. Specializing in exquisite candies handmade from Victorian molds, *Gaslight Emporium* also carries antique and reproduction jewelry, gift items, and vintage clothing for women, children, and occasionally men. The small selection of vintage garments covers the Victorian period through the 1940's, with each item a perfect work of art. If you are over 21 you can ask to visit the tiny room featuring bawdy bonbons. (Go on, you deserve a treat after all that bargain hunting.) Besides, prices are not as high as you might imagine—I bought a white chocolate cameo for 75¢.

Antiques; collectibles; candy; clothing for men, women, and children

LAUREN'S CLOSET

2302 Encinal Ave., Alameda 94501, (510) 865-2219. Mon–Sat 10 am–5:30 pm. Cash, checks, MC/VISA.

Kid's clothes, sizes 0–14, for cheap prices is what's in store for you when you visit *Lauren's Closet.* Triple-hung racks along the wall allow the shop to be packed full of merchandise and still maintain an open, airy feel. They also stock baby furniture and equipment, although supply was low the day we visited.

Consignment: Anytime; mostly buys outright, but accepts more expensive items on consignment of 60% consignor/40% store
Children's clothing, furniture, and equipment

MASTIC SENIOR CENTER THRIFT SHOP

1155 Santa Clara Ave., Alameda 94501, (510) 748-4587. Tues and Sat 10 am–2 pm. Cash, checks.

This two-room thrift shop is a real jewel that not too many bargain hunters outside of Alameda know about. Their hours are brief, so it might be worth your while to schedule your trip to Alameda when they are open, especially if you are interested in good clothing at unbelievably cheap prices. Vintage collectors might want to browse through the racks for some great finds. We saw a 1950's poodle-cloth coat for $5 and a vintage tuxedo shirt for 50¢. The selections of housewares, collectibles, jewelry, and books also revealed some unexpected treasures.

Charity: Mastic Senior Center
Everything except large appliances and large pieces of furniture

MOTHER'S CARE

2545 Santa Clara Ave., Alameda 94501, (510) 769-1336. Mon–Sat 10:30 am–5:30 pm. Cash, checks.

If you're a parent whose budget is spread thin, you'll love this very pretty store. It has a luxurious, upscale look to it, yet prices are low and the selection of boy's and girl's clothes, sizes 0–12, is all a mother could ask for. They also stock handmade blankets, sweaters, suits, and hats—great for gifts.

Buys: Mon and Thurs 10:30 am–5:30 pm, Tues–Wed 10:30 am–1

pm, and Fri–Sat 10:30 am–1 pm
Children's clothing, furniture, and equipment

ST. VINCENT DE PAUL
2315 Lincoln, Alameda 94501, (510) 865-1109. Mon–Sat 9 am–4:45 pm, Sun 12 am–5 pm. Cash, checks, MC/VISA.

This neat, organized *St. Vincent de Paul* has clean clothes at good prices, large appliances, and lots of furniture. We didn't see any great buys on housewares or collectibles but, as always at *St. Vincent*, best buys are on furniture.
Charity: St. Vincent de Paul
Everything

YETTA'S ANTIQUES
1908 Encinal, Alameda 94501, (510) 523-9696. Tues 11 am–3 pm, Thurs–Sat 11 am–3 pm. Cash, checks.

Stop by *Yetta's Antiques* when you're in the neighborhood and check out her eclectic offerings. You might find something you never knew you wanted—like a petit-point bag, a liqueur set, or a cloisonne box that once belonged to Yetta's mother. 86 year-old Yetta Kameny (she doesn't look a day over 65) is a vivid conversationalist and can tell you the story behind all the objects in her shop. You'll have to ask Yetta the prices, as none are marked. You'll know Yetta understands a bargain when you see her business cards…she handwrites them herself on the back of her banker's card to save money.
Antiques and collectibles

~~~~~ **Fremont** ~~~~~

BEST FOR LESS
4120 Peralta Blvd., Fremont 94538, (510) 795-7724. Mon–Fri 9 am–7 pm, Sat 10 am–6 pm. Cash, checks, MC/VISA.

Best for Less, "a quality thrift and discount store," might also call itself *Most for Less*: it's hard to beat it for quantity and prices (quality is another story). This former bowling alley has more clothing than you can shake a bowling pin at, all nicely organized by item, size, season, and color, and the prices are cheap (girls' dresses for $1.99–$7.99, men's sports jackets for $6–$20). With such a huge inventory, you're bound to find something you like. Furniture selection in the back of the store is limited, but jigsaw puzzle lovers will be in puzzle heaven.
Charity: Privately owned, supports Los Niños, the City of the Children
Everything

THE CLOTHING EXCHANGE
43460 Ellsworth St. (across from Ohlone College, Mission San Jose), Fremont 94539, (510) 657-1908. Mon–Sat 10 am–5 pm, Sun 11 am–4 pm. Cash, checks, MC/VISA.

Neatness, organization, and homey decor help make the best of the limited space in this pleasant consignment boutique. Women sizes 3–22-1/2 will find an ample selection of good labels, from the

Gap to Evan Picone, casual separates and classic work clothes outnumbering high-style designer labels and dressy dresses. The price is right on everything. *Consignment: Mon–Sat 11 am–4 pm, appointments appreciated, 50/50 split, 60-day contract*
Women's clothing and accessories

MY SISTER'S CLOSET
4050 Peralta Blvd., Fremont 94536, (510) 795-0131. Mon–Sat 9 am–5:30 pm. Cash, checks, MC/ VISA/DISCOVER.

All I ever found in my sister's closet was my sister's clothes, but this *Sister's Closet* has clothes for the whole family—Mom, Dad, the kids, even some maternity wear. Don't be put off by the cold, industrial look of the store—this is the no-nonsense approach to reselling, and it works. After 20 years in retailing and twelve years in the resale business, the owner has four *My Sister's Closets*. You pay for what you get, and what you get is a bit of everything: a man's Pierre Cardin suit for $75 or a man's Sears jacket for $7. The store philosophy is that merchandise has to be able to carry a price of a couple of bucks or it isn't worth messing with, and this applies to everything but baby clothes, which are dirt cheap and carried as a service to families. While you won't find any bridal gowns or bridesmaids' dresses in *My Sister's Closet*, you will find a surprisingly large assortment of men's tuxedoes at very good prices

(we saw several for $50–$65). *Consignment: Mon–Sat 9:30 am– 4:30 pm, 50/50 split, 60-day contract*
Clothing for men, women, and children

OHLONE COLLEGE SUPER FLEA MARKET
Ohlone College, 43600 Mission Blvd., Fremont 94539, (510) 659-6215. Second Sats 7 am–4:30 pm. Purchase method varies by dealer.

You don't have to hand over anything to attend this monthly event, but if you want to sell there get $12 out of your pocket.
Everything

ST. VINCENT DE PAUL
3777 DeCoto Rd., Fremont 94536, (510) 792-3711. Mon–Sat 10 am– 5:45 pm, Sun 12 am–4:45 pm. Cash, checks, MC/VISA.

Two thirds of the merchandise in this huge cinder-block warehouse is furniture and household goods, and the rest is clothing. Clothing for the most part is low quality for low, low prices, which go to half off every Friday, Saturday, and Sunday for all clothing hung on hangers. (Infant's clothes are 25¢ a piece, children's are 50¢ each—you couldn't expect them to halve those prices!) Furniture is, in general, of better quality, with the same low prices—

Right: Community Thrift Store, San Francisco.

sofas for $29–$69, upholstered chairs for $12–$18. Reconditioned large appliances come with a 30-day guarantee. It's clean, it's cheap, and they try hard.
Charity: St. Vincent de Paul
Everything

SALVATION ARMY
40733 Chapel Way, Fremont 94538, (510) 659-0637. Mon–Sat 9:30 am–5:30 pm. Cash, checks, MC/VISA.

Despite a plethora of admonitory signs ("Do not sit on furniture." "Do not alter price tags." "Keep children with you." "No food, drink, or pets allowed."), everyone is very friendly here. This is a medium-sized store, medium neat, with lime-green walls and your usual *Salvation Army* merchandise. Brides take note: new Jessica McClintock wedding gowns were priced around $135. We even saw a new wedding cake topper for $5, but it's probably gone by now.
Charity: Salvation Army
Everything

THRIFT CENTER
40645 Grimmer Blvd., Fremont 94538, (510) 490-0485. Mon–Sat 10 am–7 pm. Cash, checks, MC/VISA with a minimum of $25.

One of six Bay Area *Thrift Centers*, this one located in a former grocery store has the typical large inventory of clothing for men, women, and children, with a few pieces of furniture and other household items in the back. Quality is generally low, with enough goodies thrown in to keep you interested. Prices are low with no surprises.
Charity: Privately owned, supports Cerebral Palsy
Everything

TRI-CITY VOLUNTEERS
37350 Joseph St., Fremont 94536, (510) 793-4583. Mon–Fri 8 am–5 pm, Sat 9 am–4 pm. Cash, local checks.

If you want to see your thrift shopping dollars at work, try *Tri-City Volunteers*. The large one-room thrift shop and the social service agency it supports sit side by side. As you go in to check out the bargains, you may see one of the 6000 individuals who rely on *Tri-City* for emergency services coming out, perhaps with a three-day supply of food for a hungry family. Started 20 years ago by Grace Draper, a retired school teacher who wanted to help Mexican farm workers, *Tri-City Volunteers* now provides emergency services—food, clothing, shelter, and housing assistance—for any family or person in need.

The shop itself, staffed by the friendliest volunteers around, is a jumble of merchandise ranging from a table of stuffed animals for 25¢ each to an oak armchair for $20 to a 1940's child wardrobe. Clothing is very cheap, and there is always a box of free stuff sitting outside.
Charity: Tri-City Volunteers, a non-profit multi-service agency
Everything but large appliances

∿ Fremont/Niles District ∿

Tucked away in the foothills of Fremont lies the picturesque, historic Niles district, its main street lined with antique shops. I've listed only two. If you love antiques but hate parting with a week's salary to own a bit of the past, you'll love Niles. Charlie Chaplin fans will adore it; in 1915, Chaplin shot five films here, including "The Tramp," and his presence is still felt. The Niles Flea Market, held every year on the last Sunday of August, is purported to be a modern-day Mecca for bargain hunters and antique collectors.

BITE & BROWSE COLLECTIVE
37565 Niles Blvd., Fremont 94536, (510) 796-4537. Mon–Sat 10 am–5 pm, Sun 11 am–5 pm. Purchase method varies by dealer.

With 25 dealers offering you a bite out of history and a browse through the past, you can find just about anything…and the prices look good, too.

Antiques and collectibles

DOLORES' FASHION COTTAGE
37138 Niles Blvd., Fremont 94536, (510) 793-0688. Mon–Sat 9 am–5:30 pm. Cash, checks, MC/VISA.

Three rooms full of women's fashions come in styles suitable for everyone from high-school girls to senior citizens. At Dolores' immaculate *Fashion Cottage* you get quality, variety, a big selection, and good prices. Women who wear larger sizes will be happy to know that Dolores has four racks full of garments size 18 and over. Shoe fanatics will appreciate Dolores' fussiness when it comes to shoes—she only accepts those in perfect repair, and no soiled insides either.

Consignment: Tues–Sun 9 am–5:30 pm, 50/50 split
Women's clothing and accessories

EAGLES NEST
37581 Niles Blvd., Fremont 94536, (510) 792-6532. Fri–Tues 11 am–5 pm (closed Wed–Thurs.) Cash, checks.

Located in the historic State Bank Building which was built in 1906, *Eagles Nest*, an unusual, affordable thrift shop, has a bit of everything—from fishing gear to tools, from collectibles to jewels. Check it out.

Antiques and collectibles

NILES ANTIQUE FLEA MARKET
Niles Business District, Fremont 94536, (510) 792-8023. Last Sunday in August 7 am–4 pm. Purchase method varies by dealer.

Admission to this furniture mecca is free, and the seller's fee is $75.
Furniture, collectibles

 Hayward ∿

CHABOT COLLEGE FLEA MARKET
2555 Hesperian Blvd., Hayward 94545, (510) 786-6918. Third Sats

8 am–4 pm. Purchase method varies by dealer.

Admission is free, and the seller's fee is $12 in advance or $15 the day of the big event.
Everything

GOODWILL
893 W. A St. (at Hesperian), Hayward 94541, (510) 785-3967. Mon–Sat 10 am–6 pm, Sun 11 am–6 pm. Cash, checks, MC/ VISA.

Not one of the glamour shops, the Hayward *Goodwill* is neat, clean, organized, and filled with the usual good values. According to the manager, the big sellers here are furniture, mattresses, and women's clothing.
Charity: Goodwill
Everything

GRAND ILLUSIONS
938 B St., Hayward 94541, (510) 537-5595. Tues–Fri 10 am–5:30 pm, Sat 10 am–4:30 pm. Cash, checks.

For the past nine years *Grand Illusions* has specialized in renting and selling vintage fashions from the 1800's through the 1960's. In addition to an impressive inventory of authentic vintage wear, *Grand Illusions* also carries a line of historical patterns and supplies for historical costumes. They will also reproduce antique wedding gowns to your specifications .

The store has recently begun to accept contemporary clothing—formal and office wear, no jeans or t-shirts—and plans to continue the trend toward contemporary consignment. If you live in the area and are planning a murder mystery party, Halloween costume affair, theme wedding, or a gala night out, you won't want to miss *Grand Illusions.*
Consignment: By appointment, 50/50 split, also buys outright
Vintage and contemporary clothing for men and women

HAYWARD FULL GOSPEL MISSION MINISTRIES THRIFT STORE
306 A St., Hayward 94541, (510) 881-0811. Mon–Sat 9 am–5:30 pm. Cash.

Big and bright with bold graphics painted on the white walls, this store is full of clean, well organized, and pleasingly displayed merchandise (especially in the Kiddy Corner). Quality is medium to low; prices are uniformly low. The biggest drawback we noted was a lack of merchandise. In operation since 1990, the site also serves as a home for participants in the Mission's program. The soup kitchen in back serves a free lunch Mon–Sat 12 am–1:30 pm.
Charity: Hayward Full Gospel Mission Ministries program for alcoholics and drug addicts
Everything except large appliances

LARC THRIFT SHOP
22809 Mission Blvd. (corner of D next to library), Hayward 94541, (510) 582-1922. Mon–Fri 10 am–4 pm, Sat 11 am–3 pm. Cash.

The Ladies Aid to Retarded Children of Hayward has been operating this thrift shop since 1967 (they moved a few doors down from the original site three years ago.) It's cluttered and a bit of a jumble, but the volunteers and the paid handicapped employees are friendly and the prices are low on everything. Clothes are cheap and half off the first and seventh of each month, collectibles are cheap, and housewares are cheap, cheap, cheap (dinner plates for 50¢). If your idea of a good time is poking around in dark corners in search of the great find, you'll like *LARC Thrift Shop.*

Charity: Ladies Aid to Retarded Children of Hayward
Everything except furniture and large appliances

PURPLE HEART THRIFT SHOP
825 A St. (at Watkins), Hayward 94541, (510) 581-8094. Mon–Fri 9:30 am–6 pm, Sat 10 am–6 pm, Sun 10 am–5 pm. Cash.

This huge two-story building could use a coat of paint and a bit of spiffing up to make it as nifty inside as it looks from the outside. Yet someone there has a good eye for display, the windows are trendy, and the floor displays and cute signage try to liven things up. The problem is too much floor space for too little merchandise. Clothing is abundant and cheap, and there's a big selection of large-size garments. The housewares located upstairs are less abundant, but also cheap. The few antiques and collectibles

we saw were the only items with medium to high prices. This is a good place to dress the family on a tight budget.

Charity: Purple Heart Veterans Rehabilitation Services
Everything except large appliances

RAINBOW'S END THRIFT SHOP
22683 Main St. (across from the fire department), Hayward 94541, (510) 888-0300. Mon–Sat 10 am–4 pm. Cash, checks.

The Hayward branch of *Rainbow's End* (they have another store in Walnut Creek) had just opened the day of our visit, which perhaps accounted for the dearth of merchandise. The newly redecorated store is big, bright, neat, organized, very clean, and filled with attractive displays. They call themselves an upscale thrift shop, but the prices seemed more upscale than the merchandise. They were asking $25–$35 for women's suits and $125 for a set of Diane porcelain dishes made in Japan. You can find about the same merchandise for less elsewhere. However, they may just need a little time to get their thrift store bearings, so give it a try.

Charity: Fern Lodge Nursing Home in Castro Valley
Everything except large appliances

ST. VINCENT DE PAUL
22331 Mission Blvd., Hayward 94541, (510) 582-0204. Mon–Sat 9:30 am–5:15 pm, Sun 12 am–5

pm. Cash, checks, MC/VISA.
This is not your typical *St. Vincent de Paul*: no dirt, no clutter, no chaos. This place is so clean you could eat off the floor, so neat and so organized they probably alphabetize their garbage. The big old building, formerly a theater, has one half full of furniture, appliances, and mattresses and the other half full of clothing. Like every other *St. Vincent de Paul*, prices are low and quality is medium to low. We liked the barrels full of golf clubs and crutches, but we missed the sense of adventure and possible discovery you usually get at the *St. Vincent* stores.
Charity: St. Vincent de Paul
Everything

SALVATION ARMY
22500 Foothill Blvd., Hayward 94541, (510) 538-2698. Mon–Sat 9:30 am–5:30 pm. Cash, checks, MC/VISA.
Located in a big downtown corner store, the Hayward *Salvation Army* was featuring wedding clothing the day of our visit. All the windows displayed wedding attire, and they not only had one of the biggest selections of new Jessica McClintock wedding gowns we've seen (priced in the $200 range), but they also had an ample selection of men's formal wear, including dove gray tails for $19.50. The rest of the merchandise was typical, solid, well-priced Army goods. Note that the appliances at *Salvation Army* are sold as is, without guarantees. If you're in the market for a vacuum cleaner, this store will give you a lot to choose from.
Charity: Salvation Army
Everything

SAVERS
20812 Hesperian Blvd., Hayward 94541, (510) 783-0101. Mon–Wed 9 am–7 pm, Thurs–Fri 9 am–9 pm, Sat 10 am–6 pm. Cash, checks, MC/VISA.
In addition to the six Bay Area *Savers*, there are over 30 more in the rest of the United States and even more in Canada. Located in a former supermarket, the Hayward *Savers* brings you a huge selection of clothing for the whole family in a neat, clean, bright, well organized, and cheerful atmosphere. Quantity comes before quality and prices are good to great, although there is more clothing to choose from than furniture or housewares. The "Labels" department features new merchandise—department store returns, close-outs, and discontinued items—at prices often below manufacturers' cost.
Charity: Privately owned, supports HOPE rehabilitation services, which work with developmentally handicapped children and adults
Everything except large appliances

THRIFT CENTER
29498 Mission Blvd., Hayward 94544, (510) 881-0222. Mon–Sat 9 am–7 pm. Cash, checks, MC/VISA with a minimum of $25.
Clean but not pristine, organized

but not neat, *Thrift Center* has large scale organization down pat, but it's not so good on the details. You can rely on the store for great buys on clothes for the family. Prices range from cheap to dirt cheap on everything but collectibles, which are overpriced. You can find great buys in housewares, especially small appliances—check out the special small room where you can find electric can openers for $2.99, an old Sunbeam mixer for $14.99, toaster ovens for $6.99. They also have a great selection of books and toys.

Charity: Privately owned, percentage of sales goes to United Cerebral Palsy
Everything

~~~~~ Newark ~~~~~

SALVATION ARMY
35201 Newark Blvd., Newark 94560, (510) 791-9198. Mon–Wed 9:30 am–5:30 pm, Thurs 9:30 am–7:30 pm, Fri–Sat 9:30 am–5:30 pm. Cash, checks, MC/VISA.

In addition to your typical Army fare, the Newark *Salvation Army* boasts an in-store boutique, "The Treasure Chest," which is complete with circle racks and a three-way mirror and features better women's apparel. The clothes are the best the Army has to offer and the price is right.

Charity: Salvation Army
Everything

~~~~~ San Leandro ~~~~~

THE FLEA SHOP
601 East 14th St., San Leandro 94577, (510) 568-1087. Mon–Sat 9 am–6 pm. Cash, checks, MC/VISA.

Like an indoor flea market, *The Flea Shop* carries a bit of everything, from high-priced antiques, art, and collectibles to basic everyday sorts of things, including large appliances, linens, used furniture, and housewares, priced anywhere from 25¢ to $5000.
Everything

GOODWILL
14750 East 14th St. (at 148th), San Leandro 94578, (510) 352-6966. Mon–Sat 10 am–6 pm, Sun 11 am–6 pm. Cash, checks, MC/VISA/DISCOVER.

Although not on a par with some of the more upscale *Goodwill* stores, the San Leandro *Goodwill* is bright, clean, and attractive. New shipments come in every other day, and merchandise which stays on the floor for 30 days is reduced by 25% (with the exception of clothing). There are no dressing rooms, but a corner is reserved for trying on items over your own clothes. Electrical items carry a 24-hour guarantee; if they are not in working order they may be exchanged for other merchandise.

Charity: Goodwill
Everything except large appliances

GOODWILL

14410 Washington Ave. (at Floresta), San Leandro 94578, (510) 614-9658. Mon–Sat 10 am–6 pm, Sun 11 am–6 pm. Cash, checks, MC/VISA.

This one is San Leandro's upscale *Goodwill.* They don't carry furniture (with the exception of mattresses and box springs) or large appliances, and very few household goods, but the clothing selection is excellent and extensive.

Charity: Goodwill
Everything except furniture and large appliances

MY SIZE NOW

1320 Ottawa, San Leandro 94579, (510) 351-3303. Tues–Sat 11 am–5 pm. Cash, checks, MC/VISA.

My Size Now hadn't opened yet when we paid our visit, but we did peek in the window and it looked very elegant, organized, and well stocked with merchandise. Owner Dorothy Arrow told me she carries better quality clothing in sizes 12–50 at prices 25%–50% of retail. I know of only one other consignment store in the Bay Area which caters exclusively to larger women, so I would say *My Size Now* would be worth a visit, even though I didn't get to make one.

Consignment: Call for appointment, 50/50 split, contract of 60–90 days, also buys outright
Women's large-size clothing

~~~~~~~~~~~~~~~~~~~~~~~~~~~~~~

Left: Goodwill As Is, Oakland.

NEW TO YOU

16330 East 14th St. (at 164th), San Leandro 94578, (510) 276-5767. Mon, Wed, Fri 10 am–3 pm. Cash.

Women's clothing predominates in this large, well-organized store. Prices are low on the selection of miscellaneous items as well as clothing—men's suits for $10, sports jackets for $3–$7. We saw bolts of fabric selling for $2 a yard, with plenty of trims to go with them.

Charity: Children's Hospital/ Oakland
Everything except furniture and large appliances

SALVATION ARMY

2179 East 14th St. (at Easterbrook), San Leandro 94577, (510) 895-0602. Mon–Sat 9:30 am–5:30 pm. Cash, checks, MC/VISA.

Some *Salvation Army* stores seem to get all the best stuff, and this is one of the lucky ones. It doesn't look too promising from the outside, but inside—WOW! The housewares and bric-a-brac are the most exciting and least expensive I've seen in any *Salvation Army* store. The furniture selection, which included several remarkable antique pieces, is excellent and also priced to sell. The unique in-store boutique features men's classic clothes and fine collectibles. If you're an Army fan, put on your walking boots and march on over. You won't be disappointed.

Charity: Salvation Army
Everything

TEDI'S CONSIGNMENT BOUTIQUE

1634 East 14th St. (at Dolores), San Leandro 94577, (510) 895-2367. Tues–Fri 10 am–5:30 pm, Sat 10 am–4:45 pm. Cash, checks.

Women interested more in dependable fashion basics and reasonable prices than in high style and designer labels will feel comfortable at *Tedi's Consignment Boutique*, which stocks sizes 4–22. Tedi is big on bargains: in the front she has a 50¢ basket and in the back she has a sale room featuring a half-off rack and a $1 rack.

Consignment: By appointment, 50/50 split, contract of 60–90 days
Women's clothing

THRIFT TOWN

16160 E. 14th St., San Leandro 94578, (510) 278-1766. Mon–Fri 9 am–8 pm, Sat 10 am–8 pm, Sun 11 am–6 pm. Cash, checks, MC/VISA.

What's bigger than a garage sale and better than a flea market? *Thrift Town*! According to the people at *Thrift Town*, where thrift shopping equals big business, their store has exactly the size, quantity, and selection you need. Fresh merchandise comes in daily to this 22,000 square-foot store; over 2000 different items are put out each weekday. 800 feet of women's fashions are on display. They have something for everyone in price ranges to suit many pockets— including women's dresses for $7.99–$25. They know their antiques and collectibles—we saw kid's lunch boxes going for up to

$20. The "Old Fashions" labels designate the vintage garments, which have surprisingly low prices (a 1940's wool suit in perfect condition was only $10). The store is big on self-promotion, and we like the philosophy: SECONDHAND DOESN'T MEAN SECOND BEST!!!

Charity: Privately owned, supports CARH (Community Assistance for the Retarded and Handicapped)
Everything except large appliances

VESPER SOCIETY THRIFT STORE

378 Davis (at Hayes), San Leandro 94577, (510) 483-7977. Mon–Sat 10 am–3 pm. Cash.

Vesper Society Thrift Store is a must for treasure-seeking bargain hunters and lovers of the serendipitous discovery. The cases and shelves of this small one-room store are loaded with collectibles, from antique pressed glass to fine china teacups, all at ridiculously low prices. Ordinary housewares are also good buys, as is the clothing; we found Ann Taylor and Lanz amid the ubiquitous Sears polyesters.

Charity: Vesper Hospice and Vesper Home Health Care
Everything but large appliances and large pieces of furniture

~~~ San Lorenzo ~~~

MARINO'S SECOND TIME AROUND

17279 Hesperian Blvd. (at

Hacienda), San Lorenzo 94580, (510) 276-8705. Mon–Sat 10 am–5 pm, Sun 11 am–4 pm. Cash, checks, MC/VISA.

Whether you already have kids or are planning for one on the way, you'll thank us for telling you about *Marino's Second Time Around.* Perfection seems to be a preoccupation with Pat Marino—everything in her shop is perfect, plus the shop itself is clean, organized, and cheerful, with a beautiful Victorian crib to make you feel like you're in I Magnin's baby department. You just can't beat the prices on baby clothes—sleepers for 99¢ (limit six per customer), undershirts for 79¢– 99¢ (limit eight), rubber pants for 39¢, and so on and so on. The maternity shop in the back of the store has a great selection, including nursing bras and nightgowns. Everything looks fresh, stylish, and well-priced.

Buys: Appointment necessary for children's clothing
Children's clothing, toys, and furniture; maternity clothing

THRIFT CENTER
1311 Bockman Rd., San Lorenzo 94580, (510) 481-1930. Mon–Sat 10 am–7 pm. Cash, checks, MC/ VISA with a minimum of $25.

Green cement floors, dingy yellow walls, fluorescent lights, and dressing rooms with gold lame curtains are what you get at the San Lorenzo branch of *Thrift Center.* Clothes are plentiful and cheap, furniture and housewares less so. For even lower prices, come on Saturday, when you can take 30% off any piece of used merchandise.

Charity: Privately owned, supports United Cerebral Palsy
Everything except large appliances

ALAMEDA COUNTY (Partial)	Appliances/large	Bridal	Clothing/children	Clothing/men	Clothing/women	Collectibles	Furnishings/children	Furniture	Housewares	Maternity	Tools, etc.	Toys	Vintage	Page number
ALAMEDA, CITY OF														
Alameda Market	X	X	X	X	X	X	X	X	X	X	X	X	X	1
Clothes Encounters					X									1
Garment Bag					X					X				1
Gaslight Emporium			X	X	**X**								X	1
Lauren's Closet			X			X						X		2
Mastic Sr. Center)			X	X	X	X		X	X			X	X	2
Mother's Care			X			X					X			2
St. Vincent de Paul	X	X	X	X	X	X	X	X	X	X	X	X		3
Yetta's Antiques						X								3
FREMONT														
Best For Less	X	X	X	X	X	X	X	X	X	X	X	X		3
Clothing Exchange					X									3
My Sister's Closet			X	X	X									4
Ohlone Flea Market	X	X	X	X	X	X	X	X	X	X	X	X	X	4
St. Vincent de Paul	X	X	X	X	X	X	X	X	X	X	X	X		4
Salvation Army	X	X	X	X	X	X	X	X	X	X	X	X		6
Thrift Center	X	X	X	X	X	X	X	X	X	X	X	X		6
Tri-City Volunteers		X	X	X	X	X	X	X	X	X	X	X		6
FREMONT/NILES														
Bite & Browse							X		X	X				7
Dolores' Cottage					X									7
Eagles Nest							X		X	X		X		7
Niles Flea Market					X	X								7
HAYWARD														
Chabot Flea Market	X	X	X	X	X	X	X	X	X	X	X	X	X	7
Goodwill	X	X	X	X	X	X	X	X	X	X	X	X		8
Grand Illusions		X		X	X								X	8
Full Gospel Store			X	X	X	X	X	X		X	X			8
LARC Thrift Shop			X	X	X	X		X		X	X			8
Purple Heart	X	X	X	X	X	X	X	X	X	X		X		9
Rainbow's End	X		X	X	X	X	X	X	X			X		9
St. Vincent de Paul	X	X	X	X	X	X	X	X	X	X	X	X		9
Salvation Army	X	X	X	X	X	X	X	X	X	X	X	X		10

ALAMEDA COUNTY (Partial)	Appliances/large	Bridal	Clothing/children	Clothing/men	Clothing/women	Collectibles	Furnishings/children	Furniture	Housewares	Maternity	Tools, etc.	Toys	Vintage	Page number
Savers		X	X	X	X	X	X	X	X	X	X	X		10
Thrift Center	X	X	X	X	X	X	X	X	X	X	X	X		10
NEWARK														
Salvation Army	X	X	X	X	X	X	X	X	X	X	X	X		11
SAN LEANDRO														
Flea Shop	X					X	X	X	X		X			11
Goodwill (E. 14th)		X	X	X	X	X	X	X	X	X	X	X		11
Goodwill (Wash.)		X	X	X	X	X	X		X	X	X	X		13
My Size Now					X									
New to You			X	X	X	X	X		X	X		X		13
Salvation Army	X	X	X	X	X	X	X	**X**	X	X	X	X		13
Tedi's Boutique					X									13
Thrift Town		X	X	X	X	X	X	X	X	X	X	X	X	14
Vesper Store		X	X	X	X	X	X	X	X			X		14
SAN LORENZO														
Marino's Time		X				X			X			X		14
Thrift Center		X	X	X	X	X	X	X	X	X	X			15

ALBANY

BACKSTAGE CLOTHIER

1224 Solano Ave. (between Talbot and Evelyn), Albany 94706, (510) 527-5540. Tues–Sat 11 am–7 pm, Sun 12 am–6 pm. Cash, checks, MC/VISA.

This fun-filled uptempo store will appeal to anyone with a theatrical bent and to shoppers in their 20's, 30's, and 40's who go for the arty look of one-of-a-kind, unusual pieces (at good prices). The eclectic merchandise ranges from beaded and painted army jackets to Calvin Klein, and it includes a wonderful assortment of hats and vintage shoes. Half the pieces are vintage, half are contemporary, and 10% are on consignment. They do a big business in rentals with most outfits—even men's formal wear—renting for $25–$35, including costume jewelry and accessories. (They're trying to have the lowest prices anywhere.) The shop seems smaller than it is; be sure you ask to see the great costume collection stored in the back room.
Consignment: Buys vintage and contemporary clothing outright, call for appointment and consignment terms
Men's and women's clothing

IT'S A BIG DEAL

918 San Pablo Ave. (1/2 block south of Solano), Albany 94706, (510) 527-5533. Mon–Sat 10:30 am–5:30 pm, Sun 12 am–5 pm. Cash, checks, MC/VISA/AM EX.

When a new baby is on the way and the only thing stretched tighter than your regular clothes is your budget, it's time to head for *It's A Big Deal*. This shop specializes in quality gently-worn maternity clothes, especially upper-end designer lines like Japanese Weekend, available in sizes petite–large. They also carry a large selection of new maternity clothes, all seconds and over-runs, which are discounted 30%–70% off retail price. You can fill all your maternity wardrobe needs, from sportswear to formal wear, and when the baby is born you can make extra cash by putting your clothes on consignment. It's a good deal.
Consignment: By appointment, 50/50 split, 60-day contract
Maternity clothing

KIDZOO

1201-C Solano Ave., Albany 94706, (510) 525-3488. Mon–Sat 10 am–5:30 pm. Cash, checks.

If it doesn't make sense to you to spend a fortune on kid's clothes, take your kids to *Kidzoo*. They can amuse themselves in the play area while you shop for bargains.

Kidzoo's new owner Lisa Jaramillo sells everything (sizes 0–12) from Sears to Saks for what she thinks her customers can afford (i.e. reasonable prices). She also carries new basics, like shirts and leggings and RIKI designs.

Children's clothing, books, and toys

SALVATION ARMY
1382 Solano Ave., Albany 94706, (510) 524-5100. Mon–Sat 9:30 am–5:30 pm. Cash, local checks, MC/VISA.

This bright, clean *Salvation Army* fits right in on trendy Solano Avenue. The upper level of the store features clothes: a big selection and great prices, but no dressing rooms. The lower level has furniture, including some wonderful pieces and terrific buys.
Charity: Salvation Army
Everything

SECOND HAND ROSE
111 Solano Ave., Albany 94706, (510) 527-7742. Tues–Sat 11 am–6 pm. Cash, checks, MC/VISA.

Smart women have been wearing secondhand clothes from *Second Hand Rose* on Solano Avenue since 1967. The store also carries a smattering of men's and children's clothes. About 1/3 of the merchandise is vintage clothing from the 1890's to the 1960's, and the rest is contemporary work and casual clothing. You never know what you'll find in this crowded store...one day it may be a Joan Crawford hat for $95, or the entire wardrobe from "Peggy Sue Got Married," or a beaded top and harem pants from "The King and I" for $25. You can spend anywhere from $5 to $500 on an outfit or a nifty piece of vintage jewelry.
Consignment: By appointment, 50/50 split, 90-day contract
Women's clothing and accessories; knickknacks; gifts

SERENDIPITY CONSIGNMENT
567 San Pablo Ave., Albany 94706, (510) 524-8865. Wed–Fri 11 am–5 pm, Sat 10 am–5 pm. Cash, local checks.

Career women, graduate students, work-at-home moms, and any woman who is tired of paying department store prices will enjoy shopping in the clean, pleasant surroundings of *Serendipity Consignment*. Owner Gloria Jean carries a little bit of everything—sporty, casual, dressy, and career—all at very reasonable prices. Merchandise is crisp, pretty, and up-to-date, with labels like Liz Claiborne, Chaus, Paquette, Talbots, and Leslie Faye in sizes 7/8–16/18. Gloria Jean's passion for departments makes it easy to find whatever you're looking for. She also has beautiful jewelry.
Consignment: Wed–Sat 10 am–12 am, or by appointment; 50/50 split; contract of 60–90 days
Women's clothing

SOLANO AVENUE CLOTHING STORE (S.A.C.S.)
1419 Solano Ave. (at Santa Fe), Albany 94706, (510) 525-9520.

Mon–Sat 10:30 am–6 pm. Cash, checks, MC/VISA.

If you're not into fashion extremes, S.A.C.S. is a great place to shop for casual and work clothes. There are a few dressy outfits, but no formals. Everything is in good shape and a current style, sizes 6–22, selling for 1/3 or less of the original cost. Hardly anything in the store is over $50. You'll also find new salesman's samples, new socks, and We Be Bop, a clothing line from Indonesia which is 30% off retail.

Consignment: Tues–Sat 11 am–3 pm, 50/50 split, 30-day contract
Women's clothing

TOY GO ROUND

1361 Solano Ave., Albany 94706, (510) 527-1363. Mon–Sat 10 am–5 pm. Cash, checks, MC/VISA.

"Keep your toys in the play stream and out of the waste stream" reads the poster. Founded in 1976 by two dedicated environmentalists, *Toy Go Round*'s dual purposes are to teach kids the value of recycling and put money in their pockets at the same time. Packed with toys, books, and equipment, the store's best sellers are basic universal toys like Leggos, blocks, and Tinkertoys. You will also find Ninja Turtles and other hot fads, but no guns, war toys, or electric cars, trains, or games. Prices are 30% less than any found at Kmart.

Consignment: 10 am–4 pm, 50/50 split
Children's toys and equipment

US KIDS...AND MOM TOO

1410-A Solano Ave., Albany 94706, (510) 528-3306. Mon–Sat 10 am–6 pm, Sun 11 am–7 pm. Cash, checks, MC/VISA.

This tiny store specializes in adorable handmade outfits for younger children. Originally a resale shop for kid's clothes and maternity wear, the new children's merchandise has taken over 2/3 of the business and maternity wear has been discontinued altogether. *Us Kids* carries sizes 0–4T for boys and 0–6X for girls, all at prices 30% or more off retail. Look for resale items in the back; they specialize in very cute dresses, all freshly washed and ironed.

Buys: Mon–Sat 10 am–4 pm, 40% customer/60% store in cash or 60% customer/40% store in trade
Children's clothing

BERKELEY

Downtown

CAROUSEL CONSIGNMENT

1955 Shattuck Ave., Berkeley 94704, (510) 845-9044. Mon–Sat 10:30 am–5 pm. Cash, checks, MC/VISA.

A collection of clowns and carousels lends a festive air to this otherwise down-to-earth store. For the past eleven years *Carousel Consignment* has been a resource for women looking for good quality sports and business wear. An expensive designer piece or dressy outfit pops up now and then, but by and large the store sticks to the basics in sizes 4–18. A short consignment period makes for good turnover in merchandise. *Consignment: Mon–Sat 11 am–3 pm, 50/50 split, 30-day contract* **Women's clothing**

NEARLY NEW SHOP OF THE EAST BAY
2145 University Ave. (between Shattuck and Oxford), Berkeley 94704, (510) 841-3954. Mon–Fri 10:30 am–3 pm. Cash, checks.

Staffed by a delightful volunteer group of senior ladies, *Nearly New Shop* should be a regular stop on your treasure hunting rounds. Something wonderful is bound to turn up with each visit—antique linens one day, a piece of jewelry the next, or maybe that small appliance you've been looking for. Prices are low on everything, especially on clothing. You may not find the latest hot styles, but if you're into high-quality classics or 1950's and 1960's vintage this may be just your place. I once saw two racks of long gowns from the 1960's selling for $5–$8, a Lanvin suit from Paris for $12, and a Christian Dior original for $4. *Charity: PEO (Philanthropic Education Organization), which benefits a senior retirement home* **Everything except furniture and large appliances**

NEW TO YOU THRIFT SHOP
2480 Shattuck Ave., Berkeley 94704, (510) 540-7778. Mon, Wed, Fri 10 am–3 pm. Cash, checks.

Of the three *New to You Thrift Shops* in the Bay Area, the Berkeley store is by far the most upscale. This big beautiful shop offers a little bit of everything—antiques, collectibles, furniture, books, household goods, jewelry, and clothing. Quality is high and prices are reasonable. The best buys are women's clothing. The shop is very selective about what they keep; volunteers take items home to wash and the shop's steamer makes everything look fresh and new. A shopaholic recently donated 200 dresses...all good-as-new designer labels priced to sell (I saw an Albert Nipon silk for $15). *Charity: Children's Hospital of Oakland* **Everything except large appliances**

STOP THE CLOCK
2140 Center (between Shattuck and Oxford), Berkeley 94704, (510) 841-2142. Mon–Sat 10:30 am–6:30 pm. Cash, checks, MC/VISA/AM EX.

Vintage fanciers who want to stop the fashion clock in the 1940's, 1950's, and 1960's will find these decades well represented at this Berkeley store. Women can choose from a big selection of day dresses in good condition, priced $17–$24. Very little in the store is priced over $40. Owner Cindy Vorte, a devoted vintage collector, will extol the

virtues of older garments for
everyday wear as well as dress up.
Check out the selection of hats.
Men's and women's clothing

TROUT FARM
*2179 Bancroft Way, Berkeley
94704, (510) 843-3565. Mon–Sat
12 am–6 pm, Sun 12 am–5 pm.
Cash, checks.*

Trout Farm could be either your
fondest dream come true or your
worst nightmare come to life,
depending on how you feel about
1950's kitsch. Here is a whole store
full of rare and weird objects from
that much-maligned era. They claim
to have more chrome dinette sets
($50–$200) than the rest of the Bay
Area combined. This is not your
regular thrift store; you can expect
to pay up to $900 for a classic
Charles Eames chair and other
designer pieces. But it might be fun
to check on the prices of items just
like the ones you recently donated
to the Salvation Army.
Furniture and collectibles

～～ South Berkeley ～～

BERKELEY FLEA MARKET
*Ashby Bart Station, Ashby
Avenue and Martin Luther King
Jr. Way, Berkeley 94703, (510)
644-0744. Sat–Sun 8 am–7:30 pm.
Payment varies with vendor.*

Admission is free to this hip and
funky flea market; the seller's fee is
$11 per day.
Everything

PEOPLE'S BAZAAR
*3258 Adeline, Berkeley 94703,
(510) 655-8008. Mon–Sat 9 am–
5:30 pm. Cash, checks, MC/VISA.*

Antique shop or secondhand store?
It's a toss-up, but we felt we had to
include this high-end treasure
palace because it is possible to
walk away from it with the bargain
of the century. Filled with an
eclectic mix of exquisite pieces,
from Victorian oak tables to Art
Deco highboys to carved Chinese
chests, prices here undersell
uptown antique dealers by 20%.
And, according to owner Sam Dyke,
there's always room for adjust-
ment. So check it out, and don't be
intimidated by the sticker prices—
they're not set in cement (more like
jello).
**Furniture, antiques, and
collectibles**

～～ UC Campus Area ～～

BUFFALO EXCHANGE
*2512 Telegraph Ave. (at Dwight),
Berkeley 94704, (510) 644-9202.
Mon–Sat 10:30 am–6:30 pm, Sun
12 am–6 pm. Cash, checks, MC/
VISA.*

One of several Bay Area locations,
the Berkeley *Buffalo Exchange*
follows the mold of this successful
used clothing chain by selling a
great selection of contemporary
and vintage garments at good
prices. Store managers have
autonomy in the purchasing
department, so you're apt to find
more funky fashions and ethnic

garb in this store than the one in Pleasant Hill. Leather jackets, black hightops, and embroidered skirts from India abound, and there is often a selection of new merchandise on the racks as well. The atmosphere is uptempo, the staff is friendly, and you'll find good values for your shopping dollar (we saw a pair of White Mountain suede shoes for $15 and a woman's leather jacket for $35).
Buys: Anytime, 40% customer/ 60% store in cash, 55% customer/ 45% store in trade
Men's and women's clothing and accessories

CELLAR THRIFT SHOP
2345 Channing Way (at Dana), Berkeley 94704, (510) 644-3262. Wed 10 am–2 pm, Sat 10 am–4 pm. Cash.
Parking can be a problem around the UC campus and ten shopping hours per week does not give you a lot of time, but don't let these difficulties keep you away from the *Cellar Thrift Shop.* Staffed by volunteers from the First Congregational Church of Berkeley, this little-bit-of-everything thrift shop is a bargain hunter's delight. Clothes, books, jewelry, linens, sewing notions, and goodies of all kinds are plentiful and very inexpensive. Collectors may find their heart's desire on the 25¢ table; we were captivated by a lacy sandalwood fan and a stack of embroidered handkerchiefs. The shop is too small to accommodate large pieces of furniture, so look for a sign

announcing available items. They often have sofas and chairs, and once they even had a car.
Charity: Outreach work of the First Congregational Church of Berkeley, including the Berkeley Area Interfaith Council, the Berkeley Emergency Food Project, and the Berkeley Free Clinic
Everything except large appliances

FUTURA
2374 Telegraph Ave. (between Durant and Channing), Berkeley 94704, (510) 843-3037. Mon–Thurs 11 am–6:30 pm, Fri–Sat 10:30 am–9 pm, Sun 12 am–6 pm. Cash, checks, MC/VISA.
The downstairs is devoted exclusively to new clothing, but you can take your chances upstairs. You will always find a selection of used Levi's 501 jeans for $27–$40; finding 1940's–1960's vintage is iffier. The few pieces they had on our visit were clean, in good condition, and cheap. Sometimes, we were told, there is a lot more to choose from.
Women's clothing

SHARKS
2505 Telegraph Ave. (at Dwight), Berkeley 94704, (510) 841-8736. Mon–Sat 10:30 am–6:30 pm, Sun 12 am–6 pm. Cash, checks, MC/ VISA.
Sharks used to be *Aardvark's* until Doug Ballou bought it and changed the name to propitiate the vicious creatures so they don't bite him

when he surfs. ("Sharks" also rhymes with "Aardvarks.") More than just a cheap used clothing store, *Sharks* specializes in the unusual, catering to the strange needs of UC theme parties. They also stock the usual men's and women's vintage, aloha shirts, Levi's 501 jeans ($12–$18), jeans dyed black, and tuxedos. Doug claims that they play the best music and carry only the best most avant-garde vintage. After many years of business the people at *Sharks* have come to know what people want, and they maintain a steady inflow of good stuff at reasonable prices.

Men's and women's vintage clothing

SLASH CLOTHING

2840 College Ave. (at Russell), Berkeley 94704, (510) 841-7803. Mon–Sat 11:30 am–7 pm. Cash, checks.

The theme here is pants. The pants, which are stacked from the floor to the ceiling of this subterra-nean shop, include Levi's 501 jeans for $15 and under, genuine army surplus pants (worn first by soldiers in the American, Canadian, Swed-ish, German, and Spanish armies), working pants from the 1940's, tuxedo trousers, shorts, cut-offs.... Owner Carla Bell has every kind of pants you could imagine in every size; it just depends on how much you want to dig. (And she has 400 more at home.) Hats and wigs hang from the ceiling, and you can buy a new dress shirt for $20 or a used one for $5. Carla doesn't like

dresses (they take too much thinking), but there's a rack of them anyway, some in vintage styles and some in new and ageless ones. This is a remarkable shop and Carla Bell is an extraordinary woman. It's worth a visit just to see her in action with the softest sell in town...she calls it "jean therapy."

Men's and women's clothing

WASTELAND

2398 Telegraph Ave. (at Channing), Berkeley 94704, (510) 843-6711. Mon–Fri 11 am–6 pm, Sat 11 am–7 pm, Sun 12 am–6 pm. Cash, checks, MC/VISA.

Although it's smaller than the San Francisco store and the atmosphere is quieter, Berkeley's *Wasteland* offers the same great mix of contemporary and vintage pre-owned clothing. Downstairs you can find men's sports coats for $25 or satin bathrobes for $20. Up the funky staircase you'll find the women's department, which has a lot to choose from, including Jones New York skirts for $20. Every decade from the 1920's through the 1970's is represented, as well as more recent styles. Quality varies from "as is" to fine. *Consignment: Buys outright 12 am–4 pm, 40% customer/60% store in cash or 60% customer/ 40% store in trade; consignment for leathers only, 60% consignor/ 40% store in cash or 70% con-signor/30% store in trade*

Men's and women's clothing

THE WEDDING TRUNK

3084 Claremont Ave., Berkeley 94705, (510) 547-7343. Wed–Sat 11 am–5 pm, Sundays by appointment only. Cash, checks.

I can't imagine shopping for wedding gowns without checking out *The Wedding Trunk* first. This serene and lovely shop is my idea of the perfect bridal salon—the owner Sue Bloomquist couldn't be more knowledgeable or more charming, the atmosphere and decor calm even the most nervous bride, the gowns are to die for, and, best of all, the prices are extremely reasonable. My personal favorites are the vintage gowns—dating from the early 1950's and before, every gown is a unique creation in perfect condition and priced at a fraction of what you'd pay for a new dress at a department store. *The Wedding Trunk* also carries one-of-a-kind wedding gowns made from vintage fabrics. For brides who prefer contemporary styles, Bloomquist carries new samples selling for half of the original cost. Many of the gowns are appropriate for informal weddings or other occasions.
Wedding gowns

~~~ **West Berkeley** ~~~

DRESSING UP

1615 San Pablo Ave. (at Cedar), Berkeley 94710, (510) 559-8855. Mon–Sat 11 am–6 pm. Cash, checks.

When Donna Verner recently opened a second *Dressing Up* in

Berkeley (the original is on Grand Avenue in Oakland), she changed the focus from vintage to contemporary fashions. She still stocks selected vintage pieces from the 1940's and earlier, but now she concentrates on high-quality garments from the last two years. It's easier to shop in the new, smaller store, and every piece of clothing is a winner, whether casual or dressy, sports or career wear. Prices are moderate (low considering the quality), and a monthly Sunday auction of sale merchandise makes for some fabulous deals. Added bonuses include wonderful hats, new and vintage jewelry, and a few glitzy new items like jeweled bustiers for $42 and sequined dresses for $32.95.
Consignment: Mostly buys outright, Tues–Fri 11:30 am–3:30 pm, Sat by appointment, limited consignment on upper-end items for 50/50 split
Women's clothing

ST. VINCENT DE PAUL

2009 San Pablo Ave. (at University), Berkeley 94710, (510) 841-1504. Mon–Sat 8:30 am–5 pm. Cash, local checks, MC/VISA.

Clean, organized, cheap...another fine *St. Vincent de Paul* selling everything from ovens to overcoats. Books and records are upstairs.
Charity: St. Vincent de Paul
Everything

Above: Urban Ore, Berkeley.

TIDDLYWINKS
1302 Gilman, Berkeley 94706, (510) 527-5025. Mon–Thurs 10 am–5 pm, Fri–Sat 10 am–5:30 pm, Sun 12 am–5 pm. Cash, checks, MC/VISA.

Before it was really chic, four young mothers opened a little shop on Solano Avenue in Albany to introduce East Bay parents to the concept of children's resale. The high quality of the merchandise and the delightful atmosphere made the store an instant hit. Recently relocated to a much bigger, brighter, and more beautiful store in Berkeley, *Tiddlywinks* is as cheery and colorful as ever, with the same high-quality merchandise for low prices. They carry sizes newborn–12 for boys and girls, as well as a few new shirts and art supplies.
Consignment: By appointment; for clothing, 40% cash or 50% trade; for books and toys, 50% cash or trade; for equipment, 60% cash or trade
Children's clothing, toys, and equipment

URBAN ORE
1333 Sixth St., Berkeley 94710, (510) 559-4450. Mon–Sun 8:30 am–5 pm. Cash, checks, MC/ VISA.

Urban Ore defies description. First-time visitors are likely to stagger when confronted with its sea of sinks, wall of windows, terrain of toilets, and dozens of doors...and that's just outside in the building materials exchange yard. Inside, in the large warehouse known as the "general store," you'll find furniture, rugs, housewares, books, records, art, antiques, tools, bicycle parts, and anything else you can think of. A recent visit, for example, turned up a pinball machine for $400, an antique dental chair for $375, chandeliers, a dog house, street signs, 3 foot-high letters, and even some funky clothes.

Begun in 1979 as a salvaging operation, Urban Ore's primary purpose is to keep reusable things from being wasted. They divert them from landfill before they are dumped, or salvage them from the City of Berkeley's transfer station after they are dumped. They promote reuse (using something again in its original form) over recycling because it conserves more energy and materials: objects need not be chemically or mechanically broken down and formed into new products.

Builders and remodelers save money by shopping at the building materials exchange, where you can buy vintage and modern doors for $8–$150, windows for $15–$75, toilets, sinks, bathtubs, water heaters, and what-have-you. Antique dealers, artists, collectors, flea-market vendors, and bargain hunters comb though the general store merchandise (much of it thrift store rejects) and find treasures.

Everything

ALAMEDA COUNTY (Albany and Berkeley)	Appliances/large	Bridal	Clothing/children	Clothing/men	Clothing/women	Collectibles	Furnishings/children	Furniture	Housewares	Maternity	Tools, etc.	Toys	Vintage	Page number
ALBANY														
Backstage Clothier				X	X								X	18
It's a Big Deal										**X**				18
Kidzoo			X									X		18
Salvation Army	X	X	X	X	X	X	X	X	X	X	X	X		19
Second Hand Rose					X	X							X	19
Serendipity					X									19
S.A.C.S.					X									19
Toy Go Round							X					**X**		20
Us Kids			X											20
DWNTWN BERKELEY														
Carousel Cnsgnmnt.					X									20
Nearly New Shop			X	X	X	X			X			X		21
New to You			X	X	X	X	X	X	X			X		21
Stop the Clock			X	X									X	21
Trout Farm					X		X							22
SOUTH BERKELEY														
Berkeley Flea Market	X	X	X	X	X	X	X	X	X	X	X	X	X	22
People's Bazaar						X	**X**							22
UC CAMPUS AREA														
Buffalo Exchange				X	X								X	22
Cellar Thrift Shop			X	X	X	X	X	X	X		X	X		23
Futura					X									23
Sharks				X	X								X	23
Slash				X	X									24
Wasteland				X	X								X	24
Wedding Trunk		**X**												25
WEST BERKELEY														
Dressing Up					X								X	25
St. Vincent de Paul	X	X	X	X	X	X	X	X	X	X	X	X		25
Tiddlywinks			X				X						X	26
Urban Ore	X					X	X	X	X		X	X		26

OAKLAND

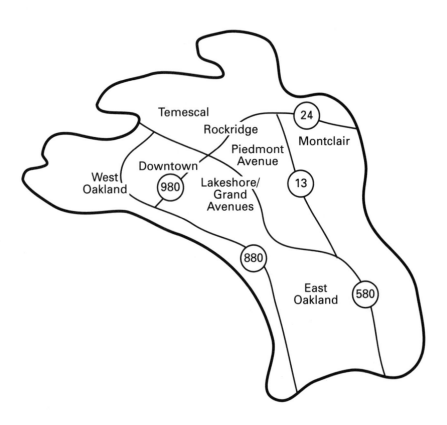

～～ Downtown Oakland ～～

BEEHIVE THRIFT SHOP
*1840 San Pablo Ave., Oakland
94612, (510) 465-2018. Tues–Sat
11 am–3 pm. Cash.*

The *Beehive Thrift Shop* has been around—I remember visiting its original location on College Avenue before it moved to its splendid two-story shop in a less elegant neighborhood. *Beehive* still offers the same wonderful treasures it always did. A star on any thrift shopper's map, this large well-organized store always seems to have more than its fair share of prize items, especially antiques and collectibles. Many an antique dealer has walked out with a smiling face and a rare find: a valuable work of art, a lovely vase, a piece of delicate china, or a Victorian piano shawl. These kinds of lovely goodies find their way to *Beehive* on a regular basis.

More mundane items like furniture, housewares, clothing, sewing notions, books, and picture frames are also available at bargain prices. You'll always find good buys in the selection of women's clothes, where large sizes are well represented and past-style I Magnin classics outnumber trendier fashions. The selection of kid's clothes is smaller, but also more up-to-date. New merchandise is put on the floor every Tuesday morning. Sales are frequent, and the half-off table is always worth checking out.

Charity: Lincoln Child Center, which provides residential and day treatment for emotionally disturbed children
Everything except large appliances

ECONOMY CORNER #2
2440 Telegraph Ave. (at 25th St.), Oakland 94612, (510) 451-0266. Tues–Sat 11 am–3 pm. Cash.

Like *Economy Corner #1* on College Avenue, *Economy Corner #2* carries a bit of everything. Although the College Avenue store gets a better grade of merchandise, according to one volunteer *Economy Corner #2* gets all the furniture, which is housed in the annex, located a few doors away and open only on request. The selection is not large, but talk about great buys. We saw a beautiful wing chair for $10, six sets of brass fireplace implements for $15 each, an exercise bike, a glass table and four chairs, bicycles priced $7–$10, and an assortment of sporting equipment.

The main store is crowded with clothes and knickknacks. As we were walking in a steady customer was walking out with an exquisite Bakelite dresser set, including a working clock, for $20. "My name is Jack," he told the volunteer at the desk, "I come here every day at 11." With finds like that, it's no wonder.

The jewelry section also always has something to offer, but the best finds are toys. Toys were once a staple of thrift store shopping, but with so many thrift stores saving them up for special holiday sales, toys are getting harder and harder to come by. Fortunately, *Economy Corner #2* specializes in them, keeping their window full of a tempting assortment. Thanks to a local toy wholesaler who donates seconds or out-of-season items, they almost always have a good supply at great prices. The low prices on all merchandise are enhanced by a half-off-everything sale twice a year and a $2.50-a-bag sale every three months.
Charity: Children's Home Society of California
Everything

ENCORE THRIFT SHOP
545 19th St. (between Telegraph and San Pablo), Oakland 94612, (510) 465-9788. Tues–Fri 10 am–3 pm, first and third Sats 10 am–3 pm. Cash.

You can count on *Encore* for something bizarre in addition to the usual thrift-store jumble. Once I opened a drawer to find hundreds of doll parts. (All those staring eyes and detached limbs gave me quite a start.) They also may actually specialize in appliances with unknown functions, but I'm not sure. Weak on clothes but strong

on stationery and party supplies, *Encore* can be trusted to have at least one table full of cards, paper plates, napkins, streamers, and tablecloths commemorating an approaching or recently passed holiday. (I saw marshmallow eggs for 25¢ a dozen the week after Easter.) The bookshelves are well organized, new toys and games are usually on hand, and the locked case almost always has an appetizing, if overpriced, collectible or two.
Charity: Oakland East Bay Symphony
Everything except furniture and large appliances

GOODWILL
1220 Broadway, Oakland 94612, (510) 834-6123. Mon–Sat 10 am–6 pm. Cash, checks, MC/VISA.

The opening of *Goodwill* in the redeveloped section of Oakland caused a bit of a flurry a few years back. Downtown merchants need not have worried. This *Goodwill*, as upscale as any fine store in the area, was bustling with well-dressed shoppers the afternoon I visited. Clothes are in front, a small selection of housewares and books is in back. You won't find any furniture or appliances.
Charity: Goodwill
Clothing, housewares, books

ST. VINCENT DE PAUL
2272 San Pablo Ave. (at West Grand), Oakland 94603, (510) 834-4647. Mon–Sat 9 am–4:45 pm, Sun 12 am–4:45 pm. Cash, local checks, MC/VISA.

According to one veteran thrift shopper, St. Vincent de Paul has the best furniture bargains in town. After I investigated this store and the St. Vincent in East Oakland, I found that the claim proved true. For sheer quantity, this St. Vincent de Paul has all other Oakland stores beat. A visit turned up no fewer than fifty sofas, twenty of which were on sale for $25.95 each. Non-sale sofas included a rolled arm 1930's classic for $49 and a twelve-foot olive-green monstrosity for $39.95. An army of over-stuffed arm chairs for $12–$15 bivouacked next to five-piece dinette sets for $89–$99. Straight chairs set out on a high shelf encircle the store. A gentleman purchasing two beauti-fully turned wood chairs for $4 each and two adorable miniature benches on sale for $1.50 each confided that he was buying them to resell in his antique shop. You can buy used mattresses and box springs, sterilized and recovered, individually or by the set. St. Vincent also has a good supply of large appliances—washers, dryers, refrigerators, and stoves—in all makes and models, priced $99–$299.

The clothing section is distin-guished primarily by the quantity. Racks and racks of men's and women's clothing are arranged by type and color, and two play pens filled with a tangled mass of baby clothes offer great buys. If your taste runs to high fashion or vintage funk, this is not the place to expand your wardrobe. But if you're looking for good prices, this is it. I once watched a young woman standing in the aisle (they have no dressing rooms) trying on one long dress after another other over her jeans. "What are you looking for?" I asked her. "I'm going to Prague," she answered, "and I'll need something to wear to the theatre." Suddenly the typical bridesmaid's taffeta with puffed sleeves took on a fairy-tale glow and I could see her looking absolutely elegant as she glided into the opera house. Cost to her—$3.50 (dresses were half off that day).

It's difficult to imagine some-thing you couldn't find in this giant warehouse of a store, and there is usually some kind of sale going on to further enhance the low, low prices. Thursday is Senior Citizens Day, when everything except upholstered furniture is 30% off. For a $10 charge St. Vincent will deliver large items anywhere in Alameda county.

Charity: St. Vincent de Paul. A free dining facility feeding the poor and hungry every day of the year is around the corner.
Everything

THE SHOP
268 14th St. (at Harrison), Oakland 94612, (510) 451-2704. Mon–Sat 10 am–4 pm. Cash.

PLEASE, they begged me, please don't put this one in your book! My neighbor, my friends, the women I've interviewed for this book, everyone wants to keep *The Shop* run by the Oakland/East Bay Junior

League a secret from the rest of you. I can't blame them. This is the crème de la crème; thrift shops just don't get any better than this one. The formula is simple: two large sunny rooms staffed by Junior League volunteers and three extraordinary professional staff members who sell merchandise of the highest quality at very low prices.

The Shop specializes in women's clothes. Wait till you see them—immaculate silk and cotton blouses, suits and dresses from the finest stores, fun sports wear. You'll think you've walked into the well-stocked closet of one of the league members. (Members are required to make donations as well as volunteer in the shop.) The dressiest outfits are saved for holidays, when *The Shop* has more glamorous gowns than Imelda Marcos has shoes. Prices are laughably low, especially considering the consistently high quality of the merchandise. Men's and children's clothing, although less abundant, is equally wonderful.

You can always find great buys on first-rate housewares, linens, knickknacks, and costume jewelry. Now and then an entire estate is donated, and the antiques and collectibles fly out of the store. Markdowns are frequent. Twice a year the shop closes briefly for a complete change of merchandise, and the week before (mid-February in spring and mid-August in fall) all merchandise goes to 50% off, then 75% off, and then comes Bag Day,

which means you pay only $2 for a whole bag. All toys are saved up for the spectacular toy sale held the first Saturday in December. (Some smart families do all their Christmas shopping then.)

The Shop owes much of its success to the good taste and merchandising skill of manager Liz Tonge, who keeps it looking fresh and new. Customers can't resist the charms of Liz and assistant manager Ginny Rolph, whose warmth and good humor make *The Shop* the friendliest thrift store in town. You can tell the regular shoppers—they're the ones with The Card, which entitles you to $5 off after ten $10 purchases. Ask for your own card. You're sure to make use of it.

Charity: Junior League projects in the arts, education, environment, and family services

Everything except large appliances and large pieces of furniture

YVETTE'S BOUTIQUE

340 14th St., Oakland 94612, (510) 271-0132. Mon–Fri 10:30 am–5 pm, Sat 11 am–5:30 pm. Cash, checks, MC/VISA.

Nothing in *Yvette's Boutique* sells for more than $16.99. So what, you're thinking, it's probably full of Sears polyester specials. Not so! Labels like Liz Claiborne, Albert Nipon, and Jones of New York, just to mention a few, adorn many of the stylish garments we saw on the racks. With the ridiculously low prices merchandise turns over

pretty quickly, so the smart shoppers pop in frequently to snap up the buys. Half of the floor space is devoted to new uniforms (not included in the $16.99 price); consignment items are in front.
Consignment: By appointment, 50/50 split
Women's clothing

~~~~ **East Oakland** ~~~~

COLISEUM SWAP MEET
Oakland Coliseum Drive-In, 5401 Coliseum Way, Oakland 94601, (510) 534-0325. Thurs–Sun 6:30 am–4 pm. Purchase method varies by dealer.

This four-day event begins with a free day on Thursday. On Friday admission is 50¢, and on the weekend it's 75¢. The seller's fees start at $7.50/day on Thursday, jump to $10 on Friday, and then up to $15/day on Saturday and Sunday.
Everything

FRED FINCH THRIFT SHOP
3800 Coolidge Ave. (at Madeline next to Bret Harte Jr. High), Oakland 94602. (510) 482-4093. Wed and Sat 10 am–3 pm. Cash, checks.

Only the most determined thrift shoppers know about this off-the-beaten-track thrift shop. Located in the former caretaker's cottage of the Fred Finch Youth Center, its four-plus rooms are filled with a haphazard collection of either junk or treasures, according to your likes. The store is staffed by volunteers from the Methodist Church which sponsors it. "Everybody marks," one charming elderly volunteer explained, "so we have the cheapest prices in town." She may be right. One man's junk may be another man's treasure, but these markers seem to consider almost everything junk and mark it accordingly. They have radios for $3, working clocks for $1–$2, and dishes for 5¢–10¢.

You will find more clothing than anything else. Nothing is particularly high style, but everything is cheap. Although an occasional vintage treasure does sneak through, the volunteers have no use for old (vintage) clothes and send them along to the Salvation Army with all the other rejects. The ladies will often take extra special things home to wash and iron, but otherwise everything is sold as is. If you're willing to dig through a lot of junk, there is a distinct possibility of making that great discovery thrift shoppers dream of. To add to the already great bargain prices, everything is half off in July, since the shop is closed for the month of August and reopens in September with all new merchandise. As final bonuses, *Fred Finch* charges no sales tax and has a table with free coffee and cookies.
Charity: Fred Finch Youth Center, a residential treatment center for boys and girls with emotional, psychiatric and medical problems
Everything except large appliances and large pieces of furniture

GOLDSTEEN'S

5219 Foothill Blvd., Oakland 94601, (510) 533-5850. Mon–Sat 12 am–6 pm. Cash, checks.

You'll find a diverse assortment of goods at *Goldsteen's*, ranging from fine antiques to balloons, with costume jewelry and ordinary housewares in between.

Everything except clothing

GOODWILL

2925 East 14th St. (at 29th), Oakland 94601, (510) 534-3037. Mon–Sat 10 am–6 pm, Sun 11 am–6 pm. Cash, checks, MC/ VISA.

Of the two Oakland locations, the East 14th St. *Goodwill* is larger and less upscale, but it offers the same great buys.

Charity: Goodwill

Clothing and housewares

GOODWILL AS IS

2925 East 14th St. (at 29th), Oakland 94601, (510) 534-3037. Mon–Fri 8:30 am–9 am. Cash.

Only confirmed thrift shoppers (or students of humanity) will want to check this one out. Every weekday morning, beginning exactly at 8:30 am, Lucky McGilbert auctions off Goodwill "as is" merchandise by the cartload. A cartload could be anything from a closet-full of clothing to a zoo-full of stuffed animals to a brace of bicycles or a herd of appliances. You never know what's going to be on the block; the only thing you can be sure of is that the bargains will knock your socks off. Try fifteen working refrigerators for $60. You can't beat that (if you have use for fifteen refrigerators). The show starts promptly at 8:30 am, so be sure to be there on time!

Charity: Goodwill

Everything

LYDIA THE PURPLE MERCHANT

3129 High St., Oakland 94619, (510) 532-9149. Tues–Fri 4 pm–8 pm, Sat 12 am–6 pm. Cash, checks, MC/VISA/AM EX.

At the end of a long, hot day we popped into *Lydia The Purple Merchant*, expecting to be on our way home shortly. But we found ourselves so enchanted that we stayed for hours. To begin with, we fell in love with Lydia (dressed, as always, from head to toe in purple) and her contagious enthusiasm for all things old and lovely. First, she showed us her treasured collection of beaded purses. And then we needed to examine a wardrobe of exquisite dresses from the 1930's and 1940's and read what the original owner had written about each garment—where and when she wore it, what accessories she wore with it, and when she retired it. Next, we had to check out Lydia's Afro-centric wares and get a brief lesson in African textiles. Every time we prepared to leave, Lydia uncovered new treasures; once she opened an armoire stuffed with Victorian garments, including a lovely wedding dress

Right: Goodwill As Is, Oakland.

with a nineteen-inch waist. Another time she presented us with a box of silk undergarments, all in perfect condition, from the 1920's. Lydia confessed that her store is just an excuse to collect. She finds it hard to part with her treasures, but she is more than happy to rent all gowns, formal wear, and day dresses. Lydia specializes in vintage (especially 1950's) garments for men, women, and children, and she also creates reproduction poodle skirts, as well as Afro-centric hats and jewelry of her own design. Prices are not marked; ask Lydia for her estimate.
Men's and women's clothing

OAKLAND PENIEL MISSION
3550 East 14th St., Oakland 94601, (510) 532-5144. Mon–Sat 9:30 am–4:30 pm. Cash, local checks.

This is what I would call a hard-core thrift shop: a big gloomy store with the paint peeling off the walls, scarred linoleum curling up to show the cement subfloor beneath, and prices so low it's scary. Lots of thrift stores tell you they carry a little bit of everything, but when manager Kevin Williams says it, he really means it. Besides the usual—clothing, furniture, knickknacks, and housewares—he even sells drums of paint. There are no set prices...everything's negotiable and sometimes things are just given away. A working color television set was going for about $50, sofas for $50–$75, and clothing (you'll find it upstairs) is priced cheap, from 50¢

for t-shirts to $5 for a man's suit. Dresses and shirts are $1, pants and shoes are $2. Kevin was selling all the eating utensils for 10¢ a piece, but Jobyna and I tried to convince him that the silver ones should cost more than the plastic. *Charity: Oakland Peniel Mission, a non-denominational organization which provides food, clothing, and shelter for the homeless*
Everything except large appliances

OVER & OVER THRIFT
5926 Foothill Blvd. (at Seminary), Oakland 94605, (510) 638-2447. Mon–Sat 10 am–5 pm. Cash, local checks.

Another proprietor with a strong emotional attachment to her wares, Agnes Bye vows she'll sell anything, regardless of what it is, if it's usable and in good shape. The merchandise in her big, crowded store attests to that. You name it, she sells it: furniture, both antique and just old; toys; television sets; old radios; clothes; bric-a-brac....There are no prices. "Make an offer, we'll bargain," says Agnes. We saw a women on her way to a funeral stop off to pick up a suitable black dress for $4. We bargained for a pair of stuffed ducks from a taxidermy shop and reached a price of $20, and then we looked at a teak pineapple-shaped hors d'oeuvres tray...well, we didn't reach a price on that one. I was especially intrigued by a 3-foot-high terra-cotta vase covered with a

collage of magazine photos, but Agnes wasn't interested in selling. Most things are for sale, and the price is usually right.
Everything

RALPH'S THRIFT SHOP
3700 Foothill Blvd. (between Harrington and 38th), Oakland 94601, (510) 534-9534. Mon–Sat 11 am–5 pm. Cash.
Formerly *La Gallinita, Ralph's* could use a little organization. Everything is there, but the question is whether it's worth the effort it takes to find it. No marked prices (you have to ask), but according to the owner's pleasant daughter they're flexible.
Everything

ST. VINCENT DE PAUL
9235 San Leandro (between 92nd and 98th), Oakland 94603, (510) 638-1996. Mon–Thurs 8:30 am–4:15 pm, Fri 8:30 am–3:55 pm, Sat 9 am–4:45 pm, Sun 12 am–4:45 pm. Cash, checks, MC/VISA.

ST. VINCENT DE PAUL AS IS
9235 San Leandro (between 92nd and 98th), Oakland 94603, (510) 638-1996. Tues–Fri 12 am–3 pm, Sat 9 am–4:30 pm. Cash.
Come at lunchtime Tuesday through Friday and you are guaranteed to find at least a dozen people lined up waiting for the doors to open at St. *Vincent de Paul As Is.* Prepare yourself for the mad rush when the whistle blows at high noon—die-hard thrift shoppers bring their own box and grab what

they want from the extraordinary selection. Among the thousands of items you might find (to just touch the surface) are shoes, puzzles, skis and ski boots, water skis, thermos jugs, medicine chests, windows, doors, sinks, toys, books, bowling balls, and more. New merchandise is put out each day. The price list on the wall singles out a dozen or so items; shoes are $1, puzzles are 10¢. For anything else, you show what you found to the manager and she names her price. The going rate seems to be $3 a box, so the more you get, the better the price. Evaluations offered by happy shoppers: "It's a great pastime." "This is my favorite place." "I come here every day!" If you are a serious thrift shopper—be there!

Maybe you're not thrift shopping for the thrill of it; you're just someone with needs bigger than your budget. In that case, you can't go wrong at the more sedate *St. Vincent* store on the same premises. Like the downtown Oakland store, this enormous warehouse excels in furniture values. With sofas going for $20, upholstered chairs for $15, and tables for $15, you really can furnish a house with almost no money. Their big selection of new furniture is a bit more expensive, but it's still a good buy. Half of this huge store features clothing.
Charity: St. Vincent de Paul
Everything

THE PUMP HOUSE
Salem Lutheran House, 2361 East 29th St. (at 23rd Avenue),

Oakland 94606, (510) 261-1406.
Tues and Thurs 10 am–3 pm.
Cash, checks.

Get out your map and plot a course
to this out-of-the-way little jewel. A
temporary reduction in size during
construction at the Salem Lutheran
Home only means that the goodies
are more tightly packed in this
shop, formerly a pump house. I
could tell it was full of bargains in
housewares, clothing, and knickknacks, but my niece Eden, who
came along for the ride, ended up
with an armful of treasures: a
wicker suitcase for storing linens
for $1, a necklace of beautiful gold
and Venetian glass beads for $1,
enamel chrysanthemum earrings
for her aunt for $1, a Fathers' Day
card for her grandfather for 10¢,
and two 1950's aluminum drinking
glasses for 10¢ each. She passed
up a classic 1950's arm chair for
$10 and several pieces of 1950's
jewelry. The jewelry was all under
$1 and, Eden explained to me, the
latest style. Exactly what they're
showing in Macy's today, she said.
*Charity: Provides programs to
add to the comfort and pleasures
of the residents of Salem Luthren
House senior retirement home*
**Everything except large
appliances**

Lakeshore Avenue/ ~~~ Grand Avenue ~~~

**AMERICAN CANCER SOCIETY
DISCOVERY SHOP**
3241 Grand Ave., Oakland 94610,

*(510) 452-2201. Mon–Fri 10 am–5
pm, Sat 10 am–4 pm. Cash,
checks, MC/VISA.*

You might walk right by their
windows featuring the latest styles
with no idea that the *Discovery
Shop* is a thrift store. Inside,
elegantly displayed merchandise
confirms the impression that you
are in a boutique. The *Discovery
Shop* is one of the most elegant
thrift shops in Oakland, and
probably one of the most expensive. If you are looking for something funky, or you're on a tight
budget and looking for well-made
garments under $10, the *Discovery
Shop* is not for you. But if you're in
the market for a designer gown that
retails for $500, you may find it
here for $50. Fashion-conscious
women who know and love
designer clothes but are not
prepared to pay the exorbitant
prices will find superbly made
garments and elegant accessories
at a fraction of what they cost new.

The best selection is in women's
clothing. The smaller selections of
men's and children's clothing offer
excellent quality for prices in a
slightly lower range. All garments
are steamed before they are put on
the floor. Local merchants and
manufacturers occasionally donate
seconds or end-of-season items, so
you can usually find a smattering of
new clothes: a rack of leather
jackets, last year's workout togs, or
samples from the Gap. A local
hatmaker periodically donates
marvelous hats (around $20 each).
The last week of the month all

clothes that have been on the floor for two months are reduced to half off. At the end of the week, everything that hasn't sold goes to the $1 rack, and then off to the Salvation Army. *Discovery Shop* also carries furniture, books, records, and housewares. There are rarely spectacular bargains, but they do get unusual and beautiful pieces of furniture and collectibles. *Charity: American Cancer Society, which supports cancer research, education, and direct service to patients* **Everything except large appliances**

CLOTHESPORT
3702 Grand Ave., Oakland 94610, (510) 893-8194. Tues–Sat 11 am–4 pm. Cash, checks, MC/VISA.
Women who want to do well while doing good consign their clothes at the *Clothesport*, the oldest consignment shop on Grand Avenue, where 50% of the selling price supports charitable projects. Whatever your size or style, you'll have plenty of shopping options at this tastefully arranged shop. Good buys on upscale clothing are the rule here; a designer specials rack features Laura Ashley for $38, Lily Ann for $48, Diane Fries for $62, and Albert Nipon for $68. A corner devoted to larger sizes had elegant suits and MOB (mother of the bride) dresses. They stock sports wear, career wear, and dressy outfits year round and formals and long gowns for the holidays. There is always a half-off rack, and half-

off-everything sales happen twice a year.
Consignment: Tues–Fri 11 am–4 pm, Sat by appointment, 50/50 split
Charity: Women's American ORT, which supports the World ORT Union, a world-wide vocational and technical education program **Women's clothing**

COLLECTABLE DESIGNS
3344 Grand Ave., Oakland 94610, (510) 444-2953. Mon–Fri 11 am–6 pm, Sat 11 am–5 pm. Cash, checks, MC/VISA, 30-day layaway with 50% down.
Oakland's Grand Avenue is fast becoming a mecca for secondhand bargain hunters; a new resale store seems to open every day. Women with a taste for designer clothes who are fed up with paying four figures for a single item of clothing should head for Corella Ford's *Collectable Designs*, the Avenue's most upscale resale boutique, which features designer fashions by the likes of Bill Blass, Albert Nipon, Oscar de la Renta, Valentino, and Victor Costa. This clothing once hung on the racks of I Magnin, Saks Fifth Avenue, Neiman-Marcus, and Irene Sergeant. Brown, a reformed shopaholic, feels it is important to provide the same gracious setting and personalized service you would expect to find in a downtown department store or exclusive boutique. Low prices, 30% less than retail, are the only indication that you are in a consignment shop. *Collectible Designs* features shoes

that are just like new; fabulous hats; accessories; and dressy, career, and formal wear in sizes 2–26.

Consignment: By appointment, 40% consignor/60% store
Women's clothing

DRESSING UP

3231 Grand Ave., Oakland 94610, (510) 893-0123. Tues–Fri 10 am–6 pm, Sat 10 am–5:30 pm. Cash, checks, MC/VISA.

For a small store, *Dressing Up* has a lot happening. The friendly staff can help you find the perfect outfit, whether it's from the stock of both used and new current clothing, a vintage garment from the 1920's through the 1960's, or a costume from their huge supply. You can become a flapper, pirate, French maid, Cleopatra, clown, nun, monk, priest, devil....Costumes rented by the day may be reserved in advance.

Dressing Up specializes in vintage women's clothing from the 1930's and 1940's; draped rayon crepe dresses ($75–$125); cocktail hats; bakelite and rhinestone jewelry; and alligator, beaded, and mesh handbags. Some pieces were formerly owned by movie stars and celebrities. *Dressing Up* also carries new glitzy party dresses. As vintage items become harder to find, owner Donna Verner predicts the percentage of new garments will steadily increase.
Women's clothing

IT'S YOUR SECRET

3421 Grand Ave., Oakland 94610, (510) 444-0872. Tues–Fri 11 am–6 pm, Sat 10 am–6 pm. Cash, checks.

A new kid on the block, *It's Your Secret* was welcomed to Grand Avenue by smart women shopping for bargains in barely worn finery. Stocking a little bit of everything, from casual to very dressy in sizes 2–24, this elegant resale boutique usually has new and used wedding gowns, evening gowns, MOB (mother of the bride) dresses, and cruise-wear. Owner Rosemarie Morton (who prefers to buy from clients' homes) delights in finding the exact item a customer is looking for. Her shop is small, but very select, and gets extra points for personal service.
Women's clothing

JAZZIROB

3704 Grand Ave., Oakland 94610, (510) 834-2226. Tues–Sun 10 am–6 pm. Cash, checks, MC/VISA.

A pink and blue confection named for the proprietor's children Jasmine and Robi, *Jazzirob* had been open for all of two weeks when we made our visit. It sells new and used clothing for boys and girls sizes newborn–12, as well as children's equipment and furniture. The new items outnumber the used, but owner Dorit Tomelden expects the ratio to change as parents learn about this darling store. A kid's corner, complete with a VCR showing kid's films, keeps children occupied while you shop.

Consignment: Fri and Sat 10 am–
6 pm, mostly buys outright,
furniture taken on consignment
**Children's clothing and
equipment**

UHURU FURNITURE ETC.
*3742 Grand Ave., Oakland 94610,
(510) 763-3342. Mon–Sat 10 am–7
pm. Cash, checks.*
You can usually depend on the
sidewalk display in front of *Uhuru* to
tempt you inside. Featuring mostly
used furniture for home and office
as well as some seconds and
overruns donated by local busi-
nesses, they seem to get their fair
share of attractive almost-antiques,
as well as the regular secondhand
stuff. *Uhuru* recently opened up a
back room which stocks clothing
and books to add their odd assortment of thrift shop junk, but the
best buys here are clearly furniture.
They gladly pick up donations.
*Charity: Uhuru House, which
defends the democratic rights of
the African Community*
Everything

VIRGIE'S RAGS
*3419 Lakeshore Ave., Oakland
94610, (510) 444-RAGS. Mon–Sat
10 am–6 pm. Cash, checks, MC/
VISA.*
Since opening the first resale store
on upscale Lakeshore Avenue,
Virgie Devera has built up a client
base of working women, many of
them single parents who can't
spend all their pay on clothing for
themselves and their children.

Selling most items at 1/4 of retail
price or less, *Virgie's* has merchandise so moderately priced that
customers claim she undersells
local thrift stores. All merchandise
in the back room of this long,
narrow shop is half off. Stock is
evenly divided between kids'
clothing (sizes newborn-12) and
women's sports and work wear
(sizes 3-18). She carries a few new
items, mostly dressy dresses for
little girls.
*Consignment: Tues–Sat 10 am–
12:30 pm, 50/50 split, 60-day
contract*
**Women's and children's
clothing**

~~~~~ **Montclair** ~~~~~

CAN YOU KEEP A SECRET
*1986 Mountain Blvd., upstairs
(across from Lucky parking lot),
Oakland 94611, (510) 339-9068.
Mon–Sat 10 am–5:30 pm. Cash,
checks, MC/VISA.*
Although her second-time-around
shop is the first of its kind in the
high-rent business district of tony
Montclair Village, proprietor Glenda
Yates has had no trouble attracting
customers and consignors to her
upscale consignment boutique.
Yates only carries items that will
sell in her area, and that means
good labels on recent styles in top
condition (sizes 2–24). Casual to
dressy, her clothes bear labels like
Rothschild, Liz Claiborne, Hana
Sung, and Ann Taylor. It's a
pleasure to browse through the

racks in this light, airy second-story shop. The clothes are lovely and Yates is charming and friendly. While prices may seem high, if you shop labels you'll know what a great deal you're getting. This is an especially good place to shop for holiday party outfits, theater and opera gowns, and special occasion clothing like dresses for brides-maids and mothers of the bride.
Consignment: Anytime, 40% consignor/60% store
Women's clothing

∿∿ Piedmont Avenue ∿∿

CRACKERJACKS
14 Glen Ave. (off Piedmont), Oakland 94611, (510) 654-8844. Mon–Fri 10 am–5:30 pm, Sat 1 pm–5 pm. Cash, checks, MC/ VISA.

Because kids grow so fast, more and more smart parents are heading to *Crackerjacks*, where they can buy their kids' fine-quality used merchandise for half the cost of new (if not less). Clothing fits boys and girls sizes 0-14. The store is large, cute, and well stocked. New items from local artists and designers are almost irresistible.
Buys: 40% customer/60% store in cash, 50/50 split in trade
Children's clothing, furniture, toys, books

DRESS BEST FOR LESS
3820 Piedmont Ave. (between Yosemite and Rio Vista), Oakland 94611, (510) 658-8525. Tues–Sat 11 am–4 pm. Cash, checks.

As one would expect from a thrift store supported by residents of ritzy Piedmont, *Dress Best for Less* features quality goods. The major portion of the merchandise in this small, very neat shop is clothing, all cleaned and pressed, boasting labels like Norma Kamali, Liz Claiborne, Jones New York, Diane Fries, and Adolfo that can be found in finer Bay Area stores. Prices run higher than most thrift stores—men's suits go for $35, sports coats are $30–$34, and children's dresses $12–$15—but everything goes to half price after one month. Check out the 50¢ box for small bargains.
Charity: Piedmont Education Foundation, which supports Piedmont schools
Housewares; clothing for men, women, and children

SOPHISTICATED LADY
4020 Piedmont Ave., Oakland 94611, (510) 654-1718. Mon–Sat 10 am–6 pm. Cash, check, MC/ VISA.

Pampering and bargain hunting don't usually go hand in hand, but *Sophisticated Lady* is the exception that proves the rule. Best described as the Nordstrom of consignment shops, this elegant boutique spares no effort to make you feel like a spoiled darling. The dressing rooms, for example, not only boast chairs, flowers, and three-way mirrors, but each one also provides a lovely kimono for you to don so you can go back out to the selling floor without having to get dressed. Good service is guaranteed by having at least two sales people on the floor at all times. *Sophisticated Lady*'s merchandise reflects the broad client base, which includes young working women as well as Piedmont matrons. They stock everything from casual sportswear to bridal gowns, all selling at 1/4 to 1/3 retail. Their astounding selection of formal wear—much of it never-been-worn designer gowns on consignment from a Bay Area formal attire rental store—includes designers like Victor Costa, Holly Harp, Tadaski, and a host of others. These are the truly spectacular bargains—$900 dresses for $135.

Budget-minded brides will be pleased to learn that *Sophisticated Lady* is helping *Clausen House Thrift Shop* sell its bonanza of beautiful, never-been-worn Jessica McClintock wedding dresses, all priced under $200. You can have your dream wedding dress and support a worthy cause at the same time. The final note of grace: your purchase will be wrapped in lavender tissue paper and sealed with a silver sticker.
Consignment: Mon–Sat 11 am–5 pm by appointment, 50/50 split, 10-week contract
Women's clothing

~~~~ Rockridge ~~~~

ALTA BATES SHOWCASE
5615 College Ave., Oakland 94618, (510) 653-1527. Mon–Sat 10 am–2:45 pm. Cash, checks.
Aptly named, this large airy store is a showcase for first-class second-hand goods. Overall, clothing for the whole family is top quality and extremely reasonably priced. You can always find some designer labels; a friend recently came away with a stunning Ellen Tracy suit for $7. Furniture, when available, gets snapped up quickly, as it is usually high quality and a good value. Prices on antiques and collectibles can be on the high side, but you can count on the selection to offer temptations you'll find hard to resist. This is a large store with a lot of merchandise, but don't neglect the everyday household goods, books, and costume jewelry.
Charity: Alta Bates-Herrick Hospital and Hospice
Everything except large appliances

BABY WORLD
5854 College Ave., Oakland 94618, (510) 655-2950. Mon–Fri 10 am–6 pm, Sat 10 am–5 pm, Sun 12 am–5 pm. Cash, check, MC/VISA.
This crowded store sells children's toys, equipment, furniture, and some clothing for boys and girls sizes newborn–10. They pay cash up front and will pick up items from your home by appointment.
Buys: By appointment, 40% customer/60% store in cash, 60% customer/40% store in trade
Children's clothing, equipment, and furniture

BIZARRE BAZAAR

5634 College Ave., Oakland 94618, (510) 655-2909. Mon–Sat 11 am–6 pm. Cash, checks, MC/ VISA.

From the patterned carpet on the floor (rescued from the defunct T & D theatre in downtown Oakland) to the art deco mirror on the wall (a relic from the old Fillmore), *Bizarre Bazaar*, a 26-year veteran in the vintage business, is long on atmosphere. The vintage garments, dating from the Victorian era through the early 1960's, are all firsts—no "as is" here. Sports clothes, day wear, evening dresses, and even wedding gowns—you'll find everything, including a magnificent assortment of vintage jewelry. Good tuxedos go for $125–$175, evening gowns average $125.

Men's and women's vintage clothing, some children's clothing

ECONOMY CORNER #1

6042 College Ave., Oakland 94618, (510) 650-9485. Tues–Sat 10 am–2:45 pm. Cash.

Collectible lovers will thrill to the sight of the merchandise here and tremble with joy when they get a load of the incredibly low prices. Antiques of obvious value (and there are many) are locked in a case and priced only slightly higher than the knickknacks that fill shelf after shelf. A lot of good things, like artificial flowers, cameras, and party supplies, are hidden away in drawers or perched out of sight on high shelves, so don't forget to investigate every nook and cranny. There's no telling what you will find on the clothing racks: always bargains, and often genuine vintage articles mixed in with the old and tired. Small household items are great buys here—we saw a brass and crystal lamp for $1. Furniture is sold at *Economy Corner #2* on Telegraph Avenue.

Charity: Children's Home Society of California

Everything except furniture and large appliances

MADAME BUTTERFLY

5474 College Ave., Oakland 94618, (510) 653-1525. Tues–Sun 11 am–6 pm. Cash, checks, MC/ VISA.

Madame Butterfly proves the old adage about good things coming in little packages. This small store is packed full of wonderful vintage wear from the 1920's through the 1960's. Gorgeous gowns are displayed on the walls and the racks are full of first quality vintage in beautiful condition. Pre-1940's day dresses run $30–$40 and evening gowns are $40–$70, but items from the 1950's are more reasonable. Carrying both men's and women's (sizes 3–16) clothing, *Madame Butterfly* also stocks contemporary clothing on consignment. You will also find some new items and exquisite vintage jewelry.

Consignment: Tues–Fri 11 am–6 pm, 50/50 split

Men's and women's clothing

O'TOOLE'S

*5638 College Ave., Oakland
94618, (510) 428-1009. Mon–Sat
9:30 am–6 pm, Sun 11 am–5 pm.
Cash, checks, MC/VISA.*

O'Toole's has so many articles of kids' clothing for sale that the racks are stacked to the ceiling and 300–400 new pieces are added every day. For quantity in the children's resale market, you can't beat O'Toole's. You can outfit your boys and girls from head to toe, if they wear sizes 0–8. In addition to a few thousand books, O'Toole's stocks toys, equipment, and furniture, all selling at half the original price.
Buys: By appointment
Children's clothing and equipment

PIERRE'S ONCE UPON A TIME

*5332 College Ave., Oakland
94618, (510) 653-2924. Mon–Sat
11:30 am–7 pm. Cash, checks,
MC/VISA.*

Once upon a time a cool princess pledged her troth to a hip prince, after which they hopped into their coach and cantered down to Pierre's, where she found the vintage wedding gown of her dreams for only $150 and he picked up a nifty 1950's evening jacket embellished with hand-painted squiggles. Commoners can also find vintage fashions in this bright, spacious store, mostly clothing from the 1940's through 1960's, with a few older "as is" items thrown in. Vintage dresses run $18–$100; shoes are $15–$30. *Once Upon a Time* also carries contemporary clothing, custom designs, lingerie, and accessories.
*Consignment: By appointment,
55% consignor/45% store*
Men's and women's clothing

ROCKRIDGE RAGS

*5711 College Ave., Oakland
94610, (510) 655-2289. Mon–Sat
10 am–6 pm, Sun 11 am–5 pm.
Cash, checks, MC/VISA.*

Savvy Bay Area bargain hunters who were shopping in consignment stores before the rest of us knew what the word meant were probably snapping up the good buys at *Rockridge Rags*. One of the first consignment stores in the East Bay, the eleven year-old veteran pioneered men's resale in the area. Expanded now to three stores, *Rockridge Rags* offers a huge inventory without feeling crowded. They specialize in contemporary casual and career wear for men and women, geared to the middle market, although you will find upper-end items and MOB (mother of the bride) dresses year round and cocktail dresses during the holiday season.
*Consignment: Tues–Sat 10 am–
12:30 pm, Thurs 5 pm–7 pm, 50/
50 split, 7-week contract*
Men's and women's clothing

~~~~ Temescal ~~~~

CLAUSEN HOUSE THRIFT SHOP

*5000 Telegraph Ave., Oakland
94609, (510) 653-4831. Mon–Sat
10 am–4 pm. Cash.*

Crowded but organized, *Clausen House* specializes in household items like bric-a-brac, dishes, linens, games, small appliances, art objects, and books, as well as clothing for men, women, and children. Everything is sold at low prices for rapid turn-over.
Charity: Clausen House, which provides education and training of mentally handicapped adults
Everything but large appliances and large pieces of furniture

CONSIGNMENTS UNLIMITED
6020 Adeline St., Oakland 94608, (510) 652-6036. Tues–Fri 10 am–6 pm, Sat 10 am–5 pm. Cash, checks.

They really do carry everything here except large appliances, weapons, and cameras. You will find furs, pressure cookers, lawn mowers, floor polishers, tricycles, drafting tables, and clothes. The clothes are real cheap, and the rest is reasonable. Prices are firm (no negotiating), but reductions occur on a regular basis. The merchandise in this large room lit by sky lights is so varied it's impossible to define the scope. The staff is friendly and the resident pooch, an Afghan/shepherd mix wearing a lace collar, is as exotic as the merchandise.
Consignment: Tues–Sat 10 am–2

~~~~~~~~~~~~~~~~~~~~~~~~~~~~~~~~~

Left: Bonnie Simon at Felino's Vintage Clothing, San Francisco.

pm, 50/50 split, 60-day contract
Everything but large appliances

GRANDMA'S ATTIC
354 42nd St. (next to Oakland Tech High school), Oakland 94609, (510) 654-3764. Tues and Fri 11 am–3 pm. Cash.

A small sign lettered in Old English script is the only indication that this little jewel exists. A short walk down a tree-shaded drive will lead you to a quaint red building primly trimmed in white. The door, flanked by benches and planters, even sports a horseshoe above. Inside, you will find a large front room holding clothing, books, records, shelves of bric-a-brac, and locked cases with jewelry and valuables. The smaller back room offers an assortment of kitchen goods, toys, games, luggage, sporting equipment, and an occasional pair of crutches or a wheelchair. If you are setting up a first kitchen, you can't beat their bargain prices on everyday household goods. A nickel can buy you a mug, a dime brings a cup and saucer, a quarter will get you a dinner plate, and five dollars gets a working waffle iron. The best selection and greatest buys are to be found in women's clothing; everything is in good to excellent condition. Without high fashion or funk, *Grandma's* garments stand out for their timeless, classic styling; quality fabrics; good labels; and great prices. A wool Evan Picone suit was $3, a long gown from Saks Fifth Avenue was $4, and an I Magnin black velvet evening coat cost $7.50. Men's clothing is of equally high quality and classic styling for good prices: suits were $6, a Pendleton robe was $7.50, a cashmere blazer cost $3, dress shirts were $2, and tuxedo shirts were $4. You can try on your picks in the spacious newly remodeled dressing room equipped with a large wall mirror, carpeting, benches, and clothes rack. Once a year *Grandma's Attic* holds a half-off-everything sale.

Charity: Matilda E. Brown Home, a non-profit retirement residence for elderly women

Everything except furniture and large appliances

SEAMS TO FIT

6577 Telegraph Ave. (between Ashby and Alcatraz), Oakland 94609, (510) 428-9463. Mon–Fri 11 am–6 pm, Sat 10 am–6 pm, Sun 12 am–4 pm. Cash, checks, MC/VISA/AM EX.

If you love the fashions but not the prices at *Says Who*, a large-size boutique on Piedmont Avenue, you will be happy to discover their clearance center, *Seams To Fit*. Well stocked with casual, career, and dressy clothing in sizes 14–28, *Seams To Fit* merchandise includes discounted seconds, new overruns from the manufacturer, final sales merchandise from *Says Who* discounted 40%–50%, and good quality consignment clothing with name brands like Elizabeth, Chaus, and Nancy Heller. The staff is friendly and flexible when it comes

to prices. You can also get your hair styled and cut to go with your glamorous new duds.

Consignment: 40% consignor/ 60% store in cash, 50/50 split in trade, 60-day contract

Women's large-size clothing

~~~~ West Oakland ~~~~

EAST BAY DEPOT FOR CREATIVE RE-USE

1027 60th St. Oakland 94608, (510) 547-6470. Tues, Thurs, Sat 10:30 am–4:30. Cash, checks.

Come dressed for combat and with an open mind to this former firehouse that has been converted into a wonderland of possibilities. Since 1970, Bay Area teachers, artists, and social workers have been coming here to sift through mountains of household, office, and industrial discards for materials to create art and science projects. You can fill a brown paper grocery bag to the brim for $3 and walk away with gorgeous stuff—paints and brushes, carpet samples, foam rubber, paper and letterhead, dried flowers, wood scraps, glitter and sequins, greeting card sample books, corks, beads, stickers and seals, wallpaper, office supplies, frames and matt boards, buckles, buttons, zippers, fabric, plastic...to name but a few. You never know what you'll find, because new stuff arrives every day. Most of it is donated by Bay Area manufacturers and retailers—Amsterdam Arts, Esprit, Jeanne Marc (quilters will be in heaven when they see the bolts of fabric and trims), Furry Folk Puppets, Precision Die Cutting, UC Berkeley, and private individuals. And everything here is recycled. *The Depot* was founded by a group of school teachers who gathered materials from local businesses and made them available for classroom needs. Now anyone can prospect for treasures in this gold mine of creative reuse. Bring the kids (they'll love it) and sign up for family art classes, including Junque Jewelry and Robots, Robots, Robots!!!

Charity: The East Bay Depot serves educational institutions, cultural organizations and non-profit agencies
Household, office, and industrial discards

GOODWILL
6624 San Pablo Ave., Oakland 94608, (510) 428-4911. Mon–Sat 10 am–7 pm, Sun 11 am–6 pm. Cash, checks, MC/VISA.

A zoo full of stuffed animals, furniture, and the usual good buys in clothing are all to be found at this *Goodwill.*

Charity: Goodwill
Everything except large appliances

ALAMEDA COUNTY (Oakland)	Appliances/large	Bridal	Clothing/children	Clothing/men	Clothing/women	Collectibles	Furnishings/children	Furniture	Housewares	Maternity	Tools, etc.	Toys	Vintage	Page number
DOWNTOWN														
Beehive Thrift Shop			X	X	X	X	X	X	X		X	X		31
Economy Corner #2	X		X	X	X	X	X	X	X		X	X		31
Encore			X	X	X	X	X		X		X	X		32
Goodwill		X	X	X	X	X			X					32
St. Vincent de Paul	X	X	X	X	X	X	X	**X**	X	X	X	X		32
The Shop			X	X	**X**	X	X	X	**X**	X		X		33
Yvette's Boutique					X									34
EAST OAKLAND														
Coliseum Swap Meet	X	X	X	X	X	X	X	X	X	X	X	X	X	35
Fred Finch Thrift			X	X	X	X	X	X	X		X	X		35
Goldsteen's	X				X	X	X	X			X	X		36
Goodwill		X	X	X	X	X			X					36
Goodwill As Is	X	X	X	X	X	X	X	X	X	X	X	X		36
Lydia the Purple			X	X									X	36
Oakland Mission			X	X	X	X	X	X	X		X	X		38
Over & Over Thrift	X		X	X	X	X	X	X	X		X	X		38
Ralph's Thrift Shop	X		X	X	X	X	X		X		X	X		39
St. Vincent de Paul	X	X	X	X	X	X	X	X	X	X	X	X		39
Pump House			X	X	X	X	X	X						39
LKSHR./GRAND AVE.														
Discovery Shop		X	X	X	X	X	X	X	X	X		X		40
Clothesport					X									41
Collectable Designs					X									41
Dressing Up					X								X	42
It's Your Secret					X									42
Jazzirob			X			X						X		42
Uhuru			X	X	X	X	X	X			X			43
Virgie's Rags			X		X									43
MONTCLAIR														
Can You Keep					X									43
PIEDMONT AVENUE														
Crackerjacks			X				X					X		44
Dress Best for Less			X	X	X	X			X			X		44

ALAMEDA COUNTY (Oakland)	Appliances/large	Bridal	Clothing/children	Clothing/men	Clothing/women	Collectibles	Furnishings/children	Furniture	Housewares	Maternity	Tools, etc.	Toys	Vintage	Page number
Sophisticated Lady	X				X									44
ROCKRIDGE														
Alta Bates Showcase			X	X	X	X	X	X	X	X		X		45
Baby World			X				X					X		45
Bizarre Bazaar			X	X	X								X	46
Economy Corner #1			X	X	X	X	X		X		X	X		46
Madame Butterfly			X	X									X	46
O'Toole's			X				X					X		47
Pierre's Once Upon			X	X									X	47
Rockridge Rags			X	X										47
TEMESCAL														
Clausen House Thrift	X		X	X	X	X	X	X	X	X	X	X		47
Consignments Unltd.	X	X	X	X	X	X	X	X	X	X	X			49
Grandma's Attic			X	X	X	X	X	X	X		X	X		49
Seams to Fit					X									50
WEST OAKLAND														
East Bay Depot						X			X		**X**			50
Goodwill			X	X	X	X	X	X	X	X	X	X		51

~~~~~ Clayton ~~~~~

EMILY'S WARDROBE
6064 Main St., Clayton 94517, (510) 672-4759. Tues–Sat 10 am– 4:30 pm. Cash, checks, MC/VISA.
A cute little house surrounded by a white picket fence in the quaint little town of Clayton holds a new (opened March 1992) upscale women's consignment shop. With its moss-green carpet, striped wallpaper, and chintz-covered slipper chair, *Emily's Wardrobe* is every bit as adorable inside as out and offers an upbeat selection of women's clothing, labels good to better in sizes 4–18, selling for 1/3 of their retail price. Emily shares the space with a design studio and gallery featuring the work of local artists and a pottery studio.
Consignment: Anytime, 50/50 split
Women's clothing

~~~~~ Concord ~~~~~

CLAUSEN HOUSE THRIFT SHOP
3616 Willow Pass Road (in Monte Gardens shopping center), Concord 94519, (510) 680-0878. Mon–Sat 10 am–4 pm. Cash, checks.
You couldn't fit another piece of merchandise into this small shop if you tried, and yet, somehow, everything seems to be in perfect order. *Clausen House* has your usual thrift store jumble of clothing, housewares, and bric-a-brac, with unusually good prices on every- thing, especially household goods—a cup and saucer set for 50¢, dinner plates for 35¢. They have their fair share of collectibles, also well priced (although I wish they wouldn't write the prices directly on the item). One satisfied customer said she was pleased with every *Clausen House* purchase she'd ever made; she singled out their jewelry and book selections for special praise. "Every day is a good day at *Clausen House*, and some days," she added, "you hit a bonanza." We did see one happy young woman walk out with one of the ubiquitous new Jessica McClintock wedding gowns under her arm. Since *Clausen House* prices for these beauties run $35– $100, we had to consider the day of our vist one of the bonanza days.
Charity: Clausen House, which provides retarded adults with day and vocational programs and residences
Everything except furniture and large appliances

THE CLOTHESLINE
3490 Clayton Rd. (rear, across from Goodwill), Concord 94519, (510) 676-8066. Mon–Sat 11 am– 4:30 pm. Cash, checks.

The Clothesline is a no-nonsense kind of place: the atmosphere is strictly utilitarian (the ceiling insulation shows) and the merchandise is mid-priced casual wear (no formals) at very good prices. You'll see more labels from the Emporium than from Nordstrom. Owner Lynn Adams, a straightforward type, describes her pricing system as "a guess and by golly. If I would pay something, I put that on." Everything is reduced by 20% after 30 days, goes to half off after 2 months, and then moves to the last chance: the $3 rack. This system keeps the merchandise moving, and the selection is good, especially in lingerie, sweats, and large sizes.
Consignment: Mon–Fri 11 am–3 pm, 50/50 split
Women's and children's clothing

CONCORD BI-ANNUAL FLEA MARKET
2000 Kirker Pass Rd., Concord 94521, (510) 798-6800. Call for dates. Purchase method varies by dealer.
Parking is $4 (free admission), and $20 will buy you a selling spot.
Everything

GILDED CAGE THRIFT SHOP
3439 Chestnut (Chestnut Square shopping center), Concord 94519, (510) 686-0324. Mon–Sat 10 am–4 pm. Cash, local checks.
Gilded Cage has more sales than you can shake a stick at. The day I was there they had just finished a three-day bag sale for clothes, so

wearable items were scarce. A friendly volunteer did inform me that clothing runs $1–$5. There was, however, an abundance of pottery from the estate of a local artist of some renown. Housewares, knickknacks, and books were also plentiful. Be sure to ask for the special sales calendar available each month.
Charity: Contra Costa Association for Retarded Citizens, which provides sheltered workshops and aid to the Lynn Center Preschool for babies with developmental disabilities
Everything except large appliances

GOODWILL
3495 Clayton Rd. (between Babel and Chestnut), Concord 94519, (510) 676-8140. Mon–Sat 10 am–6 pm, Sun 11 am–6 pm. Cash, checks, MC/VISA.
A big, clean, neat, and bright store with housewares and furniture in the back. New Jessica McClintock wedding gowns run $69–$119. Free on-site parking.
Charity: Goodwill
Everything

SOLANO FLEA MARKET
Solano Drive-In Theatre, 1611 Solano Way, Concord 94520, (510) 687- 6445. Sat and Sun 7 am–4 pm. Purchase method varies by dealer.
If you want to check out this flea market, make it there on Saturday, when admission is free. (It costs you $1 on Sunday.) Saturday is also

cheaper for sellers: sellers's fees are $5 on Saturday and $15 on Sunday.

Everything

TOY TRADER

2075 Pacheco St. (in downtown Concord), Concord 94520, (510) 676-2752. Tues–Sat 10:30 am–5 pm. Cash, checks.

A stucco bungalow with a red tile roof and a Raggedy Andy doll in the window provides just the right setting for this children's consignment shop, which has been in business since 1977. There are three cheerful rooms: one devoted to babies' and toddlers' toys and equipment; one to boys' and girls' clothing, sizes newborn–14; and one to big kids' toys, books, and furniture. All offer good quality merchandise at low prices (baby sleepers for $1.25–$2.50, blanket sleepers for $3–$4). Owner Diane Hernandez likes what she's doing and it shows—she's friendly, helpful, and willing to deal.

Consignment: By appointment, 50/50 split, items over $20 split 60% consignor/40% store

Children's clothing, toys, furniture, and equipment

~~~~~ Danville ~~~~~

MARCY'S

155-C Railroad Ave., The Railroad Centre, Danville 94526, (510) 820-8553. Tues–Sat 9 am–4 pm. Cash, checks.

After 25 years as a journalist, Marcy Bachmann recently opened an upscale resale shop in the spanking new Railroad Centre. Elegance is the keynote here, from the subtle beige and gray color scheme to the dish of chocolates on the coffee table. *Marcy's* carries better women's clothing in sizes 2–14, sportswear to evening gowns (no bridal), priced at 1/3 of their retail cost. Expect to find labels like Calvin Klein and St. John. The best buys are among the high-end items; Marcy tries not to price things out of resale range, so you may find an $800 suit going for $120. You might get a kick out of the rack of clothing donated by members of the Blackhawk Museum Auxiliary—proceeds benefit the museum.

Consignment: By appointment, 50/50 split

Women's clothing

SOMETHING OLD-SOMETHING NEW

442 Hartz Ave., Danville 94526, (510) 838-4492. Mon–Sat 10 am–5 pm. Cash, checks, MC/VISA with a minimum of $50.

Six years ago Sandra Jones took over a Century 21 real estate office, knocked out a few walls, installed dove-gray carpeting and flowered wallpaper, and turned it into a first-class consignment shop. Sandra carries women's clothing in sizes 4–18, good labels and designers, all priced at 1/4–1/3 of retail. She has something for almost everyone— fine suits for lady executives, great sportswear for work-at-home women, and a terrific selection of evening dresses for the mother of the bride or the high-school prom queen, and shoes to go with everything. For the big spenders she stocks furs and fine jewelry at bargain prices: we saw a gold and diamond wedding ring set (over one carat), valued at $3400, priced at $1700. Lovely, soft-spoken Sandra Jones is one of the nicest people you'll ever find.

Consignment: By appointment, 50/50 split
Women's clothing

THE THRIFT STATION
375 Hartz (corner of Prospect), Danville 94526, (510) 821-1988. Mon–Sat 10 am–4 pm. Cash, checks.

The Thrift Station was as busy as Grand Central Station the day we were there. It happened to be the first Wednesday of the month, which is Senior Discount Day and all clothing is half price. You can hardly beat *Thrift Station* clothing prices; even at full price, men's suits go for $8–$12.50.

But clothing is not the main attraction; *Thrift Station* has a bigger inventory of housewares. You'll find a lot of the usual at good prices, and some of the unusual— shelves of canning jars, lots of sewing notions and patterns, and stacks of jigsaw puzzles.

Charity: San Ramon Valley Discovery Center, a community counseling center
Everything except furniture and large appliances

~~~~~ **Lafayette** ~~~~~

DEJA VU
3540-A Wilkinson Lane (in La Fiesta Square), Lafayette 94549, (510) 283-4800. Tues–Sat 10 am– 4:30 pm. Cash, checks, MC/VISA.

Deja Vu, otherwise known as *The Designer Consignor Boutique*, specializes in quality consignment clothing and current-season salesman samples. They carry everything for the discerning woman, from very casual wear to business suits to ball gowns. If you are a young businesswoman, homemaker, or professional who loves designer clothing, prefers the personalized attention and lovely atmosphere of a boutique setting, and also wants a good buy, you will enjoy shopping at *Deja Vu*. Open since June 1991, it has the look and feel of an exclusive women's specialty shop. Quality is high, prices are 1/4–1/3 of retail prices, and there are many good labels, such as St. John and Armani. Salesman samples are especially jazzy but, alas, come only in medium.

Consignment: Tues–Fri 10 am–4 pm, Sat by appointment, 50/50 split
Women's clothing and accessories

THE NIFTY THRIFT SHOP
261 Lafayette Circle, Lafayette 94549, (510) 284-5237. Mon–Sat 10 am–5 pm. Cash, checks.

Nifty Thrift is, indeed, nifty—you don't want to miss this airy, expansive, well-stocked, and well-maintained shop. Since it's set up like a mini department store, you can browse in the main room for women's apparel, jewelry, and gift items (we saw an elegant display of silver-plate equestrian awards), or visit the patio, men's, home, or children's shops, each located in a separate room. Prices are low, quality is high, and all garments are cleaned and ironed. You will find the large staff, most of whom are clients of Futures Explored (the shop's charity), extremely courteous and helpful.

Charity: Futures Explored, an innovative program which provides training in work-related and life skills to developmentally disabled adults
Everything except furniture and large appliances

ROSIE'S
1020 Brown Ave., Lafayette 94549, (510) 283-6540. Mon 11 am–4:30 pm, Tues–Sat 10 am–4:30 pm. Cash, checks, MC/VISA.

Rosie's has been doing a steady business on historic Brown Avenue for eighteen years, but when new owner Sherissa Heiser took over recently, things really began to hop. Sharing the ground floor of an old house with an antique store, *Rosie's* two rooms are packed to the gills with casual to dressy women's wear in sizes 4–14, including lots of sportswear, lingerie, accessories, jewelry, and boutique items. *Rosie's* claims to be upscale resale, and it certainly is:

don't let your first glance throw you off. (I did—the store was so packed and the bargain rack at the door confused me.) I actually found the racks chock-full of goodies at very good prices—outfits by St. John for $75, Raul Blanco for $28, Diane Friez for $75–$125. *Rosie's* has something for all ages, from college students to senior citizens. Everyone will enjoy the hot cider and coffee and the fire in the fireplace.
Consignment: Tues–Sat 10 am–4:30 pm, 50/50 split
Women's clothing

WAY SIDE INN THRIFT SHOP AND COSTUME RENTAL
3521 Golden Gate Way, Lafayette 94549, (510) 284-4781. Tues–Fri 11 am–4 pm. Cash.

If you long for a thrift shop with a twist, you definitely do not want to miss this one. As quaint as it could be, located in an historic landmark (it was at one time a stagecoach stop), *Way Side Inn* offers high-quality items at low prices in a boutique setting. The volunteers really go all out to make this an attractive place to shop—unfortunately, some of the most intriguing items on display are not for sale. But there are still plenty of antiques, collectibles, and housewares, not to mention clothing for men, women, and

Right: Meg Spence at Felino's Vintage Clothing, San Francisco.

children, a lot of it high quality at good to great prices. (A good selection of women's dresses priced $8–$35 included a glamorous assortment of evening outfits. In addition to selling first-rate merchandise, *Way Side Inn* rents over 1000 costumes at the best prices you'll find anywhere. Dress up like an animal, Santa Claus, the Easter Bunny, or a character from any vintage period from the Renaissance to the roaring 20's. Whether you need it for Halloween, a murder mystery party, or a theme wedding, they have it, including a good inventory of costumes for larger sizes. Garments are cleaned after each wearing.

Charity: Assistance League of Diablo Valley Community Resource Center

Everything except large appliances and large pieces of furniture

~~~~ Pleasant Hill ~~~~

FAMILY SAVERS THRIFT SHOP
2265 Contra Costa Blvd., Pleasant Hill 94523, (510) 680-6535. Mon–Tues 9:30 am–5 pm, Wed–Fri 9:30 am–8 pm, Sat 9:30 am–5 pm, Sun 12 am–5 pm. Cash, checks.

Not to be confused with the privately owned *Savers*, *Family Savers* is difficult to find—look for it behind the Pleasant Hill Bowling Alley. A large, dark store with a rather mundane assortment of cheap but out-of-style clothing, *Family Savers* is set apart by its huge selection of NEW furniture. The good people at *Family Savers* buy furniture directly from local manufacturers—Danken, Fino, Rosalco, Best Connections, Good Bedrooms, Durometals, Royal Pacific Mattress, to name a few—and sell it to you at bargain prices. They try to concentrate on the necessities—bed frames, box springs, mattresses, chests of drawers, lamps, etc. The inventory changes, but on our visit there was an eclectic mix of high-tech Italian, brass and glass, and your basic Sunset redwood look. My personal favorite was the display of magazines of all kinds and all dates laid out in rows neater than any seen at my dentist's office, all for 10¢ each.

Charity: Contra Costa Child Care Council, Family Stress Center, and Northern California Family Center

Everything except large appliances

MOTHER AND CHILD
1916 Contra Costa Blvd. (in Pleasant Hill Plaza shopping center), (510) 676-6906. Mon–Sat 10 am–5 pm, Thurs 10 am–8 pm. Cash, checks, MC/VISA.

Carrying store close-outs, Leading Lady nursing bras, and new and recycled children's and maternity clothes, this small, pleasant, well-organized store has a definite upscale look. Owner Jackie Shikuzawa is very picky about what she takes, and as a result there is not a lot of merchandise but everything is choice. Prices are on the high end, but the quality of the maternity clothes makes this store a must for any style conscious mother-to-be. Gorgeous, stylish, name-brand maternity clothes such as Jeanne Mark and Pea in a Pod sell at 1/3 of the original price. *Consignment: Mon–Wed 10 am– 12 am, children's clothes bought outright, current season maternity accepted on consignment of 50/50 split in cash or 60% consignor/40% store in trade* **Maternity clothing and children's clothing and equipment**

ST. VINCENT DE PAUL
3325 N. Main, Pleasant Hill 94523, (510) 934-5063. Mon–Sat 9 am– 4:45 pm, Sun 12 am–4:45 pm. Cash, checks, MC/VISA.

I've seen some pretty scuzzy *St. Vincent de Paul* stores in my day, but nothing to compare to this one! You walk in the door of this barn-like structure (it was in fact a barn originally, then a lumber company), check out the collectibles in the glass case, and think, hey, this looks pretty good. Things deteriorate rapidly as you penetrate the deeper recesses of the store until you arrive at the ultimate pit, the tin-roofed yard in back. Here reigns total anarchy...bags of moldy bread share space with console television sets, upholstered furniture, a pink marble sink, and box after box of clothes, Christmas ornaments, dishes, lunch boxes... You cannot fathom the extent of the chaos. All of which is not to say that you

shouldn't go. I watched one woman patiently and systematically going through box after box and unearthing treasures. For the truly adventurous, this one is a must.

As I was walking to my car in the parking lot in back, the staff was speculating on how much to ask for a sleek, shiny speedboat that had just been donated. Don't expect to find it there—I'm sure it's long gone. I only mention it to illustrate a point...expect the unexpected at *St. Vincent de Paul.* *Charity: St. Vincent de Paul* **Absolutely everything!**

SALVATION ARMY
1806 Linda Dr., Pleasant Hill 94523, (510) 685-6900. Mon–Sat 9:30 am–5:15 pm. Cash, checks, MC/VISA.

Attractive wall displays and savvy merchandising make this *Salvation Army,* located in a former super-market, a pleasant place to shop. New Jessica McClintock wedding gowns were going for $175–$200. You can purchase gift certificates here for your thrift-shopping friends. *Charity: Salvation Army* **Everything**

~~~ Walnut Creek ~~~

AMERICAN CANCER SOCIETY DISCOVERY SHOP
1538 Locust St., Walnut Creek 94596, (510) 944-1991. Mon–Sat 10 am–5 pm. Cash, checks, MC/ VISA.

After fifteen years in their old Main Street location, in July of 1991 the *Discovery Shop* moved to these elegant new quarters, complete with their own washer and dryer. Like their sister stores, they stick to the *Discovery Shop* policy of keeping only the best merchandise to bring you upscale resale at reasonable prices.

Charity: American Cancer Society
Everything except large appliances

BEARLY WORN

1625 N. Broadway (across from Walnut Creek Library), Walnut Creek 94596, (510) 945-6535. Mon 10 am–2 pm, Tues–Sat 10 am–5 pm. Cash, checks, MC/VISA.

A cheerful little shop for little people sizes newborn–7, *Bearly Worn* carries quality recycled children's clothing, toys, equipment, books, and some handmade dresses and wooden toys. Prices are a little higher than most children's resale shops, but the selection is first class, all very clean and ironed, and includes a lot of baby designer labels.

Consignment: Wed, Thurs, Sat 10 am–12 am; buys clothing outright; consigns equipment, 60% consignor/40% store
Children's clothing and equipment

THE FASHION EXCHANGE

1422 Lincoln Ave., Walnut Creek 94596, (510) 935-5554. Mon–Sat 11 am–6 pm. Cash, checks.

We almost missed this one, which you won't want to do. (Lincoln is a one-block alley running between N. Main and N. Broadway.) Featuring better business suits, cocktail and evening wear, mother-of-the-bride attire, and prom and bridal gowns (no casual jeans or t-shirts), *Fashion Exchange* can dress you up for that special occasion when you need to knock 'em dead. Quality is high, prices are good (at least 50% below retail), and you can't beat the selection of truly glamorous outfits, including a dozen or so beaded gowns worn by a former Miss Alaska and other beauty queens. We strongly advise any Miss America hopeful to try the *Fashion Exchange* first. Why shell out $2000–$4000 at Nordstrom when you can pick up a once-worn beauty here for under $500? Do you hesitate to spend that kind of money on a dress you may wear only once? Don't worry—according to Ms. Meri Bush, the irrepressible owner, you're not married to your wardrobe. You can buy something, wear it, bring it back, and she'll resell it for you.

Consignment: Mon–Fri 11:30 am– 5 pm, 50/50 split
Women's clothing

GARRET THRIFT SHOP

1530 Third Ave., Walnut Creek 94596, (510) 932-9474. Mon–Fri 10 am–4 pm, Thurs 10 am–8 pm, Sat 12 am–4 pm. Cash, checks, MC/VISA.

We like a thrift shop that knows how to market itself. When other thrift shops were letting the

ubiquitous bounty of Jessica McClintock's gorgeous wedding dresses just sit on the racks, the *Garret Thrift Shop* announced a Wedding Faire. A special flyer and newspaper article had 70 budget-conscious brides waiting in line on the announced date of the sale. (They sold 40 gowns, priced $75–300, on the first day.) You definitely want to sign up for their regular mailings announcing sales and promotions. Forget the clothes—jewelry, furniture, collectibles, antiques, books, and art are the things to buy here. Prices are high, but the selection is terrific. Taken from a recent list of new items at the *Garret*: sterling silver chains; Zuni bolo; Czechoslovakian end table; Hammond organ; Chinese Celadon charger c. 1900; Japanese gold couched embroidery panel, Dai-Nichi Nyorai, Meiji Period; "Tippy" windup Scotty dog by Schuco. Every Monday is Senior Citizen's Day—all clothing and accessories are half off for customers over 60.
Charity: John Muir Medical Center
Everything except large appliances

THE HOSPICE SHOPPE
1550 Olympic Blvd. (corner of Locust and Olympic), Walnut Creek 94596, (510) 947-1064. Mon–Sat 10 am–4 pm. Cash, checks, MC/VISA.

This shoppe gives new meaning to the term "upscale." While many lay claim to the title, few are, but

Hospice Shoppe is the one in a million. You couldn't ask for a cleaner, brighter, more beautifully decorated store. All merchandise, from kid's clothes to furniture to housewares, is top of the line. Expect a lot of designer labels. 90 volunteers work at keeping up the high standards—every item donated is screened, and only the best is kept for the store. Rejects are donated to the *Salvation Army*, blankets and towels go to the local animal shelter. Clothing is steamed before it's put out on the floor. The price is right, the cause is good. DON'T MISS IT!
Charity: Hospice of Contra Costa, which provides medical and personal care for the terminally ill
Everything but large appliances

KATHY'S NEW & RESALE BOUTIQUE
1203 Arroyo Way (corner of Civic Drive), Walnut Creek 94596, (510) 934-6571. Mon–Sat 10 am–4:30 pm. Cash, checks, MC/VISA.

Kathy's (formerly *Judy's*, formerly *Clair's*, formerly *Nancy's*, formerly *Janice's*) has something for every occasion—work, play, and dress up—for women sizes 2–18. Three rooms full of beautiful clothes (no furs, no bridal), all mid-priced to designer and selling for 1/3 of their original price if previously worn or half price if brand new with labels still attached, mean that you'll find it impossible to leave empty handed. Go there just once and you'll keep coming back.

Above: Sydney Koliha and Wendy Monino at The Rag Doll Resale Shoppe, Walnut Creek.

Consignment: Mon–Sat 10 am–3 pm, 50/50 split, 90-day contract
Women's clothing

LEFTOVERS THRIFT SHOP
2333 Boulevard Circle, Walnut Creek 94596, (510) 930-9393. Tues–Sat 10 am–3:30 pm. Cash, local checks.

Leftovers, aptly called "Little Shop of Treasures," occupies a quaint cottage complete with a planter full of primroses, a red door, and six rooms full of treasures. These include a women's shop, a boutique for "better dresses," kids' stuff, housewares, a men's shop, the books and magazines corner, and a patio featuring shoes, luggage, men's suits, and the $2 rack. The place was jumping the day we were there; we had inadvertently chosen the first day of the February half-off sale. With half off the already low prices, customers were walking away with bags full of spectacular bargains—try a Courege suit for $12.50, a Florence Eisman dress for $2.50, an electric hand mixer for $2.50, saucers for 5¢, place mats for 12¢, games and puzzles for 50¢. These sales happen twice a year; genuine values are an everyday occurrence. *Charity: Contra Costa Crisis and Suicide Intervention Service*
Everything except furniture and large appliances

MAIN STREET RAGS
1380 N. Main, Walnut Creek 94596, (510) 943-1459. Mon–Sat

10 am–5:30 pm, Thurs 10 am–8 pm, Sun 12 am–4 pm. Cash, checks, MC/VISA.

Like its sister store, *Rockridge Rags* in Oakland, *Main Street Rags* specializes in classic sportswear and business clothing, with a top-notch inventory of pants, blouses, skirts, dresses, jackets, and suits. The selection of dressy dresses is smaller, but also first rate. The small back room holds a few pieces of maternity, lingerie, jumpsuits, larger sizes, and ski wear. A budget-minded working woman can't go wrong with *Rags*; it's a lovely store with a great selection of high-quality clothes at 1/3 to 1/2 of retail. The staff is helpful and friendly, especially manager Phyllis Hoskins.
Consignment: Mon–Sat 10 am–1 pm, Thurs 5 pm–7 pm, 50/50 split
Women's clothing and accessories

MT. DIABLO THERAPY CENTER THRIFT SHOP
1539 N. Main, Walnut Creek 94596, (510) 935-4211. Mon–Fri 11 am–4 pm, Sat 10 am–3 pm. Cash, checks, MC/VISA.

Someone at this shop is a whiz at desktop publishing; computer-generated signs are everywhere. The place is organized and compart-mentalized within an inch of its life, but on our visit we didn't find a lot of merchandise. Men's and children's clothing were short on style, but also low in price: long-sleeve shirts were $3, short-sleeve shirts were $2, suits were $9–$20.

Women's clothing was of stodgy medium quality and medium price. The shop recently celebrated its 40th anniversary, so they must be doing something right. Maybe we hit it on a bad day, so you'd better check it out for yourself.
Charity: Mt. Diablo Rehabilitation Center, Alzheimer Unit, and Adult Day Care
Everything except furniture and large appliances

THE RAG DOLL RESALE SHOPPE
1109 Bont Lane, Walnut Creek 94596, (510) 937-2344. Mon–Sat 11 am–5 pm. Cash, checks.

Hundreds of rag dolls live in this charming ivy-covered little house; they line the walls, perch on the cupboards, sit grandly on the love seat, and add a note of nursery-rhyme charm to this delightful shop. Upstairs and down, the rooms are bursting with clothes for women sizes 2–22 and boys and girls sizes newborn–12. Suits, everyday clothes, t-shirts, warm-ups, dressy dresses…some good labels, some designer pieces, something for everyone. Owner Gerrie Dodson (dressed from her shop, of course), has that casual, artsy elegance I've always admired. You see a lot of that particular style—fantasy, ethnic, unusual—as well as classic styles. With a host of artsy dresses priced $8–$20, you can indulge your fantasy and buy something you may want to wear only a few times…at these good prices you don't have to wear anything forever.

Consignment: Mon–Sat 11 am–3:30 pm, 50/50 split, 60-day contract

Women's and children's clothing and accessories

RAINBOW'S END THRIFT SHOP
1389-D Main St., Walnut Creek 94596, (510) 932-8489. Mon–Sat 10 am–4 pm. Cash, checks.

Rainbows End has taken over the rather dingy shop vacated by the Cancer Society *Discovery Shop* last July. We found prices on almost everything too high for the quality of the merchandise, although they do have a great book section. You'll find some of the best antiques and collectibles around, but be prepared to pay top dollar for them—we saw a Beleek sugar bowl going for $145 and a sterling silver soup spoon for $10.

Charity: Fern Lodge Nursing Home in Castro Valley

Everything except large appliances and large pieces of furniture

CONTRA COSTA COUNTY (Central)	Appliances/large	Bridal	Clothing/children	Clothing/men	Clothing/women	Collectibles	Furnishings/children	Furniture	Housewares	Maternity	Tools, etc.	Toys	Vintage	Page number
CLAYTON														
Emily's Wardrobe					X									54
CONCORD														
Clausen House		X	X	X	X	X			X	X		X		54
Clothesline		X			X									54
Concord Flea Market	X	X	X	X	X	X	X	X	X	X	X	X	X	55
Gilded Cage			X	X	X	X	X	X	X			X	X	55
Goodwill	X	X	X	X	X	X	X	X	X	X	X	X		55
Solano Flea Market	X	X	X	X	X	X	X	X	X	X	X	X	X	55
Toy Trader		X				X						X		56
DANVILLE														
Marcy's					X									56
Something Old					X									56
Thrift Station			X	X	X	X			X			X	X	57
LAFAYETTE														
Deja Vu					X									57
Nifty Thrift Shop			X	X	X	X	X		X			X	X	57
Rosie's					X									58
Way Side Inn			X	X	X	X		X	X			X		58
PLEASANT HILL														
Family Savers			X	X	X	X	X	X	X			X	X	60
Mother and Child		X				X				X		X		60
St. Vincent de Paul	X	X	X	X	X	X	X	X	X	X	X	X		61
Salvation Army	X	X	X	X	X	X	X	X	X	X	X	X		61
WALNUT CREEK														
Discovery Shop			X	X	X	X	X	X	X			X		61
Bearly Worn			X						X			X		62
Fashion Exchange					X									62
Garret Thrift Shop		X	X	X	X	**X**	X	X	X	X	X	X		62
Hospice Shoppe		X	**X**	**X**	**X**	X	X	X	X	X	X	X		63
Kathy's Boutique					X									63
Leftovers Thrift Shop			X	X	X	X	X	X	X			X		64
Main Street Rags					X									64
Mt. Diablo Shop			X	X	X	X	X		X			X	X	65
Rag Doll Shoppe		X			X									65
Rainbow's End			X	X	X	X	X	X	X			X		66

~~~~~ El Cerrito ~~~~~

AMERICAN CANCER SOCIETY DISCOVERY SHOP

10313 San Pablo Ave. (between Columbia and Eureka), El Cerrito 94530, (510) 527-1469. Mon–Sat 10 am–4 pm. Cash, checks, MC/ VISA.

You can always find an impressive selection of gift items and collectibles at the El Cerrito *Discovery Shop.* Unfortunately, prices are often sky high. Clothing tends to be less upscale than you usually find in *Discovery Shops,* but the prices are in keeping with the quality.

Charity: American Cancer Society
Everything except large appliances

DARLA'S BABY BOUTIQUE

10293 San Pablo Ave., El Cerrito 94530, (510) 526-KIDS. Mon–Sat 10 am–6 pm, Sun 11 am–4 pm. Cash, checks, 30-day layaway on new merchandise, MC/VISA.

Darla Courtney is a real go-getter. She'll go to your house, get furniture your kids have outgrown, and pay you for it, too. If, on the other hand, your kids are still in the newborn–6X category, take them with you to *Darla's Baby Boutique,* where you will find used furniture, clothing, and equipment selling at 1/3 the cost of new. Darla guarantees to buy any purchase back from you at half the purchase price when you're through with it. Darla is out buying every day, so merchandise turns over rapidly. Expecting wee guests for the weekend? Darla also rents baby equipment, and sells a lot of new merchandise at cheap, cheap prices, everything from clothes to baby pictures.

Buys: By appointment
Children's clothing and furniture

R & R CLOTHING EXCHANGE

11236 San Pablo Ave., El Cerrito 94530, (510) 237-5929. Mon–Fri 11:30 am–6 pm, Sat 1:30 pm–6 pm. Cash.

R & R Clothing Exchange is one of the few resale establishments I've come across where you can shop for the whole family in a cozy, boutique-like setting. Owner Prudence Russell makes the best of her small space by tight organization and romantic touches of lace. Everyone in the family will find a good selection of up-to-date basics and women sizes 5/6–16 can pick up special designer items at rock bottom prices—a Flora Kung dress for $18.95 or an Albert Nipon dress for $23.

Consignment: Women's clothing only, 40% consignor/60% store, 60-day contract
Clothing for men, women, and children

RAGS & RICHES

11072 San Pablo Ave., El Cerrito 94530, (510) 232-2024. Tues–Sat 11 am–5 pm. Cash, checks, MC/ VISA.

From jeans to evening wear, Sylvia Barandier's small store is packed with contemporary women's fashions, sizes 6–20. Priced to sell, skirts never run more than $9.50, suits are $29–$39, and dresses are $19.50 or under, unless they are really special, such as new hand-beaded dresses from India selling for $95–$395.

Consignment: Tues–Sat 11 am–4 pm, 50/50 split, also buys outright
Women's clothing

THE TURNABOUT SHOP

10052 San Pablo Ave., El Cerrito 94530, (510) 525-7844. Mon–Tues and Thurs–Sat 11 am–3 pm. Cash.

Veteran East Bay thrift shoppers will remember *The Turnabout Shop*'s annual Christmas sales, when scores of bargain hunters lined up outside the door of the old Berkeley store. Relocated in 1986 to El Cerrito, the shop is bigger and better than ever, with four rooms and an abundance of bargains and good buys. Clothing tends toward the staid, but you can't beat the prices. The book collection is extensive and well organized, and I can almost guarantee you will find an unexpected treasure among the cases of collectibles and jewelry.

The Christmas sale, held the first Saturday after Thanksgiving, is still a major event. Christmas items and especially nice articles of clothing are saved for this once-a-year bonanza, to which every member of the Berkeley Clinic Auxiliary must contribute five new collectibles.

Charity: Berkeley Clinic Auxiliary, which supports community health care
Everything except furniture and large appliances

~~~~ El Sobrante ~~~~

THRIFT TOWN

3645 San Pablo Dam Road, El Sobrante 94803, (510) 222-8696. Mon–Fri 9 am–8 pm, Sat 10 am–7 pm, Sun 11 am–6 pm. Cash, checks, MC/VISA.

Clean, organized, well lit, and full of good buys for the whole family, this enormous store is the nicest of all the Bay Area *Thrift Towns*. Vintage fanciers will definitely want to check out their "oldies" vintage selection, the best we've seen in a store of this type. Chapeau connoisseurs shouldn't miss the hat rack in front.

Charity: Privately owned, supports CARH (Community Assistance for the Retarded and Handicapped)
Everything except large appliances

~~~~ Kensington ~~~~

LUNDBERG HABERDASHERY

396 Colusa (at Colusa Circle), Kensington 94707, (510) 524-

3003. Wed–Sat 12 am–4 pm, and by appointment. Cash, checks.

According to Jon Lundberg, his *Haberdashery* is the only store in the world devoted exclusively to selling men's vintage fashions. (Over 90% of the 1000 vintage stores in this country carry 90% women's fashions.) Because men's styles change much more slowly than women's, vintage men's clothing is much scarcer. Nevertheless, Lundberg has amassed an outstanding collection of men's wear from the 1850's to the early 1950's (before lapels got narrow), including suits, tuxedoes, tails, vests, shoes, ties, hats, vintage swim wear, and some rare boy's suits and knickers. Although prices may seem high—suits and tuxedoes go for $250–$300, evening tails for $400, coats are $75, ties are $5–$50 (some rare ties go for $100), hats cost $10–$300—bear in mind that Lundberg carries only the highest quality in perfect condition. A comparable suit would sell for $500 today at Wilkes Bashford, and even at that price you couldn't match the fabric or workmanship, according to Lundberg. Lundberg numbers among his customers old car owners, Art Deco society members, theatrical groups, Hollywood production people, Ralph Lauren (who has been known to knock off the style or have a vintage fabric reproduced in Italy or England for his Polo collection), and "some guys who just like to be snappy dressers."

Men's vintage clothing

~~~~~~ **Pinole** ~~~~~~

CHILDREN'S EXCHANGE
2830 Pinole Valley Road (in Lucky Shopping Center), Pinole 94564, (510) 758-1652. Mon–Wed 10 am–5 pm, Thurs–Sat 10 am–6 pm. Cash, checks, MC/VISA.

The only way to detect that this big new store is a resale shop is to note the low, low prices. Boys' and girls' clothing, sizes newborn–10, is so clean and fresh you would swear it was new. Car seats, strollers, changing tables, and cribs also look as good as new and sell for half the retail price or less: a GRACO deluxe model stroller was marked $55, an Aprica went for $33. Although you can't exchange your teenager for a toddler, *Children's Exchange* will trade your outgrown children's clothes and equipment for new stuff or cash.

Consignment: Buys outright Mon–Sat 10 am–6 pm, 40% customer/60% store in cash or 60% customer/40% store in trade, check on terms for items over $50
Children's clothing and equipment

GOODWILL
620-G San Pablo (in Del Monte shopping center), Pinole 94564, (510) 724-0408. Mon–Sat 10 am–6 pm, Sun 11 am–6 pm. Cash, checks, MC/VISA/DISCOVER.

The Pinole *Goodwill* couldn't be cleaner, brighter, newer, or nicer. Neon signs define the different departments, each featuring good merchandise at great prices. This

Goodwill does not stock furniture, although they do sell reconditioned mattresses and box springs.
Charity: Goodwill
Everything except furniture and large appliances

THE SECOND FIDDLE THRIFT SHOP
2101 San Pablo Ave., Pinole 94564, (510) 724-7948. Mon–Sat 11 am–4 pm, closed first Thurs of every month. Cash, checks.

The 23 lovely ladies who keep this remarkable thrift shop going could use a few more volunteers, if you live in the area. If you don't, you might want to pay them a visit to check out their four rooms full of incredible bargains. They do a lot of senior business, so they like to keep their prices real, real, low: good dresses are $4, others $2–$3, and the most expensive baby item is $2.25. After a month on the floor items are reduced to half off for the first two weeks, the third week they go to 50¢ each or 3 for $1, and the fourth week to 25¢ each. Volunteers take laundry home to wash and iron; they send anything with a stain or tear to the Richmond Rescue Mission. The volunteer manager thinks *The Second Fiddle* is one of the least expensive thrift stores in Pinole; I know it's one of the cheapest stores in the Bay Area. Don't expect high fashion, but if you're looking for basic necessities at bargain prices you can't beat this shop.
Charity: Tri-Cities Discovery Center, a community counseling program for adolescents and their families
Everything except furniture and large appliances

~~~~~ Richmond ~~~~~

CENTER FOR THE AGED AND VISUALLY HANDICAPPED THRIFT BOUTIQUE
3101 MacDonald Ave., Richmond 94804, (510) 232-4336, Tues–Sat 10 am–4:30 pm. Cash.

Don't come in unless you want to save money, warned the volunteer at the desk. And don't be fooled by the front room, where better fashions and gift items are displayed in a minimalist boutique atmosphere. All the thrift store treasures are in the back. One room featuring less elegant clothes has top prices hovering around $5 for a man's suit (shirts and sweaters are 75¢). Another room is packed with furniture, collectibles, housewares, appliances (they all work), odds and ends, and unexpected delights. Furniture may be your best buy— we saw a nearly antique vanity for $45 and a sleeper sofa for $45. Any nook, cranny, chest, or drawer is apt to be hiding your heart's desire. Check them all out.
Charity: Center for the Aged and Visually Handicapped
Everything

GOODWILL
12915 San Pablo Ave. (at McBride), Richmond 94805, (510) 236-2422. Mon–Sat 10 am–6 pm,

Sun 11 am–6 pm. Cash, checks, MC/VISA.

Are you in the mood for a purple blouse? At the Richmond *Goodwill* you can pick one from the Gap, Hunters Run, Nordstrom, J.C. Penny, Moby Up…all for the low price of $2.95. Also for $2.95, you can have a high-kitsch Donald Duck painted on black velvet. With the exception of furniture and appliances, this flawlessly clean *Goodwill* sells just about everything.

Charity: Goodwill
Everything except furniture and large appliances

HOLY TRINITY THRIFT SHOP
555 37th St., Richmond 94805, (store located along the side of the church , through the parking lot on Roosevelt and 37th), (510) 236-6225. Fri–Sat 10 am–4 pm. Cash, local checks.

Holy Trinity is perfect for thrift shoppers who enjoy the thrill of the hunt. You never know what will turn up among the jumble of this three-room thrift shop. You can always be sure to find clothes for the whole family at prices so low they're almost giving them away—any blouse goes for $1.25, any skirt for $1, and so on. You take your chances on unearthing some marvelous treasure. I fell in love with a box of greeting cards from the 1930's (5¢ each), and Jobyna found a 1903 edition of *Hasluck's Recitations for Ladies* for $1. Twice a year they hold a half-off-everything sale in the parking lot.

Charity: Holy Trinity Episcopal Church and community projects
Everything except furniture and large appliances

JOYCE'S BOUTIQUE
309 23rd St., Richmond 94804, (510) 215-1255. Tues–Sat 10 am–5 pm. Cash.

Don't expect anything fancy at *Joyce's Boutique*—Joyce Johnson isn't selling atmosphere or tony decor. You will find used clothing for the whole family at rock-bottom prices: men's and women's clothing starts at $3, children's at $1, and nothing is priced higher than $12. Prices aren't marked, so you have to ask. I couldn't believe my ears—a beaded Oscar de la Renta evening gown was priced at $3, an After Six tuxedo was quoted at $5. Joyce also carries a few new items, which are priced slightly higher.

Clothing for men, women, and children

NEW TO YOU
3219 McDonald Ave. (at 33rd), Richmond 94804, (510) 234-4972. Tues and Thurs 10 am–3:45 pm. Cash.

The smallest and least upscale of the three *New to You* shops in the Bay Area, the Richmond branch recently celebrated its 42nd anniversary. This tiny store has a little bit of everything, from cheap clothes to knickknacks and everyday household items. The all-volunteer staff is friendly and helpful.

Above: Urban Ore, Berkeley.

Charity: Children's Hospital/
Oakland
**Everything except furniture
and large appliances**

ST. VINCENT DE PAUL
*1025 13th St. (between Lincoln
and Rheem), Richmond 94801,
(510) 236-5521. Mon–Sat 9 am–
4:45 pm, Sun 12 am–4:45 pm.
Cash, checks, MC/VISA.*

Furniture, furniture, furniture! If
you're tired of sleeping on a
mattress on the floor and eating off
of packing cases, but can't see
spending six months' salary at
Breuners, hightail it down to *St.
Vincent de Paul*, where the
selection is eclectic and the prices
are rock bottom. It might take
several visits, but a determined
shopper with a sense of style can
work wonders with even the

smallest budget at *St. Vincent.*
While you're there check out the
book room.
Charity: St. Vincent de Paul
Everything

SALVATION ARMY
*1430 Cutting Blvd. (at 15th across
from Kaiser Hospital), Richmond
94804, (510) 234-5181. Mon–Sat 9
am–4:30 pm. Cash, MC/VISA.*

If you don't have time to visit all of
the 823 *Salvation Army* thrift stores
in the United States, my advice is
to go to Richmond for the great
deals. A beautiful display of
clothing, furniture, and artifacts in a
jungle theme encircled the large,
organized clothing section. Good
buys included new Jessica
McClintock wedding dresses for
$85 and men's white tuxedoes and
tails for $19.50. The furniture

department offered sofas for $26–$67, desks for $25–$67, and a five-piece dining set for $142.

Charity: Salvation Army

Everything

~~~~~ Rodeo ~~~~~

COUNTY FAIR GIFTS AND COLLECTIBLES

246 Pacific Avenue, Rodeo 94572, (510) 799-1221. Fri–Sat 11 am–4 pm. Cash, checks.

Jean Woodbury finds items for her store at garage and rummage sales, where she buys anything that's a little different. Jean doesn't expect to make any money selling this fascinating collection of odds and ends (books, greeting cards, dolls, jewelry, old records, pots and pans, and lots of junk) for super cheap prices. She does it as a hobby. If your hobby is bargain hunting, you'll enjoy meeting this warmhearted, amiable lady and browsing through her store.

Housewares and collectibles

GARMENT EXCHANGE

250 Pacific Avenue, Rodeo 94572, (510) 799-7680. Tues–Sat 10 am–5 pm. Cash, checks, MC/VISA.

One of the first thrift stores in the East Bay, *Garment Exchange* has been doing business since 1943. Present owner Hazel Jones bought it in 1978 and stuck to the original owner's winning methods. She pays cash for gently worn clothing, washes and steam presses everything on site, and sells it at 1/3 of the original price. Twice a year she marks everything down to cost and donates what doesn't sell to the Salvation Army. You can dress the whole family, from baby to Grandpa, from this large immaculate store and still have money left over. The selection is extensive—from women's suits for $22 to prom dresses for $12 to men's suits up to size 50. The Jones' collections of classic car models and vintage bottles are on display, although they are not for sale.

Clothing for men, women, and children; housewares; children's furniture

KAREN & ED'S MYSTIQUE ANTIQUES

208 Parker Ave., Rodeo 94572, (510) 799-7270. Mon–Sat 11:30 am–5 pm. Cash, local checks.

The real mystique of Karen and Ed is how they can sell antiques at such ridiculously low prices. Don't be intimidated by the "antique" in the name—a sign over the door reads "Thrift Store" and the merchandise inside ranges from clothes to jewelry, collectibles, tools, kitchenware, furniture, toys, dolls, Elvis memorabilia, genuine antiques, and assorted junk. Most of the stuff has prices lower than those found in thrift shops. According to owner Karen Werth, the store sells more used necessities than antiques. They sell a lot of their antiques to dealers because, as Karen so succinctly put it, Rodeo isn't Sausalito.

Everything

ROOKIE'S DUGOUT
*209 1/2 Pacific, Rodeo 94572,
(510) Mon–Sun 11 am–4:30 pm.
Cash.*

Ed, of Karen and Ed, recently turned over his first store, *Mystique Antiques,* to his daughter Karen and her daughter Heather Crow so he could open this tiny, very personal store. Ed makes furniture (which he sells); collects cards, coins, and Coca Cola memorabilia (which he also sells); and also knows the secret to cleaning cast-iron pots and pans. You can buy spruced-up used ones as well as other assorted antique kitchen implements from Ed, or you can bring in your crusty rusted ones for him to clean. Karen and Ed are such a cheerful, chatty pair that it's worth a trip to Rodeo to meet them and check out all of their bargains.
Baseball cards, furniture, collectibles

~~~~~ San Pablo ~~~~~

MANY THINGS THRIFT AND GIFT STORE
13752 San Pablo Ave., San Pablo 94806, (510) 236-4553. Thurs–Sat 11 am–6 pm. Cash, checks.

If Melody Keating hadn't gone to the flea market and had such a good time, *Many Things Thrift and Gift Store* wouldn't exist. A former administrative professional, Keating has found happiness buying and selling anything that strikes her fancy, if the condition is good and the price is right. Only a year old, her busy store already has a loyal following (25% dealers), who come from Portland, Utah, Redding, Daly City, and Benicia to snap up her good buys. Merchandise includes contemporary to antique furniture, housewares, books, pictures, and collectibles, all at thrift store prices. Even these low prices can be negotiated.
Furniture, housewares, collectibles

MILLHOLLIN'S
2280 Giant Road, San Pablo 94806, (510) 233-8734. Mon–Sat 9 am–5 pm, Sun 10 am–5 pm. Cash, checks, MC/VISA.

"WE CARRY THE GOODS" reads their business card. The goods change every two or three days in this humongous store. The day we were there they included tires, toilets, camper tops, paint, furniture, lots more furniture, office equipment, gasoline engines, gardening tools, wheelchairs, large and small appliances, a saddle, a guitar, a sequined mariachi sombrero, books, records, organs, pianos, a snare drum, a ship model clock, and even a few articles of clothing. In your wildest dreams, you cannot imagine the quantity and variety of stuff you will find at *Millhollin's.*

Thirty years ago, Louis and Norma Millhollin opened an antique store. After a few decades, they felt they had saturated the area with antiques and decided to go back to basics. People have to have furniture and household goods, they reasoned, so they phased out the antiques and got into the unclaimed storage business. They no longer deal with unclaimed storage, but they still have plenty of secondhand furniture and what-have-you. They also still carry some antiques at good flexible prices—don't hesitate to bargain.

Everything

ST. VINCENT DE PAUL

650 El Portal Shopping Center, San Pablo 94804, (510) 620-0203. Mon–Sat 10 am–5:45 pm, Sun 12 am–4:45 pm. Cash, checks, MC/VISA.

We found this store to be a middle-of-the-road *St. Vincent de Paul*, neither pin neat nor crazily chaotic.
Charity: St. Vincent de Paul
Everything

SALVATION ARMY

13577 San Pablo Ave., San Pablo 94806, (510) 236-0847. Mon–Sat 9:30 am–5:30 pm. Cash, checks, MC/VISA.

This *Salvation Army* is so gorgeous you wouldn't believe it was a thrift store if you didn't see the familiar red and white shield. The furniture selection is first rate; the "Something Special Shop" features wedding attire and better women's clothing. One of the Army's finest!
Charity: Salvation Army
Everything

CONTRA COSTA COUNTY (West)	Appliances/large	Bridal	Clothing/children	Clothing/men	Clothing/women	Collectibles	Furnishings/children	Furniture	Housewares	Maternity	Tools	Toys	Vintage	Page number
EL CERRITO														
Discovery Shop			X	X	X	X		X	X	X		X		68
Darla's Boutique			X				X					X		68
R & R Clothing			X	X	X									68
Rags & Riches					X									69
Turnabout Shop			X	X	X	X		X	X	X	X			69
EL SOBRANTE														
Thrift Town		X	X	X	X	X	X	X	X	X	X	X	X	69
KENSINGTON														
Lundberg Haber.			X										**X**	69
PINOLE														
Children's Exchange				X				X					X	70
Goodwill	X	X	X	X	X		X		X	X	X	X		70
Second Fiddle		X	X	X	X				X		X	X		71
RICHMOND														
Center for the Aged	X		X	X	X	X	X	X	X		X	X		71
Goodwill	X	X	X	X	X		X		X	X	X	X		71
Holy Trinity		X	X	X	X		X		X		X	X		72
Joyce's Boutique		X	X	X										72
New to You		X	X	X	X		X		X		X	X		72
St. Vincent de Paul	X	X	X	X	X	X		X	X	X	X	X	X	73
Salvation Army	X	X	X	X	X	X		X	X	X	X	X	X	73
RODEO														
County Fair Gifts						**X**			X					74
Garment Exchange			X	X	X									74
Mystique Antiques	X		X	X	X	**X**	X	X	X		X	X		74
Rookie's Dugout						X			X	X				75
SAN PABLO														
Many Things						X		X	X					75
Millhollin's	X					X		X	X		X			75
St. Vincent de Paul	X	X	X	X	X	X	X	X	X	X	X	X		76
Salvation Army	X	X	X	X	X	X	X	X	X	X	X	X		76

~~~ Corte Madera ~~~

BABIES UNLIMITED
5627 Paradise Drive, Corte Madera 94925, (415) 924-3764. Mon–Sat 10 am–5 pm, Sun 12 am–4 pm. Cash, checks, MC/ VISA.

Predominantly a retail store, *Babies Unlimited* does stock about 25% used merchandise, including a limited selection of children's equipment, furniture, and clothing in sizes 0–6X. Check out the used furniture upstairs and compare prices with the new pieces downstairs. Used cribs run $59–$79; used equipment sells for about half of new prices. Be sure to ask about putting your name on the wish list, as many items go out the door before they even make it to the floor.
New and used children's clothing, furniture, and equipment

CLOTHES ENCOUNTERS OF THE 2ND KIND
5627 Paradise Drive, Paradise Shopping Center, Corte Madera 94925, (415) 927-0811. Mon–Sat 10 am–5 pm. Cash, checks.

Right next door to *Babies Unlimited*, this large one-room store boasts a mirrored wall from its former incarnation as a Tai Chi center. You will find a bit of everything on the crowded racks— casual to dressy clothing in sizes 4–18, with a variety of labels and prices of $5–$500. From a St. John knit suit for $198 to a basic black dress from Nordstrom for $34 or a Chanel skirt for $44, items are priced to move. The two racks of men's clothing had suits priced $50–$75 and a new blazer for $295. Bargain hunters should check out the half-off sale rack in the back.
Consignment: Mon–Sat 10 am–3 pm, 50/50 split
Men's and women's clothing

~~~ Fairfax ~~~

LA DONNA
1822-1/2 Sir Francis Drake Blvd., Fairfax 94930, (415) 485-0331. Mon–Sat 12 am–6 pm. Cash, checks.

No one was home the first time we stopped by, but the windows were so cute we gave it a second try. I'm glad we did. *La Donna* is a darling little shop packed full of upbeat, trendy, high-style fashions at good prices. From bathing suits to prom dresses in sizes 3/4–18, *La Donna* caters more to a youthful fashion-conscious crowd, although the more sedate can find more classic styles. Teens will like the great selection of new sample dresses from local manufacturers and

moms will appreciate the changing table and play area for tots. *Consignment: Anytime, 50/50 split*
Women's clothing

ROSS VALLEY CHILDREN'S STORE
44 Bolinas Rd., Fairfax 94930, (415) 459-7556. Tues–Fri 10 am–5 pm, Sat 12 am–5 pm. Cash, checks.

This is not your ordinary children's resale shop. For starters, it's a genderless store where boys' and girls' clothes in sizes newborn–10 hang together on the racks. You'll find a good selection of everyday clothes, some Grandma's specials (you know, those little Lord Fauntleroy suits), and unique costumes for dress up—all at good prices. And then there are the toys…among your ordinary, everyday toys are some dandy collectibles—a hand-built model of Sir Francis Drake's ship, or an antique doll with her own wardrobe trunk. And most extraordinary are the music lessons: every Friday afternoon from 3 pm to 5 pm a group of kids, ages two to twelve, shows up for free violin and cello lessons (the store provides the instruments). On Saturday afternoons you're apt to find an impromptu quartet sitting on little benches playing away.

This delightful place is as much a community center as a children's store. Kids are welcome to come in and play, and parents can just hang out. It's crowded and cozy—like Gepetto's workshop. Don't miss it!

Consignment: Tues–Fri 10 am–5 pm, Sat 12 am–5 pm, 50/50 split in trade, 40% consignor/60% store in cash
Children's clothing, toys, books, furniture

~~~~~ Larkspur ~~~~~

SAINT PATRICK'S THRIFT SHOP
457 Magnolia, Larkspur 94939, (415) 924-5393. Tues–Sat 10 am–4 pm. Cash, checks.

If you covet collectibles, love old linens, and go mad for jewelry, you will definitely want to put *Saint Patrick's* on your list of must-sees. Clean, cheerful, bright, and friendly, with traffic-stopping windows, Larkspur's only thrift shop is to die for. Forget the clothes, even though they are clean and in good shape for great prices (a St. John knit for $16.50, a genuine Panama hat for $2.50), and head straight for the glass counter, where there is always some treasure you can't live without, be it jewelry, fine china, silver, or a fabulous collectible. Although the volunteer in charge of antiques once owned an antique store and knows the ropes, prices are still good to great. You can usually find a few fabulous bargains on the open shelves and tables full of housewares and what-nots. Occasional half-off sales make for even greater bargains.
Charity: Saint Patrick's Church and School
Everything except furniture and large appliances

~~~~~ **Marin City** ~~~~~

MARIN CITY FLEA MARKET
*147 Donohue, Marin City, (415)
332-1441 weekdays, (415) 331-
6752 weekends. Sat and Sun 6
am–4 pm. Purchase method
varies by dealer.*

If you walk or drive in to buy,
admission is free. If you are
interested in buying, give the office
a call to find out the details and the
cost.
Everything

~~~~~ **Mill Valley** ~~~~~

**AMERICAN CANCER SOCIETY
DISCOVERY SHOP**
*773 East Blithedale, Mill Valley
94941, (415) 389-1164. Mon–Sat
10 am–5 pm. Cash, checks, MC/
VISA.*

A typical *Discovery Shop*, the
emphasis is on antiques; collectibles; jewelry; housewares; and
quality clothing for women, men,
and children. The shop keeps only
the best (i.e., items with 60% of
their life still left in them) and
donates the rest to the *Salvation
Army*.
Charity: American Cancer Society
**Everything except large
appliances**

A CHANGE OF HEART
*35 Reed Blvd. (next to Strawberry
Village), Mill Valley 94941, (415)
388-9854. Mon–Sat 9:30 am–5:30
pm. Cash, checks.*

You won't see yourself coming and
going if you shop in this jazzy-
looking store. *A Change of Heart*
features good to designer labels,
casual to dressy in sizes 3/4–20, at
great prices. We liked their organiz-
ing system—purple hangers
indicate higher priced items, pink
signals casual wear, and black
means designer. Executive women
will like their suits—an Evan Picone
goes for $58, a Valentino for $50,
an Ann Taylor for $36. You can find
the perfect accessory for any outfit
from their full selection of purses,
scarves, and jewelry. Consignors
will be glad to know that *A Change
of Heart* will pick up from your
home and take care of the dry
cleaning for you.
*Consignment: Mon–Sat 9:30 am–
5:30 pm, 50/50 split*
**Women's clothing and
accessories**

DOWD'S BARN
*157 Throckmorton Ave , Mill
Valley 94941, (415) 388-8110.
Mon–Sat 11 am–6 pm, Sun 1 pm–
5 pm. Cash, checks, MC/VISA.*
Mill Valley's oldest business (they
celebrated their centennial in 1992),
Dowd's Barn represents recycling
at its best. *Dowd's* buys items from
local residents and resells them to
other local residents and to anyone
smart enough to shop there. An
enormous treasure house (treasure
barn to be exact), *Dowd's* is filled to
the very rafters with used and
antique furniture, books, records,
sheet music, jewelry, crystal, china,
linens and laces, housewares, and

art. From the exquisite to the mundane at exquisite to mundane prices, *Dowd's* has it all, including considerable charm, whimsy, and a real creek flowing out in back. Looking for something special? *Dowd's* will list it in their computerized want box and notify you when it's available.

Furniture, housewares, antiques, collectibles, books

THE FAMILY STORE

448 Miller Ave., Mill Valley 94941, (415) 388-9596. Mon–Fri 11 am–4 pm, Sat 10 am–4 pm. Cash, checks.

For 25 years *The Family Store* has been selling recycled clothing, furniture, appliances, and other more esoteric items to benefit the Family Service Agency of Marin. They like to think of themselves as a community resource where people can find serviceable items for everyday use at bargain prices. Two small rooms are crammed with merchandise, but everything is organized and neatly labeled. Check every drawer…we found one full of enough tennis and golf balls to supply a country club.

Charity: Family Service Agency of Marin, which provides counseling services and programs for minority outreach, older adult services, self-help support groups and family education

Everything but large appliances and large pieces of furniture

MT. CARMEL SALVAGE SHOP

45 Lovell Ave., Mill Valley 94941, (415) 388-4332. Mon–Sat 10 am–4 pm. Cash, checks.

Started 40 years ago, *Mt. Carmel Salvage Shop* is now serving third-generation customers, many of whom come from San Francisco and the East Bay to search out funky finds. "We put out things that other shops don't," explained manager Gwen Rasella. "Unusual, unexpected things—people know they can find them here." You bet! You can find almost anything in this converted mortuary—furniture, pots and pans, toys and games, musical instruments, clocks, records, luggage, baskets, pictures and frames, greeting cards, lamps and fixtures, sporting equipment, not to mention clothing for adults and children, yardage, sewing notions, bedding, and an ample library of hard- and soft-cover books. Furniture, kids' clothes, and the unusual are downstairs. Prices are low.

Charity: Our Lady of Mt. Carmel Catholic Church

Everything except large appliances

NELLU'S ATTIC

14 Locust Ave., Mill Valley 94941, (415) 388-2277. Tues–Sat 11 am–6 pm. Cash, checks, MC/VISA.

Is this a fancy secondhand store or a bargain antique bazaar? Check it out for yourself and decide. *Nellu* has some high-priced antiques and also some funky finds—stuffed animal heads, old toys and games,

books, buttons, and jewelry. Prices are high, but still lower than you'd find in upscale antique shops in Marin. There's even a 50¢ basket full of goodies.
Furniture, antiques, collectibles, jewelry, housewares

RETHREADS
7 Throckmorton, Mill Valley 94941, (415) 388-5342. Mon–Sat 11 am–5:30 pm, Sun 12 am–5 pm. Cash, checks, MC/VISA.

Rethreads has a special look about it—maybe it's the pine panelling or the first-quality vintage displayed on the walls—that says shopping here is going to be an adventure. Vintage clothes from the Victorian era through the 1950's represent less than 10% of the merchandise, and the rest is high-quality contemporary clothing, sizes 3/4–15/16, some new, all in perfect condition. The shop is small, packed but organized. The consignment period is only 45 days, so the turnover is rapid. Prices are mid-range to high, but the selection is exceptionally fine—from Banana Republic to Ann Taylor. Choice items on one visit included a Donna Karan dress for $65, a Matsuda jacket for $125, an Italian silk jacket for $250, and a Liz Claiborne suit for $48.
Consignment: Tues and Wed 11 am–3 pm, Fri and Sat 11 am–3 pm, 40% consignor/60% store
Women's clothing, both contemporary and vintage

THE SECOND BANANA
405 Sycamore Ave., Mill Valley 94941, (415) 381-5437. Tues–Sat 10:30 am–4:30 pm, closed for vacation in July. Cash, checks, MC/VISA.

Go up the stairs to the yellow door in the Mill Valley Middle School, and behind it you'll find *The Second Banana*, where Mill Valley parents consign their kids' outgrown clothes, toys, equipment, and baby furniture. Quality ranges from fair to great, prices cheap to dear, but there is lots of everything. Look for the real bargains at the biannual rummage sale, when nothing is over $2 and a 20% discount is given on all merchandise.
Consignment: Mon–Fri 11 am–4 pm, 50/50 split
Charity: Mill Valley Schools Community Foundation
Children's clothes, furniture, and equipment; maternity clothing

SUSANS'
448 Miller Ave., Mill Valley 94941, (415) 381-3733. Tues–Sat 10:30 am–5:30 pm. Cash, checks, MC/VISA.

If you like interesting, unusual clothing, or just want to add a little spice to your wardrobe of basics, give *Susans'* a try. Formerly owned by two women named Susan, this inviting shop carries everything from casual to executive clothing, sizes 2–22, for anyone from high school age on up. Current owner Beckie Raskowsky accepts any garment as long as it's in a current

style, in good condition, and saleable. Prices start at 1/3 of the original cost and are marked down regularly on the first and 15th of the month. "She always has fun things," states one loyal customer. Accompanying men can sit in the comfy armchair and read magazines while waiting, or they can check out *The Family Store* right next door.
Consignment: Tues–Sat 10:30 am–4 pm, 50/50 split
Women's clothing

~~~~~ Novato ~~~~~

AMERICAN CANCER SOCIETY DISCOVERY SHOP
928 Grant Ave., Novato 94947, (415) 898-1149. Mon 10 am–4 pm, Tues–Sat 10 am–5 pm. Cash, checks, MC/VISA.

This *Discovery Shop* is actually two stores put together, with one devoted to clothing and the other to housewares, collectibles, etc. When we were there, the etc. included a nice array of new stationery supplies.
Charity: American Cancer Society
Everything except large appliances

CASTAWAY SHOP
967 5th St., Novato 94945, (415) 892-1609. Tues–Wed 11 am–2

~~~~~~~~~~~~~~~~~~~~~

Left: Eden Tanovitz and Angel Menendez at Felino's Vintage Clothing, San Francisco.

pm, first and third Sats 10 am–1 pm. Cash, checks.

One of the oldest thrift stores in Novato, the tiny crowded *Castaway Shop* has the cheapest prices we've seen. According to the posted price list, dresses are $1.50, slacks are $1.25, suits for men and women cost $3, purses are $1, hats are $1, and so on. Housewares and collectibles are also plentiful, wonderful and cheap. We couldn't resist a set of never-been-used Sheffield bone-handled steak knives in the original 1930's box for $6. They don't give you a lot of shopping hours, so it might be worthwhile to schedule your trip to Novato around their schedule.
Charity: Episcopal Church Women of Saint Francis Church
Everything except furniture and large appliances

THE CONSIGNMENT SHOP
818 Grant Ave., Novato 94945, (415) 892-3496. Tues–Sat 10 am–5 pm, Sun and Mon 11 am–4 pm. Cash, checks.

Sharon Hirte, the feisty owner of *The Consignment Shop*, likes to think of her store as an adoption agency for stuff. If you're looking to adopt an antique or semi-antique piece of furniture, for $395 you could end up the proud parent of a small 1930's writing desk. Objects of all kinds, periods, and styles, priced from $1 to $1000, are looking for permanent homes. A word of advice: don't tell Hirte you're planning to paint anything white. She recently refused to sell

an antique etagere to a woman who had this fate planned for it. *Consignment: Tues–Sat, 50/50 split*
Furniture, art, antiques, collectibles, jewelry

HAMILTON THRIFT SHOP
Hamilton Air Base, Novato 94947, (415) 883-5770. Tues, Thurs, Fri 10 am–1:30 pm, first Sats 10 am–1 pm. Cash, checks.
Only military personnel can consign, but anyone can shop at *Hamilton Thrift Shop*, located on the base. We found prices high for the quality of the merchandise. Best buys were household goods. Unless you're in the market for potted plants (orchids were $13), it's not worth a trip.
Everything

NOVATO SEEDLINGS
1133 Grant Ave., Novato 94945, (415) 892-5600. Mon–Sat 10 am–5 pm. Cash, local checks, MC/VISA.
A good-sized store divided down the middle with new merchandise on one side and used on the other, *Seedlings'* racks are tightly packed with girls' clothes, sizes newborn–14, and boys' clothes, sizes newborn–16. Prices are good and the selection even better, especially in hard-to-find clothing for big boys. New merchandise comes in every day. Owner O'Linda Pine advises her customers, "If you don't see it on Monday, come back on Friday." Mothers of young girls will enjoy the one-stop shopping opportunities afforded by the selection of dance supplies and official Girl Scout and Brownie paraphernalia. *Consignment: Mon–Sat 10 am–4 pm, 40% consignor/60% store*
Children's clothes, toys, furniture

SECOND CENTER THRIFT SHOP
1523 S. Novato Blvd., Novato 94947, (415) 892-2172. Mon–Fri 10:30 am–5 pm, Sat 10 am–4 pm. Cash, checks.
When you step inside this quaint little yellow house, you're in for a swell surprise. Someone with a sense of style right out of the pages of *Victoria* magazine has decorated the front room. Antiques and collectibles line the shelves; vintage hats peek out of vintage hat boxes; and old quilts lay casually across antique steamer trunks, drawers filled with antique linens and other delectable collectibles. Customers come from all over to snap up the treasures at bargain prices. You might be tempted to linger in the book room—it's so neat, well-organized, and inviting (book dealers are frequent customers, and it's no wonder with paperbacks for 10¢ and hardbacks for 25¢). But my advice is to keep going (the shop goes on and on) until you've seen it all. *Second Center Thrift Shop* may be the best reason there is to drive out to Novato.
Charity: Novato Human Needs Center
Everything except large appliances and large pieces of furniture

SECOND STORY

408 Ignacio Blvd., Novato 94947, (415) 883-2400. Mon–Sat 10 am–5 pm. Cash, checks, MC/VISA.

Second Story is a fine example of the no-frills approach to resale shopping. The store is big, ugly, and not pristine by any means. But merchandise is plentiful, with a broad range of styles, sizes, and labels. They have casual to dressy, cruise-wear to square-dance outfits, kids' clothes sizes newborn–12, and a "big and beautiful" section for larger women, all at no-frills prices.

Consignment: Mon–Sat 10 am–3 pm, 50/50 split

Women's and children's clothing

WARDROBE EXCHANGE

1531 S. Novato Blvd., Novato 94947, (415) 898-8113. Mon–Sat 11 am–6 pm. Cash, checks, MC/VISA.

Smaller and less trendy than its sister store in San Anselmo, Novato's *Wardrobe Exchange* is also less expensive. Casual wear and work clothes are stocked year round; dressier outfits appear during the holiday season. A pleasant, clean, but somewhat empty store, plans are to change over to merchandise geared to the younger crowd. Prices are moderate, with great deals on the $3 rack.

Consignment: Mon–Sat 11 am–4 pm, 50/50 split (less any cleaning costs)

Women's clothing

~~~~~~~ **Ross** ~~~~~~~

LAUREL HOUSE ANTIQUES

Marin Art and Garden Center, PO Box 437, Ross 94957, (415) 454-8472. Tues–Fri 11 am–4 pm. Cash, checks, MC/VISA.

Everyone in Marin already knows about the beautiful Marin Art and Garden Center. Uninitiated lovers of wonderful old things will definitely want to get to know this venerable Marin institution. *Laurel House,*the Garden Center's consignment shop, consists of two separate buildings—one housing Asian arts and artifacts, and the other Western antiques and collectibles.

Antique fanatics will find this place irresistible. Room after room filled with treasures—crystal, china, brass-ware, pottery, linens and laces, furniture—you name it, they have it, and the best of it. Although we're not talking thrift-store prices by any means, bargains abound in comparison to antique shops with merchandise of similar quality. New merchandise is put on the floor every Tuesday morning, when the store is packed with antique dealers looking for choice items to sell at twice the price. *Laurel House* is definitely worth a visit, even if just to browse. You might want to have lunch in the charming tea room, open 11:30 am–2 pm.

Consignment: Mon 10 am–1 pm, 73% consignor/27% store
Charity: Marin Art and Garden Center

Furniture, antiques, collectibles, jewelry

~~~~ San Anselmo ~~~~

THE CATCH-ALL
541 San Anselmo Ave., San Anselmo 94960, (415) 456-1206. Mon–Sat 10 am–5 pm, Sun 11 am–4 pm. Cash, checks, MC/VISA.

As you might expect from one of the finest private schools in Marin, *The Catch-All* is an upscale thrift shop specializing in slightly worn, high-quality used clothing. Except for men's suits, priced $20 and up, prices are a bit steep, even taking into consideration the designer labels. On our visit we found that new clothing—a high style, mid-priced junior line donated by a local manufacturer—was a much better buy.
Charity: The Branson School Scholarship Fund
Everything except furniture and large appliances

CAROL'S CONSIGNMENTS
65 Red Hill Ave., San Anselmo 94960, (415) 456-9022. Tues–Fri 11 am–6 pm, Sat 10 am–6 pm. Cash, checks, MC/VISA.

Previously known as *From Many Closets*, new ownership has recently opened *Carol's Consignments* to bring you quality merchandise (designer and middle range) for women and children (sizes newborn–12, mostly girls) at modest prices (1/3 the retail value).
Consignment: Anytime, 50/50 split unless over $80
Women's and children's clothing

HUMANE SOCIETY THRIFT SHOP
360 San Anselmo Ave., San Anselmo 94960, (415) 459-9929. Mon–Fri 10:30 am–3:30 pm. Cash, checks.

It's impossible to predict what you are going to find in this crowded little shop. One day there will be so many tempting goodies, you won't know how to choose. Not long ago someone donated an entire collection of horse figurines, all selling for $3 and under. Another day—zilch! The shop's been doing business at the same location since the 1940's, so there must be more banner days than not. Clothing is never the main attraction, but it's always cheap (men's suits run $10–$15). Books, jewelry, knickknacks, and the unexpected are the items to look for.
Charity: Marin County Humane Society
Everything except large appliances and large pieces of furniture

SAX
629 San Anselmo Ave., San Anselmo 94960, (415) 456-7655. Mon–Sat 11 am–6 pm, Sun 11 am–5 pm. Cash, checks, MC/VISA.

If you are young, trendy, and devoted to high fashion but not high prices, *Sax* is the place for you. One of the few resale shops we've seen with a clearly defined market, *Sax* carries only upscale, sporty fashions in the latest styles (sizes 2–14) for the definitely hip young woman—forget the tailored dress-for-success look. New hats, jewelry, socks, tights, leggings, and tees are available to complete any outfit. The only way you can tell the consigned clothes aren't new is by the price—half of what you'd pay retail.

Consignment: Wed–Sat, 50/50 split, pressing charge 50¢–$2 per garment
Women's clothing

SECOND CHANCE GALLERY

530 San Anselmo Ave., San Anselmo 94960, (415) 721-7275. Mon–Sat 11 am–5 pm, Sun 12 am–5 pm. Cash, checks, MC/ VISA.

Another delightful store for the younger woman, *Second Chance* carries vintage garments from the 1920's through the 1960's, stylish contemporary clothes, and bridal fashions. Before making a major investment outfitting the women in your wedding party, investigate these once-worn bridal gowns for $90–$450, bridesmaids' dresses and hats, and high-fashion dresses for the wedding guests. This pretty store also carries antique furniture and accessories for the home.

Consignment: Mon–Sat 11 am–5 pm, 50/50 split, 90-day contract
Antiques, art, bridal, and women's clothing

SHADOWS

429 San Anselmo Ave., San Anselmo 94960, (415) 459-0574. Mon–Sat 11:15 am–6 pm, Sun 12 am–5 pm. Cash, check, MC/VISA.

Do lace doilies and dried rosebuds decorate your dresser? Do you sigh for the romance of a bygone era? Then *Shadows* is your dream store. Feminine, delicate, and romantic are the operative words here. Brides with a hankering for things Victorian (Edwardian, Art Deco, etc.) can find authentic period gowns, new gowns handmade from old fabrics, or contemporary frocks made in the style of days gone by. Most wedding dresses cost $200–$600, although some vintage Victorians are higher. Old and new jewelry and vintage and contemporary day dresses complete the inventory.
Jewelry, vintage, and new bridal gowns

WARDROBE EXCHANGE

570 San Anselmo Ave., San Anselmo 94960, (415) 459-7317. Mon–Sat 11 am–6 pm. Cash, checks, MC/VISA.

Featuring casual to dressy clothing in sizes 4–14, this busy shop gives you good value for your money.

Consignment: Mon–Sat 11 am–4 pm, 50/50 split
Women's clothing and accessories

~~~~~ San Rafael ~~~~~

AMERICAN CANCER SOCIETY DISCOVERY SHOP

Northgate I, Terralinda Shopping Center, San Rafael 94903, (415) 507-0157. Mon–Sat 10 am–5 pm. Cash, checks, MC/VISA.

By the time this book goes to

press, the *Discovery Shop* will have moved to their new address listed above. We did not have a chance to visit the new store, but I'm sure it's as upscale as the rest. Go see for yourself!

Charity: American Cancer Society
Everything except large appliances

THE BARGAIN BOX
607 Irwin St., San Rafael 94901, (415) 459-2396. Mon–Sat 10 am–4 pm. Cash, checks.

Ask about thrift stores in Marin and the first one mentioned is always *The Bargain Box*—the Pacific Sun named it the best thrift shop in Marin. It's certainly one of the biggest, definitely one of the busiest, and it boasts a huge inventory of merchandise ranging from junk to funk to exquisite. Their "Owl's Attic Books" section, organized like a little local library, is one of the biggest and best in town. Clothes are plentiful and cheap, as are ordinary furniture and housewares. Artifacts, antiques, and anything anyone might consider collectible are corralled in Peacock Allee, their high-end boutique, where prices are sky-high.

Charity: Sunny Hills Children's Service, which provides residential care to children separated from their families because of abuse or neglect
Everything

DEPOT AT ST. VINCENT SCHOOL FOR BOYS
4900 Hwy 101 (Exit Marinwood), San Rafael 94903, (415) 479-0366. Tues–Fri 10 am–3 pm, first and third Sats 10 am–3 pm. Cash, checks.

The *Depot* would be worth a visit just to see the exquisite garden setting and magnificent 19th-century buildings of St. Vincent's School for Boys. Once a dormitory for 600 boys, the *Depot* now beckons thrill-seeking thrift shoppers like Circe called Ulysses. "We take anything from anybody," explained a friendly volunteer. "Anything you ever heard of we have or will have." From door-knobs to bathroom sinks, they have it all, and at ridiculously low prices, too. There are two floors of treasures and trash: downstairs you have the housewares and col-lectibles room (with a magnificent stone fireplace), the furniture room, the library (selling books, of course), and more. Upstairs, visit the basket room, a room with beds, a room of hardware, a clothes room, and so on....

Charity: St. Vincent's School, a residential school for boys from broken homes
Everything except large appliances

ENCORE
5 Mary Street, San Rafael 94901, (415) 456-7309. Mon–Sat 10 am–5 pm. Cash, checks, MC/VISA.

In business for 30 years, *Encore* has a new store with 1400 square feet and over 7000 items on consignment. Featuring casual to dressy styles in sizes 2–22/24, they are known for their upscale cocktail dresses and long gowns. A savvy salesclerk advised, "You should always look in a consignment store first." Which is just what *Encore's* loyal customers do. Socialites come from San Francisco to snap up Italian and French designer wear, while ordinary mortals are content with high quality clothing bearing a Nordstrom, Liz Claiborne, or Ann Klein label. Nothing is more than two years old. Prices start at 1/3 to 1/2 of retail; garments are marked down 25% after 30 days and then go to 50% off the original price during the last two weeks of the 60-day consignment period. *Consignment: Tues–Sat 10 am–3 pm, 50/50 split, 60-day contract* **Women's clothing and accessories**

GOODSTUFF

1942 Fourth St., San Rafael 94901, (415) 456-4227. Tues–Sat 10 am–5 pm. Cash, checks.

When you first see the black and white checkered floor and the neatly displayed assortment of knickknacks in the front room, you'll suspect another upscale thrift shop boutique. Don't be fooled by first impressions. Disorder replaces organization as you make your way through the back rooms. Although you will find ample amounts of everything from clothing to collectibles, you won't find any unbelievable bargains. *Goodstuff* is

not giving anything away, but your dollars do support a good cause. *Charity: Marin Food Bank* **Everything except large appliances**

GOODWILL

809 Lincoln, San Rafael 94901, (415) 456-5273. Mon–Fri 10 am–7 pm, Sat 10 am–6 pm, Sun 11 am–5:30 pm. Cash, MC/VISA/DIS-COVER.

From underwear (new) to exercise equipment, you'll find just about everything except large appliances in Marin's bright, cheerful *Goodwill.* We were especially impressed with the selection of classy furniture, which included a nifty 1940's sofa for $125 and a seven-piece dining set, antique or almost, for $200. Merchandise comes from the San Francisco distribution center. *Charity: Goodwill* **Everything except large appliances**

HOSPICE HODGEPODGE THRIFT AND GIFT

1541 Fourth St., San Rafael 94901, (415) 459-4686. Tues–Sat 10 am–4 pm. Cash, checks.

Aptly named, *Hodgepodge* is a thrift shopper's dream—a 2100 square-foot treasure box filled to overflowing with knickknacks, housewares, and collectibles of every description. They have very few clothes, but you won't miss them when you feast your eyes on everything else—jewelry, clocks, telephones, linens, laces, chairs, and china. When I was there, they

had recently received a collection of orientalia, which included an exquisitely carved ivory cricket cage. The near future includes plans to expand, according to manager Cinnie Potts. Let's hope nothing changes but the size. Look for half-price sales every three months.
Charity: Hospice of Marin
Everything except large appliances

MARIN GENERAL HOSPITAL VOLUNTEER THRIFT SHOP
1115 Third St. (in the arcade between A & B Street), San Rafael 94901, (415) 456-1430. Mon–Sat 11 am–4 pm. Cash, checks.

Formerly a computer store, this large two-room thrift store now sells clothing, furniture, bric-a-brac, and household items. Among the clothing you'll find overall low prices and quality running the gamut from Sears polyester to Jaeger.
Charity: Marin General Hospital
Everything except large and small appliances

MOM MATERNITY CENTER
1414 Fourth St., San Rafael 94901, (415) 457-4955. Mon–Sat 10 am–4 pm. Cash, checks, MC/ VISA.

A resource center for maternity needs, *MOM* recently expanded its services to include pre-owned maternity wear and breast pump rental. Featuring new and used maternity clothing and accessories,

MOM specializes in high-quality clothing for the professional woman and casual and special occasion outfits. Consignment clothes include top-of-the-line maternity labels like Pea in a Pod, Page Boy, Mother's Work, and Japanese Weekend, all in up-to-date styles and perfect condition. Executive suits run $69–$80. Prices may seem a bit high, but you get excellent values with such top-end merchandise.
Consignment: Mon–Fri 10 am–4 pm, 50/50 split, 90-day contract
Maternity clothing

MOTHER'S LOVE
2915 Kerner Blvd. #G (one block past UPS), San Rafael 94901, (415) 456-3542. Mon–Fri 10 am–5 pm, Sat 10 am–4 pm. Cash, checks.

Mothers—especially mothers on tight budgets—will love *Mother's Love*. It's hard to find, but once you do we guarantee you'll go back. This 1000 square-foot store shows how a little paint and carpeting, good taste, ingenuity, and hard work can take an unfriendly warehouse space and turn it into a warm, inviting store. Racks are packed with clothing, all clean, in good condition, low-priced, and in sizes to fit infants through teens. "It's a waste not to recycle," affirms owner Adelle Haran, who prices merchandise below price levels found at Mervyns. Mothers-to-be who are not looking for fancy labels or high style will love the maternity selection, which features

many items under $10.
Consignment: Anytime, 50/50
split, 90-day contract
Children's clothing, toys,
baby furniture, maternity
clothing

ONE MORE TIME/THE LOFT
1821 Fourth St., San Rafael
94901, (415) 459-6137. Tues–Fri
10 am–4:30 pm, Sat 10 am–3 pm.
Cash, checks.

Side by side, these two stores
benefit Marin Suicide Prevention
Center. *One More Time* stocks
clothes, housewares, books,
baskets, and miscellanea. Look for
great buys on everything, especially
clothing: men's suits run $12–$25,
sports coats go for $4–$12, and
jeans (which were on special during
our visit) cost $1.49. Women's
clothes, including some high-end
labels like Leslie Fay and Joanie
Char, are also great bargains. All
antiques and collectibles received
as donations are sold in *The Loft*,
along with items on consignment.
You can expect to find a wealth of
beautiful pieces at almost antique-
store prices.
Consignment: Mon 12:30 am–3
pm and Tues, Thurs, Fri 10 am–
12:30 am; 70% consignor/30%
store
Everything except large
appliances and large pieces
of furniture

OUTGROWN
1417 Fourth St., San Rafael
94901, (415) 457-2219. Mon–Sat
10 am–4 pm. Cash, checks, MC/
VISA.

Below: Crackerjacks, Oakland.

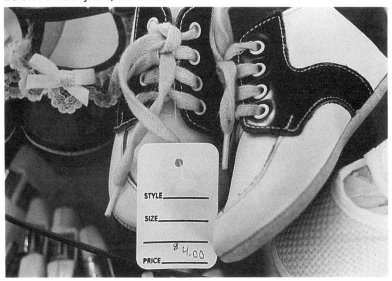

Sydne Robinson opened the first children's consignment store in Marin 15 years ago, and it has been going strong ever since. In addition to gently worn maternity clothes and new and used baby furniture, the store is packed with high-quality, reasonably priced clothes in sizes newborn–14. For the Osh Kosh crowd there's an excellent selection priced $4–$8; Levis cost $6–$8; and best of all, you'll find an impressive array of the rarest of all resale finds—clothes for older boys. Moms, check here before you shell out big bucks for that classy blue blazer at Young Man's Fancy which, if you're lucky, he'll wear twice before he outgrows it.

Consignment: Mon–Fri 10 am–3 pm, 40% consignor/60% store on clothing and toys, 50/50 split on furniture

Maternity clothing, children's clothing and furniture

PLAY IT AGAIN

967 Grand Ave. (1 blk. north of Montecito Center), San Rafael 94901, (415) 485-0304. Mon–Sat 10 am–5 pm. Cash, checks.

The crème de la crème of children's resale, *Play It Again* carries only the best, sizes newborn–14, for your precious darlings. The selection is smaller and prices are slightly higher than other children's resale shops, but the quality is unsurpassable. Owners Steffi Shekar and Sally Kornhauser are very selective about what they buy, so you don't have to waste your time looking at a lot of things you

don't want. Grandmas will love this place. Their new baby clothes from France are to sigh for.

Consignment: Mostly buys out right by appointment, consigns equipment for 50/50 split

Children's clothing and equipment

SALVATION ARMY

350 Fourth St., San Rafael 94901, (415) 454-7201. Mon–Sat 9:30 am–5 pm. Cash, checks, MC/ VISA.

My first thought when I drove up to the handsome ranch-style complex housing the *San Rafael Salvation Army Community Center and Thrift Store*: only in Marin. Even the unenlightened who disdain thrift shopping as grimy and grungy would have to change their tune if they saw this beautiful complex. The inside is almost as nice as the outside. Half of the store holds clothing—new Jessica McClintock wedding gowns were $60–$85, bridesmaids' dresses were $20. The other half holds furniture—a five-piece formica dinette set was $89.50, a white kitchen table was also $89.50, and a four-burner Magic Chef oven was $135. This big, bright store is filled with the best the Army has to offer.

Charity: Salvation Army

Everything

SEEK AND FIND THRIFT SHOP

1815 Fourth St. (across from Yard Birds), San Rafael 94901, (415) 456-7353. Mon–Sat 11 am–4 pm. Cash, local checks.

Seek and Find is a two-room store, but only one room is open to the public—unless you see something you like in the window. Then you can go into the closed room, the marking room, to get it. (We just stuck to the small public room, so I can't speak with authority about the other room.) What we found was mostly clothes at unbelievably low prices: men's suits for $9, sports jackets for $5, women's dresses for $3–$8, blouses for $3. Although I saw many good labels, nothing was particularly new or high style. Vintage collectors, this is your place: they clearly don't know old from vintage here. Seek and I guarantee you'll find at least one classic piece at a price you can't pass by. We did pass up a 1940's quilted satin robe for $3 and some 1950's housedresses, also $3.

Charity: San Francisco Theological Seminary of the Presbyterian Church

Everything except furniture and large appliances

SUCH A DEAL!

638 Fourth St., San Rafael 94901, (415) 453-BUYS. Mon–Sat 11 am–6 pm. Cash, checks, MC/VISA.

The new kid on the block, *Such a Deal!* has been making deals only since September 1991. Eye-catching windows give you a preview of high-quality merchandise inside. 80% of the stock is clothing, much of it high quality for low prices. Kids' items are $1, men's suits are $15, sports coats cost $10, pants and shirts cost $4,

women's suits are $12, dresses are $6, sweaters and pants are $5, and shoes cost only $4. All the appliances work, thanks to a handy volunteer who can fix anything from a printer to an answering machine. On our visit we found plenty of collectibles, including vintage linens and chenille spreads from the 1940's—wonderful, but not such a deal price-wise.

Charity: Osher Marin Jewish Community Center

Everything except large appliances and large pieces of furniture

TWICE IS NICE

1015 Second St. (at A), San Rafael 94901, (415) 453-0690. Mon–Sat 10 am–6 pm, Sun 2 pm–5 pm. Cash, checks, layaway, MC/VISA.

Quite a few antique dealers are going to hate to see this secret told. Sorry, but this one is too good to keep quiet. If you love period furniture, fine antiques, quality 20th-century pieces, and unusual collectibles, you'll want to shout with joy when you see the splendid selection Daisy Samoun has put together in her charming shop. Unique, one-of-a-kind pieces go for fabulous bargain prices. We're talking dollars here, not pennies, but still half of what you'd pay in an antique store. (Her secret is consignment. Low overhead allows her to pass on great deals to you.) DON'T MISS THIS ONE!

Consignment: Mon–Sat 10 am–6 pm, 50/50 split on most items,

60% consignor/40% store on high-priced items. Also buys outright.
Furniture, antiques, collectibles

YOURS FOR THE EVENING
1327 Fourth St., San Rafael 94901, (415) 456-5516. Mon–Sat 10 am–5 pm. Cash, checks, MC/ VISA.
Been invited to the Academy Awards but haven't a thing to wear? Don't fret. Visit *Yours for the Evening* and experience their collection of gorgeous designer gowns, sizes 2–26, and rent the dress of your dreams. Proms, cruises, the Academy Awards, even the Nobel Prize ceremonies—these exquisite, unique creation have been everywhere. Rental prices start at $60. All gowns are retired after a season and sold at bargain prices. Check it out—unless you regularly attend opera openings or gala charity balls, you've probably never seen so many spectacular gowns in one place. The store is a knockout also.
Women's formal wear

~~~~ Sausalito ~~~~

SAUSALITO SALVAGE SHOP
19 Princess, Sausalito 94965, (415) 332-3471. Mon 1 pm–4 pm, Tues–Fri 10 am–4 pm, Sat 12 am– 4 pm. Cash.
Started in 1939 as *Bundles for Britain*, *Sausalito Salvage* lays claim to the title of Marin's oldest thrift

shop. It is certainly one of the best. Located in a former pool hall (you can still see the dents in the wooden floor made by the pool tables), it is chock-a-block with intriguing merchandise, from designer toilets for $75 to Dresden china. "Whatever it is, it will arrive sooner or later," stated one confident volunteer. Because the shop supports fifty different charities, it collects merchandise from a large donor base. (Being Sausalito's only thrift shop doesn't hurt either.) Clothing prices couldn't be better: children's clothes, toys, and shoes are all priced at 50¢. If the thrill of the hunt is what excites you, be sure to put this one on your list.
Charity: Supports 50 local charities (ask to see the list)
Everything except large appliances and large pieces of furniture

~~~~ Tiburon ~~~~

SECOND GENERATION
1 Blackfield Drive (Cove Shopping Center), Tiburon 94920, (415) 388-8313. Mon–Sat 10 am–5 pm, Sun 12 am–4 pm. Cash, checks, MC/VISA.
The best-dressed woman I know consigns her clothes here. (No, she doesn't shop here also, thank goodness. Someone has to support I Magnin and Saks Fifth Avenue.) With white walls and minimalist, neat-as-a-pin decor, *Second Generation* doesn't waste any

effort on creating ambience. But with their merchandise, they don't have to. From jeans to Jeanne Marc, from Gap to Gucci, from completely casual to dynamite dressy, all in sizes 4–16, they cover the fashion map with a range of prices to match almost any budget. Although prices at times seem inconsistent, you can find consistently great buys on gorgeous pieces from their designer rack—we saw a Louis Feraud suit for $150 and a three-piece Parigi tuxedo for $95.

Consignment: Mon–Sat 10 am–3 pm, 50/50 split, 60-day contract
Women's clothing

TIBURON THRIFT SHOP
1101 Tiburon Blvd., Tiburon 94920, (415) 435-6050. Tues–Sat 10 am–4 pm. Cash, checks.

A one-room shop carrying a bit of this and a bit of that at little bitty prices. Sheets are $2, place mats and pillowcases are 50¢. You get a tie free when you buy a man's suit ($25–$35).

Charity: Community Congregational Church, Saint Hillary's, Westminster Presbyterian, St. Stephen's, and Reed Union School District
Everything except large appliances and large pieces of furniture

MARIN COUNTY	Appliances/large	Bridal	Clothing/children	Clothing/men	Clothing/women	Collectibles	Furnishings/children	Furniture	Housewares	Maternity	Tools, etc.	Toys	Vintage	Page number
CORTE MADERA														
Babies Unlimited			X				X							79
Clothes Encounters			X	X										79
FAIRFAX														
La Donna					X									79
Ross Valley Store			X					X				**X**		80
LARKSPUR														
Saint Patrick's			X	X	X	**X**	X	X	X			X		80
MARIN CITY														
Marin City Market	X	X	X	X	X	X	X	X	X	X	X	X	X	81
MILL VALLEY														
Discovery Shop			X	X	X	X	X	X	X			X		81
Change of Heart					X									81
Dowd's Barn						**X**		X	X					81
Family Store			X	X	X	X		X	X		X	X		82
Mt. Carmel Shop			X	X	X	X	X	X	X		X	X		82
Nellu's Attic						X		X	X					82
Rethreads					X								X	83
Second Banana			X				X		X			X		83
Susans'					X									83
NOVATO														
Discovery Shop			X	X	X	X	X	X	X	X		X		85
Castaway Shop			X	X	X	X			X			X		85
Consignment Shop					X			X	X					85
Hamilton Shop	X	X	X	X	X	X	X	X	X	X	X	X		86
Novato Seedlings			X				X					X		86
Second Center			X	X	X	X	X	X	X		X	X		86
Second Story			X		X									87
Wardrobe Exchange					X									87
ROSS														
Laurel House						X		X	X					87
SAN ANSELMO														
Catch-All			X	X	X	X			X			X		88
Carol's Cnsgnmnts.			X		X									88

MARIN COUNTY	Appliances/large	Bridal	Clothing/children	Clothing/men	Clothing/women	Collectibles	Furnishings/children	Furniture	Housewares	Maternity	Tools, etc.	Toys	Vintage	Page number
Humane Society Shop			X	X	X	X		X	X			X	X	88
Sax					X									88
Second Chance		X			X	X		X	X				X	89
Shadows		X			X								X	89
Wardrobe Exchange					X									89
SAN RAFAEL														
Discovery Shop			X	X	X	X	X	X	X			X		89
Bargain Box	X	X	X	X	X	X	X	X	X	X	X	X		90
Depot at St. Vincent			X	X	X	X	X	X	X			X	X	90
Encore					**X**									90
Goodstuff			X	X	X	X	X	X	X			X	X	91
Goodwill		X	X	X	X	X	X	X	X	X	X	X		91
Hospice Hodgepodge			X	X	X	**X**	X	X	X			X	X	91
Marin Hospital Thrift		X	X	X	X	X	X	X	X	X	X	X		92
MOM Maternity										X				92
Mother's Love			**X**			X			X			X		92
One More Time			X	X	X	X	X	X	X	X		X		93
Outgrown			X			X			X			X		93
Play it Again			**X**			X								94
Salvation Army	X	X	X	X	X	X	X	X	X	X	X	X		94
Seek and Find		X	X	X	X	X	X		X				X	94
Such a Deal!		X	X	X	X	X	X	X	X	X		X		95
Twice is Nice						X		**X**						95
Yours for the Evening					**X**									96
SAUSALITO														
Salvage Shop			X	X	X	X	X	X	X			X	X	96
TIBURON														
Second Generation					X									96
Tiburon Thrift			X	X	X	X	X	X	X				X	97

SAN FRANCISCO

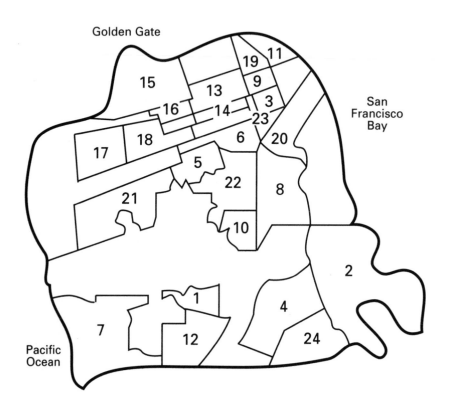

Golden Gate

San Francisco Bay

Pacific Ocean

1. Balboa Terrace	13. Pacific Heights
2. Bayview	14. Pacific Heights/Lower
3. Downtown	15. Presidio
4. Excelsior	16. Presidio Heights
5. Haight Ashbury	17. Richmond/Central
6. Hayes Valley	18. Richmond/Inner
7. Lakeshore	19. Russian Hill
8. Mission/Inner	20. South of Market
9. Nob Hill	21. Sunset
10. Noe Valley	22. Upper Market
11. North Beach	23. Van Ness/Civic Center
12. Ocean	24. Visitation Valley

〰 Balboa Terrace 〰

ST. FRANCIS CHURCH MOUSE THRIFT STORE

St. Francis Church, Ocean Ave and San Fernando Way, San Francisco 94112, (415) 587-1082. Tues, Thurs, Sat, 10 am–3 pm. Cash, checks.

The church mice must be working overtime to keep this pleasant shop in such apple-pie order. Whatever you're looking for in the way of men's, women's, and children's clothing is easy to find in this highly organized store. Prices are low, quality is medium to high, and great finds pop up all the time. I couldn't resist a men's gabardine shirt from the 1940's in perfect condition for only $3. I sent it to my fashion-designer niece in New York, who changed the buttons and wears it everywhere. These shirts go for $40 in downtown vintage shops (and more in New York).
Charity: St. Francis Church
Everything but furniture and large appliances

〰 Bayview 〰

GOODWILL

3801 3rd St. (in Bay View Plaza), San Francisco 94124, (415) 641-4470. Mon–Sat 1 am–6 pm, Sun 12 am–6 pm. Cash, checks, MC/VISA/DISCOVER.

This beautiful store looks more like Macy's than any other *Goodwill* in San Francisco, and carries the same fine selection of clothing at the same great prices.
Charity: Goodwill
Everything except large appliances

〰 Downtown 〰

COMMUNITY HOSPICE THRIFT SHOP

1173 Sutter (at Larkin and Polk), San Francisco 94019, (415) 673-3030. Tues–Sat 10 am–4 pm. Cash, layaway, MC/VISA.

Yes indeed, they do have everything. The variety of merchandise is truly outstanding. Dressers and dresses, vases and vintage, tapes and toys—collectors of just about everything will have a field day excavating for funky and fabulous trash and treasures in this crowded store. Better clothes and vintage are kept behind the counter, best clothing buys are on the floor. You'll have to sift through a lot to find the real bargains, but they're there. A fishbowl full of handkerchiefs, a French nightstand for $65, a sofa for $50, a set of five wine glasses for $5.50. If you like the item but

not the price, talk to the manager Gail Acevedo. She might be able to do something for you, or she might not. See for yourself.
Charity: Hospice by the Bay
Everything

GOODWILL
922 Geary (between Hyde and Larkin), San Francisco 94109, (415) 922-0405. Mon–Sun 10 am–6 pm. Cash, checks, MC/VISA.
A clean, pleasant Goodwill.
Charity: Goodwill
Everything except large appliances

LOVE PROJECT
766 Geary, San Francisco 94109, (415) 928-3773. Mon–Fri 1 pm–6 pm. Cash.
Knickknacks, antiques, and oddities perpetually circle on the revolving display in the window of this small thrift shop. Clothing (most of it men's), knickknacks, housewares, and odds and ends make up the majority of the merchandise you'll find inside. Prices are quite reasonable—men's pants are $4–$10, suits are $14–$30, sports coats are $7–$14—and not at all firm. Bartering is expected. We admired a fur muff trimmed with fox heads and some matching earmuffs, and they were instantly reduced in price from $10 to $8 before we had a chance to say a word.
Charity: Shanti project
Everything except large appliances and large pieces of furniture

RAFAEL HOUSE
1065 Sutter, San Francisco 94109, (415) 474-4621. Thurs–Sat 10 am–4 pm. Cash, checks.
Rafael House prices are the best in the city, according to manager Brother John of Christ the Savior Brotherhood. Looking at the $1 price tags on pants, shirts, and blouses, you have to believe him. Residents of Rafael House, a home for San Francisco homeless, shop at the store for free. Children's clothing, furniture, and any household goods that would be useful for a family setting up a new home are reserved for the program. Volunteers get second pick, then staff members, then the rest of us. But not to worry, there are always great bargains left in clothes, books, knickknacks, and crafts made by the Seniors' Sewing Circle. Brother John has a knowing eye for collectibles, antiques, and special treasures, and he reserves these for the general public. One look at the delightful window display (also the work of Brother John) lets you know that there are always plenty of treasures.
Charity: Rafael House
Everything except large appliances and large pieces of furniture

~~~~ **Excelsior** ~~~~

DEMELLO'S FURNITURE WAREHOUSE
4352 Mission (at Silver), San Francisco 94112, (415) 587-0320.

Mon–Sat 10 am–6 pm. Cash, checks.

New, used, antique, and modern; from catalogs, estates, offices, and hotel liquidations...they have furniture to suit every taste in this large warehouse. While we're not talking bargain-basement prices (the less expensive pieces get sent to *Aron Furniture*, their other store in the Mission), you can still find good deals. Two beautiful refinished turn-of-the-century dining sets were going for $1000 and $1295. For my money, I'd take the older used pieces any day. However, if you prefer the new stuff, you can order from a catalog or buy off the floor at good savings.
Furniture

~~~ Haight Ashbury ~~~

AARDVARK'S ODD ARK
1501 Haight St., San Francisco 94102, (415) 621-3141. Mon–Sun 11 am–7 pm. Cash, checks, MC/ VISA.

Contrary to popular belief, *Aardvark's* DOES NOT buy or trade clothing. Everything—vintage, reproductions made from bolts of vintage fabrics, used, new—comes from the warehouse in Los Angeles. They have stores in Hollywood, Venice, and Canoga Park as well. Placing themselves somewhere between a boutique and a thrift store in terms of prices and atmosphere, *Aardvark's* stocks good quality men's and women's clothing at reasonable prices. With a black and white checkered floor, walls lined with black leather jackets, a unisex approach to merchandising, and a plethora of signs ("Save your soul," "Don't you dare shop lift," and "It's cool to look like a penguin"), *Aardvark's Ark* has style. The staff is decidedly unfriendly—or maybe they were all having a bad day.
Men's and women's clothing

BUFFALO EXCHANGE
1555 Haight St. (between Ashbury and Clayton), San Francisco 94102, (415) 431-7731. Mon–Sat 11 am–7 pm, Sun 12 am–6 pm. Cash, checks, MC/ VISA.

If you're looking for casual day wear, you can't beat *Buffalo Exchange* for quantity, selection, and price—put it on your list of regulars. Most of the stock (90%) is used garments (contemporary or pre-1950's vintage) with an average price of only $11. Based in Arizona, *Buffalo Exchange* has been doing business in the Bay Area since 1986. This large San Francisco store, geared to a younger crowd, is fun and uptempo, with a friendly, helpful staff.
Consignment: Accepts only leather jackets on consignment, 50/50 split. Buys outright, 40% customer/60% store in cash or 55% customer/45% store in trade.
Men's and women's clothing

HELD OVER
1543 Haight St. (between Ashbury and Clayton), San

Francisco 94102, (415) 864-0818. Mon–Sat 10 am–7 pm, Sun 11 am–7 pm. Cash, MC/VISA.

Held Over will pay you up to $10 for your used 501 Levis. If you don't own a pair, this is the place to buy them. Levis are their big seller, but you will also find a great selection of men's and women's vintage clothing from the 1940's through the 1970's, as well as contemporary used garments. Check out their huge selection of uniforms, vintage overcoats, tuxedo shirts for $10, and tuxedo jackets and pants for $20 each or $60 for the set.
Men's and women's vintage clothing

LA ROSA
1711 Haight St. (at Cole), San Francisco 94102, (415) 668-3744. Mon–Sat 11 am–7 pm, Sun 11 am–6 pm. Cash, checks, MC/VISA/AM EX.

Werner Wervie, captain of San Francisco's vintage industry, owns Held Over, Vintage Boutique, Clothes Contact—but none of these can hold a candle to La Rosa, the flagship of his fleet. A true collectors' store featuring high-end, top-of-the-line vintage from the 1940's and earlier, La Rosa is the place members of the Art Deco Society head when they need a knock-'em-dead outfit. They specialize in formal wear to rent or buy. A

~~~~~~~~~~~~~~~~~~~~

Left: Leftovers, Walnut Creek.

woman can drop $250–$750 on a perfect vintage gown (even more if it's designer), and men's tuxedos start at $200. Rentals go for 1/3 the retail cost.
Consignment: By appointment, 50/50 split, 60-day contract
Men's and women's vintage clothing

THE NEW GOVERNMENT
1427 Haight St., San Francisco 94117, (415) 431-1830. Mon–Sat 12 am–7 pm, Sun 1 pm–6 pm. Cash, MC/VISA.

Remember platform shoes, Nehru jackets, psychedelic polyester shirts, and hot pants? Some people would just as soon forget these fashions. If you're not one of them, climb into your Corvette and hightail it down to The New Government, where you will find an entire store full of original 1960's and 1970's vintage garments still in perfect condition. Platform shoes will set you back $35–$200, pants are $30–$65, and dresses cost $30–$75. (Don't forget to bring your false eyelashes, black eye liner, and white lipstick.)
Men's and women's vintage clothing

ST. VINCENT DE PAUL
1519 Haight St. (near Ashbury), San Francisco 94117, (415) 863-3615. Mon–Fri 9:30 am–4:45 pm, Sat 9 am–4:45 pm, Sun 12 am–5 pm. Cash, checks, MC/VISA.

Not your typical St. Vincent de Paul, the Haight store is smaller, cleaner, and more organized than most, but

with the same great buys. A small furniture selection is in the back, and the rest of the store is devoted to clothing (including great shoes), books, records, and housewares. *Charity: St. Vincent de Paul*
Everything except large appliances

SPELLBOUND
1670 Haight St. (between Belvedere and Cole), San Francisco 94117, (415) 863-4930. Mon–Fri 11 am–6:30 pm, Sat 11 am–7 pm, Sun 12 am–6 pm. Cash, checks, MC/VISA.

Vintage aficionados looking for a softer, more sedate atmosphere will be spellbound by this classy store. Concentrating on high-end vintage couture from the late 1800's to the mid 1960's, *Spellbound* offers a wide range of men's and women's fashions in top condition, with an outstanding selection of cocktail and evening dresses, men's formal wear (to buy or rent), and collectible costume jewelry. Expect to pay $40–$100 for dresses; evening gowns can go higher. The friendly staff will help you coordinate your outfit.
Men's and women's vintage clothing

SUGARTIT
1474 Haight St. (at Ashbury), San Francisco 94117, (415) 552-7027. Mon–Sat 11 am–5 pm, Sun 12 am–5 pm. Cash, checks, MC/VISA/AM EX.

This isn't an X-rated adult store—in the South, "sugartit" is a name for a baby's pacifier. Up north, if you're an adult and you get upset, you go shopping at *Sugartit* on Haight—Alex McMath's version of a pacifier for grown-ups. This small, crowded store specializing in art deco memorabilia carries a mixture of authentic originals and new reproductions of everything from ashtrays to jewelry and clocks to candlesticks. High-end vintage clothing for men and women includes fashions from the Victorian era though the 1970's. This is definitely a collectors' store—good for the gift for someone who has everything. Prices are high: $100–$1000, except for the *Sugartit* mugs and t-shirts for $10. For answers to the ten most asked questions about tattoos, you can also rent or buy "Tattoos are Forever," a video produced by *Sugartit*'s enthusiastic sales clerk Rebecca Halas.
Collectibles, men's and women's clothing

WASTELAND
1660 Haight St. (at Ashbury), San Francisco 94117, (415) 863-3150. Mon–Fri 11 am–6 pm, Sat 11 am–7 pm, Sun. 12 am–6 pm. Cash, checks, MC/VISA.

Eighty years ago, when San Francisco's entertainment district was located in the Haight, the heart of it all was the theatre at 1660 Haight. Today, the best shopping entertainment you can find in the city is still at the very same spot. The 5000-square-foot vaudeville and silent movie palace has been converted into the *Wasteland*, an exciting, outrageous, upbeat resale emporium reeking of incense, blasting loud music, and featuring 8000 items which range from funky fashions to vintage furniture. Specializing in pre-1970's clothing, *Wasteland* also carries contemporary fashions from the past three years. This is not the place to go for conservative office wear, but if you want casual street clothes and sportswear, this is it!

Wasteland also has a wholesale outlet, which sells clothes from the 1940s–1960s (especially Levi's 501s and jackets, men's sports and trench coats, and cowboy boots) to wholesale buyers at discount prices *Consignment: Buys outright Mon–Sun 12 am–4 pm; 40% customer/60% store in cash, 60% customer/40% store in trade; jewelry 35% customer/65% store in cash, 50/50 split in trade; will consign leather garments or higher-priced items for 60% consigner/40% store in cash, 70% consigner/30% store in trade* **Furniture, men's and women's clothing**

~~~~ Hayes Valley ~~~~

COUNTESS OLIZAR
146 Fillmore St. (at Waller), San Francisco 94117, (415) 861-7691. Tues–Sat 11 am–7 pm, Sun 12 am–5 pm. Cash, checks, MC/VISA.

Talk about gentrification—Hayes Valley is going upscale faster than

you can read this entry. So if you're looking for bargains in secondhand goods, you'd better hustle down there before prices go out of your range. A good place to start among the dozen or so trendy shops is *Countess Olizar*. Fair warning: once here you won't want to leave. Even if you don't wear vintage, I guarantee you won't be able to resist the spell. From the red floral carpet to the purple fainting couch, the period perfection will convince you you've stepped back in time to an exclusive salon of the 1940's. And if you do wear vintage clothing, this is the dream boutique. Nothing here is "as is;" every coat, dress (priced $50–$75), hat, pair of shoes, or tuxedo is of superior quality. Specializing in the 1940's and 1950's, the *Countess* also offers a smattering of 1920's and 1930's fashions. Loretta DePorceri is the sorceress who put this enchantment together; her sister is the Countess.
Women's vintage clothing

JINX
735 Haight St. (between Scott and Pierce), San Francisco 94117, (415) 552-3604. Tues–Sat 11 am–7 pm, Sun 12 am–6 pm. Cash, checks, MC/VISA.

At the other end of the spectrum—night to *Countess Olizar*'s day—*Jinx* is wonderful in its own way. Anything but subtle with its red, blue, and purple walls, orange ceiling, and border of stars, *Jinx* sells vintage thrift from the Victorian era through the 1970's.

Unique, one-of-a-kind garments, many from the 1880's, were so inexpensive we couldn't believe our eyes. Granted, you'll find a lot of "as is" tags, but never the less we're talking cheap! *Jinx* also carries well-priced collectibles, new and antique jewelry, magic oils, incense, and penny candy, which sells for a nickel (still cheap).

Vintage clothing, relics, penny candy

SHARP BROTHERS TRADING POST

525 Hayes (between Laguna and Octavia), San Francisco 94102, (415) 864-2756. Mon–Sat 8:30 am–5:30 pm. Cash.

No one would ever accuse Mr. Sharp of going upscale. Take your white-gloved neatnik aunt's worst fears of what you might encounter in those nasty secondhand places you insist on frequenting, multiply it by 10,000, and you'll come close to *Sharp Brothers Trading Post*. This place makes the funkiest, filthiest thrift shop look like an operating room by comparison. We loved it! The original junk shop—lit by one naked light bulb—is packed with stuff that fills every corner of the store, save two narrow aisles. Stacked from floor to ceiling on either side are sinks, beds, truck tires, old mimeograph machines, wheelchairs, telephones, hub caps, chairs, tables, refrigerators....To extract your selection might bring the whole inventory crashing down about your ears. Mr. Sharp carries whatever he can fix that looks like it might be worthwhile. And he can fix anything; the knowledge just comes to him as a gift of God. Mr. Sharp seems more interested in passing the time than making money, so we found it difficult to get an idea of prices. This is a trading post, after all, and they do more trading than anything. An experience you won't want to miss—just don't bring your mother.

Everything

VELVET PELVIS

531 Haight St. (between Fillmore and Steiner), San Francisco 94117, (415) 864-7034. Mon–Sun 12 am–8 pm. Cash, checks, MC/ VISA.

OK, let's get this straight: this used to be *The Rehaberdashery*, now it's the *Velvet Pelvis*, but the sign says *Gabardine's*? Well, the store changed owners, who changed the name to the *Velvet Pelvis* but fell in love with the *Gabardine's* sign. Whatever, this is an upbeat shop carrying late 1930's through mid 1960's fashions, with an emphasis on the 1940's and 1950's. Loud music, floors made of clean fir wood, and a neon cowboy hat gracing a brick wall contribute to the clean, trendy look. There's not a lot of merchandise, but what there is is choice. Cowboy boots, vintage denim, western wear, and cocktail dresses are the specialties. Expect to pay $20 for used Levis, $85–$225 for vintage tuxedos, and $36 for vintage gabardine shirts.

Men's and women's vintage clothing, some furniture

～～～ Lakeshore ～～～

LAKE MERCED FLEA MARKET
Doegler Center, 101 Lake Merced Blvd., San Francisco 94132, (415) 991-8012. Second Suns June–November, 8 am–3 pm. Purchase method varies by dealer.
If you make it down to this summer and fall event, you'll be able to enter for free. If you want to make some money by selling, you'll have to have $15.
Everything

～～～ Mission/Inner ～～～

ARON FURNITURE COMPANY
657 Valencia St., San Francisco 94110, (415) 626-3567. Mon–Sat 2:30 pm–6 pm. Cash, local checks.
The ultimate dark and dingy secondhand store, *Aron Furniture Company* gets the rejects from *De Mello's Furniture Warehouse* in Excelsior (same owner). What it lacks in ambience, it makes up for in good buys...I saw some attractive armoires and almost-antique dressers for under $200. Bring a flashlight—this place is really dark.
Furniture and large appliances

COMMUNITY THRIFT STORE
625 Valencia St. (between 17th and 18th), San Francisco 94110, (415) 861-4910. Mon–Sun 10 am–7 pm. Cash, MC/VISA with a $25 minimum.

One of the biggest (9,000 square feet) and certainly one of the best thrift stores in San Francisco, *Community Thrift* is a must for anyone who loves the thrill of the hunt. Formerly a motorcycle repair shop and a surf store, you can still see the surfing mural painted by Prairie Prince of the local rock group The Tubes on the back wall. Possibilities for great finds are almost unlimited here. It could be clothing (so much is donated they can only put out the very best), furniture (the supply is endless), bric-a-brac (a collector's paradise), books (best book section in town, kept in apple-pie order), records (they do over $3000 a month in the record section), and star stuff. Ann Rice donated her library when she moved, and Barbara Streisand gave them a houseful of furniture (they kept her bamboo bar). They recently sold a coffee table custom-made for William Holden to display his Oscar from "Stalag 17." All this and low, low prices, too.
Charity: Donors select the benefits of their choice from a list of 240 non-profit organizations.
Everything except bedding and large appliances

CLOTHES CONTACT
473 Valencia St. (at 16th), San Francisco 94110, (415) 621-3212. Mon–Sat 11 am–7 pm, Sun 11 am–6 pm. Cash, check, MC/VISA with $15 minimum.
If *La Rosa* is the alpha, than *Clothes Contact* is the omega in Werner Wervie's vintage empire. At

Clothes Contact you buy your vintage by the pound...the regular price is $6/lb, but everything was on sale for $3 /lb the day I was there. In this large store with an industrial look to it you'll find old garments from the 1950's–1980's that couldn't make the grade for Wervie's other stores—the cheap stuff with a little stain or a broken zipper or a too-tiny size. First quality, class-A items are hard to come by, but a persistent forager and a person handy with a needle and thread could end up with a really great deal. Jeans are $5 when you buy by the pound

Men's and women's vintage clothing

COTTRELL'S
150 Valencia St. (near Market), San Francisco 94103, (415) 431-1000. Mon–Fri 9 am–5:30 pm, Sat 9 am–4:30 pm. Cash, local checks, MC/VISA.

The Cottrell family has been buying, selling, moving, and storing furniture since 1905. Their humongous warehouse as big as a football field offers a smorgasbord of household and office furniture to suit every decor, from vintage Victorian to brass-and-glass modern to wood-grain metal monstrosities. Prices are fair, with the best buys on "as is" pieces. We saw sofas for $50–$295 and a nine-piece 1950's dining set for $695. Prices are firm unless you are willing to forgo the free delivery...then they'll bargain.

Furniture, housewares

FELINO'S VINTAGE CLOTHING
3162 16th St. (between Valencia and Guerrero), San Francisco 94103, (415) 863-5706. Mon–Sat 11 am–6 pm. Cash, checks, MC/VISA.

Felino's nostalgic clothing fills the favorite shop of the vintage fanciers I know. They tell me owner Jose "Felino" Campos has the best selection and best prices in town for 1940's, 1950's, and 1960's fashions. Top-grade 501's are only $14.99, dresses and women's suits run $12–$14, tuxedo jackets are $15–$45, tuxedo suits cost $95–$125, sports coats are $15–$28, and men's suits run $95–$125. Everyone likes the laid-back atmosphere: no hassles, only friendly, helpful service. I adored the ubiquitous slinky black panthers and bold pink flamingo decor, the gorgeous vintage bathrobes, and the wit and charm of the owner. Plan to spend time checking out trunks and corners for hidden bargains. You won't be disappointed.

Men's and women's vintage clothing, some furniture

GOODWILL
2279 Mission St. (between 18th and 19th), San Francisco 94110, (415) 826-5759. Mon–Sat 9:15 am–6:15 pm, Sun 8:30 am–5:30

Right: Jose "Felino" Campos, owner, Felino's Vintage Clothing, San Francisco.

pm. Cash, checks, MC/VISA/ DISCOVER.

The two-storied Mission *Goodwill* is not as elegant as some of the other stores, but it stocks the same good merchandise at the same great prices.

Charity: Goodwill

Everything but furniture and large appliances

HARRINGTON BROS. MOVING & STORAGE

599 Valencia St. (at 17th), San Francisco 94110, (415) 861-7300. Mon–Sat 8 am–6 pm. Cash, checks, MC/VISA/AM EX.

John Harrington started this enterprise in 1930, and in 1966 Jarlath O'Connor bought it from him with $1000. It's primarily a moving business; O'Connor buys furniture from his moving customers, model homes, and hotels to sell to you for less than half of what you'd pay for new goods. If you have the taste for fine new furniture (nothing from Furniture USA here) but not the budget, and if you can live with a few nicks you'd put on yourself in six months anyway, *Harrington Bros.* should be your first stop. O'Connor claims he can furnish an entire house for $2000, including never-been-slept-in beds from model homes. I was skeptical until he pointed out a stylishly elegant sofa and love seat ensemble for $750. This is also a good place to pick up knickknacks and accent pieces.

Furniture, housewares, antiques, collectibles

HOCUS POCUS

900 Valencia St., San Francisco 94110, (415) 824-2901. Tues–Fri 11 am–7 pm, Sat 10 am–6 pm, Sun 12 am–6 pm. Cash, checks.

The *San Francisco Chronicle* named *Hocus Pocus* one of the ten best secondhand stores in the city. A middle-of-the-road shop somewhere between an antique store and a thrift shop, you can find antiques, collectibles, and used items priced from 50¢ to $2000.

Furniture, antiques, collectibles

JIM'S USED FURNITURE

1499 Valencia St. (at 26th), San Francisco 94110, (415) 285-2049. Mon–Sat 11 am–6 pm. Cash.

Jim's Used Furniture seems tiny in comparison to the huge *Salvation Army* across the street. The place is packed like a tin of sardines with what looks like a lot of junk, but could turn out to be some great buys. No prices are marked because everything is negotiable. Jim quoted me $45 for a nice wing chair, $15 for a handsome sewing box, and $12 for a padded, studded trunk/bench…and these prices came without negotiating. Certainly worth a visit if you're shopping at the Army.

Furniture and collectibles

KERNAN'S MOVING & FURNITURE SALES

819 Valencia St. (at 19th), San Francisco 94110, (415) 647-9300. Mon–Sun 10:30 am–5:30 pm. Cash.

Carrying anything and everything, antiques and just old stuff, *Kernan's* is a place to look for good serviceable furniture. Prices are reasonable with room to bargain, "depending on how desperate we are," says owner John McCaffrey. New merchandise comes in two or three times a week, so check back if you don't find what you're looking for the first time.

Furniture

NO NAME COLLECTIBLES

603 Valencia St. (at 17th), San Francisco 94110, (415) 864-5743. Mon–Fri 12 am–5 pm, Sat 10 am–5 pm, Sun 12 am–6 pm. Cash, checks.

Moving or redecorating? Call *No Name Collectibles*. They'll pick up what you don't want and pay you to haul it away. All sort of things end up in their shop this way—from 1960's movie magazines to 1920's vanity tables to 1980's television sets—all priced to compete with their thrift shop neighbor *Community Thrift*. "We don't sell to people who are going to spend a lot of money," explained a personable sales clerk. Unless it's a large piece of furniture, they avoid the expensive stuff and keep the shop well-stocked with interesting affordable pieces.

Furniture and collectibles

PINK PARAFFIN

3234 16th St., San Francisco 94103, (415) 621-7116. Mon–Sun 12 am–6 pm. Cash, checks, AM EX.

According to Wess Graham, religious knickknacks are their forte. *Pink Paraffin's* late owner was a Jesuit and the current owners are all collectors of religious artifacts. So if you share their enthusiasm for retablos, altar pieces, Jesus statues, and the like, *Pink Paraffin* is an answer to your prayers. For the secularly minded they also carry furniture, collectibles, some vintage clothing, and a few new rugs and throws at prices ranging from 50¢ to $500.

Vintage clothing, furniture, collectibles

PURPLE HEART VETERAN'S THRIFT STORE

1855 Mission St. (at 15th), San Francisco 94103, (415) 621-2581. Mon–Fri 9 am–8 pm, Sat and Sun 10 am–6 pm. Cash.

Merchandise tends to get lost in this enormous warehouse of a store. But there is plenty of the usual thrift store fare—furniture, books and records, large and small appliances, cheap clothes, and also many items that don't show up regularly. Typewriters, toilets, treadmills, and trunks, as well as lawn mowers, bicycles, medical equipment, and assorted odds and ends I couldn't identify, but I'm sure are useful. No dressing rooms are to be found.

Charity: Purple Heart Veterans Rehabilitation Services, which provide counseling, job training and placement, and medical assistance to veterans

Everything

SALVATION ARMY

1509 Valencia St. (at Army), San Francisco 94110, (415) 695-8040. Mon, Wed, Fri 9:30 am–9 pm; Tues, Thurs, Sat 9:30 am–6 pm. Cash, MC/VISA.

The mother of all thrift stores, the *Salvation Army* giant on Valencia has to be the biggest nonprofit store in San Francisco. Give yourself plenty of time to look over the goodies in the two huge rooms. They have more clothing than Carters has liver pills, all neatly organized and priced to sell. You can even find Levi's 501's for $4 (if you beat the professional Levi's buyers) and new Jessica McClintock wedding gowns for $45. There's enough furniture, appliances, and housewares to rival Macy's. If the enormity over-whelms you, you can stick to "The Inn Shoppe," a small in-store boutique featuring better clothes, leather items, almost-new shoes, and collectibles. It's open Monday through Friday 11 am–3 pm and Saturday 11 am–4 pm.
Charity: Salvation Army
Everything

THRIFT TOWN

2101 Mission St. (corner of 17th), San Francisco 94103, (415) 861-1132. Mon–Fri 9 am–8 pm, Sat 9 am–6 pm, Sun 11 am–6 pm. Cash, MC/VISA.

It's hard to imagine a thrift store bigger than the *Salvation Army* giant on Valencia, but *Thrift Town* is indeed. Housed in the landmark Reelick Building since 1973, *Thrift Town* offers 1000 square feet of clothing on the main floor and 5000 square feet of furniture up on the mezzanine. Best buys are in clothing. Every weekday, two trucks full of merchandise bring in 2000 fresh items, including furniture, toys, kitchenware, collectibles, jewelry, books, 100 different pairs of shoes, and more. Clothing prices start at 95¢; baby clothes at 65¢. *Thrift Town* advises shoppers that there is hardly an item in the store that isn't priced too high or too low. If it's too low, buy it FAST! If it's too high, be patient—everything in the store will eventually be marked down. When it reaches a price level you consider acceptable, buy it. Sales are frequent; there's a 30% senior discount every Tuesday, and half-off-everything (except furniture) sales happen four times a year.
Charity: Privately owned, merchandise bought from Aid to Retarded Citizens
Everything except large appliances

UPSTAIRS, DOWNSTAIRS

890 Valencia St. (at 20th), San Francisco 94110, (415) 647-4211. Mon–Sat 11 am–6 pm, Sun 1 pm–5 pm. Cash, checks, MC/VISA.

Since this is really more of an antique store, check out the gorgeous antiques and collectibles upstairs and downstairs. Nothing's priced for the budget-minded, but everything is fun to dream about.
Furniture, antiques, collectibles

~~~~~ Nob Hill ~~~~~

THE ATTIC SHOP
1040 Hyde St. (at California), San Francisco 94109, (415) 474-3498. Tues–Sat 10 am–4:30 pm. Cash, checks.

Don't be deterred by the lovely and pricey antiques in the window; *The Attic Shop* is a thrift store. Step inside, where you'll find they have bargains as well as beautiful linens, costume jewelry, and collectibles. Among the usual run-of-the-mill thrift shop clothing we saw a St. John knit for $42, a classic Evan Picone suit for $18, and a velvet Jaeger suit for $22. The 95¢ clothing rack is in the back room, along with books, records, bicycles, men's clothing, and great shoes.
Charity: St. Francis Memorial Hospital
Everything (furniture and large appliances only occasionally)

BUFFALO EXCHANGE
1800 Polk (at Washington), San Francisco 94109, (415) 346-5726. Mon–Sat 11 am–7 pm, Sun 12 am–6 pm. Cash, checks, MC/VISA.

Fashion at fair value is the whole concept of *Buffalo Exchange*. Your closet is their warehouse; they buy your clothing in current styles, and you buy their recycled (or new) fashions, accessories, jewelry, and shoes at a fair price. With four successful stores located throughout California and six more in Arizona and New Mexico, they must be doing something really right. The daily crowds also say a lot. Geared to a younger market, they have high energy, friendly sales people and a ton of wonderful stuff to choose from.
Men's and women's clothing

CATHEDRAL SCHOOL SHOP
1036 Hyde St. (at California), San Francisco 94109, (415) 776-6630. Tues–Sat 10 am–6 pm. Cash, checks, MC/VISA.

A long time favorite of San Francisco thrift shoppers, *Cathedral School Shop* is a fine place for family clothing, books, housewares, and children's items. Wonderful, unpredictable collectibles show up all the time, too. Stop in on your way to Chinatown.
Charity: Cathedral School for Boys scholarship fund
Everything

~~~~~ Noe Valley ~~~~~

ALWAYS AND FOREVER
3789 24th St. (between Church and Dolores), San Francisco 94114, (415) 285-7174. Mon–Sat 11 am–6 pm. Cash, checks, MC/VISA.

A diamond may be forever, but the rhinestones at *Always and Forever* are definitely for now. If you're serious about glitter, you'll find some fabulous new friends at George Esparza's gorgeous vintage store. His collection of classic rhinestone clip earrings and necklaces is to die for, and the rest

of the merchandise isn't so bad either. Specializing in glamorous evening wear of the 1940's and 1950's, *Always and Forever* carries only the best these decades had to offer. Classic tuxedos go for $150–$195, one-of-a-kind evening dresses for $65–$125. Esparza also stocks vintage ties, hats, Hawaiian shirts, and day wear. For authentic period atmosphere and high quality fashions, this is one of the best.
Men's and women's vintage clothing

THE CHAMAELEON
Noe Valley Mall, 3915 24th St., San Francisco 94114, (415) 550-8112. Tues–Sun 11 am–6 pm. Cash, checks, MC/VISA.

Bonnie Black has a thing for chameleons—maybe because she likes change. In her professional life she's gone from fine arts to criminal investigation to used clothing, and she likes to keep changing the looks of her store. Geared to the young hip look, *Chamaeleon* emphasizes fun clothes (no business suits) and carries men's and women's new and used garments, from casual to dressy, both vintage and contemporary. If you like the idea of an ever-changing wardrobe, *Chamaeleon's* good prices will allow you to garb yourself in leathers one day and a funky old dress the next. The shop is in a hard-to-find courtyard down an alley...look for the very inconspicuous "Noe Valley Mall" sign.
Men's and women's clothing

MARY'S EXCHANGE
1414 Castro St. (between 25th and Jersey), San Francisco 94114, (415) 282-6955. Mon–Fri 12 am–5:30 pm, Sat 12 am–6 pm. Cash, checks.

A wisteria-covered lattice adds a charming touch to this mini (400 square feet) consignment shop. Opened two years ago, *Mary's* stocks new samples and irregulars and used women's clothing, sizes 2–22, all in good condition and moderately priced at around 50% of retail. Fun sports clothes are a favorite here, but "anything nice and good" will be accepted on consignment.
Consignment: Mon–Wed 12:30 am–3 pm, Fri 12:30 am–3 pm, Sat by appointment, 50/50 split
Women's clothing

NATURAL RESOURCES
4081 24th St. (at Castro), San Francisco 94114, (415) 550-2611. Mon–Fri 10:30 am–6 pm, Sat 11 am–4 pm. Cash, checks, MC/VISA.

A community-based resource center focusing on pregnancy, childbirth, and early parenting, *Natural Resources* offers services and products for prospective and new parents. Their small selection of used maternity clothes features contemporary styles in natural fibers. They also carry seconds from Japanese Weekend and other local manufacturers. They get extra points for friendliness, enthusiasm, and the box of free maternity and baby clothes (can't beat that price).

Consignment: Wed and Thurs 2 pm–6 pm, 50/50 split in cash, 60% consignor/40% in trade (may be applied to books, classes, etc.)
Products and services for pregnancy, childbirth, and parenting

ONE MORE TIME
4156 24th St. (between Castro and Diamond), San Francisco 94114, (415) 282-8819. Mon–Sat 1 pm–6 pm. Cash, checks, MC/ VISA.

Taren Sapienza, who calls her store "a fun place to shop," combines a Nordstrom attitude with dress-for-the-recession merchandise. Three rooms are stocked with a range of sizes, styles, and prices, to better appeal to the diversity of the Bay Area. You'll find men's and women's contemporary and vintage fashions—women's dresses in the front of the store, shoes and sportswear in the middle, and men's apparel in back (men's suits go for $45–$90). Everything goes to half off after 60 days. Prices are negotiable.
Consignment: Mon–Sat 1 pm–6 pm, 50/50 split
Men's and women's clothing

PEEK-A-BOOTIQUE
1306 Castro (at 24th), San Francisco 94114, (415) 641-6192. Mon–Sat 10:30 am–6 pm, Sun 12 am–5 pm. Cash, checks, MC/ VISA.

Paul Morgan and Barbara Ellis, the helpful couple at *Peek-a-Bootique*, gave up jobs in the corporate rat

race to open this store five years ago. Expertise from their previous life translates here to an organized, convenient place to buy kid's stuff. They carry children's furniture, equipment, and clothes, all both new and used. Boys' clothing (sizes 0–6X) and girls' clothing (sizes 0–7/8) sells for 1/3 the original price; furniture and equipment go for 1/2–2/3 the original price. A good supply of kid's staples—bath tubs, potty seats, safety items—make for easy, one-stop shopping.
Consignment: Mon, Wed, Thurs 11 am–12:45 am and 2 pm–3:45 pm, Sat by appointment; 40% consignor/60% store in cash or 50/50 split in trade for clothes, 50/50 split in cash or 60% consignor/40% store in trade for furniture
Children's clothing, furniture, and equipment

~~~ **North Beach** ~~~

OLD VOGUE
1412 Grant St. (between Green and Union), San Francisco 94133. (415) 392-1522. Mon 11 am–7 pm, Tues–Thurs 11 am–10 pm, Fri and Sat 11 am–11 pm, Sun 12 am–8 pm. Cash, checks, MC/VISA.

What could be more San Francisco than shopping for classic clothing right in the heart of North Beach (if you can find parking)? Men: if leather jackets, Levis's, and 1950's fashions represent your idea of sartorial splendor, hop on your Harley and hightail it down there. You'll find a store full of vintage

1950's fashions, new leather jackets and hats, and more Levis and jeans than you can shake a stick at for $15–$25. Women: head to the back for the beaded sweaters, hats, dresses, etc.

Men's clothing, some women's clothing

ST. FRANCIS OF ASSISI THRIFT SHOP

610 Vallejo St. (corner Vallejo and Columbus), San Francisco 94133, (415) 421-4095. Mon and Sat 12 am–5 pm. Cash.

The outgrowth of a church rummage sale, the *St. Francis of Assisi Thrift Shop* has been operating in the church's gymnasium since 1976. Working against the odds— parking in North Beach is close to impossible and ten hours a week are pretty short business hours— *St. Francis* manages to attract a following of loyal customers. Bargain hunters are drawn by the extremely low prices on clothing and housewares, vintage lovers come for the serendipitous surprise like a 1950's business suit in perfect condition for $3, and collectors love the treasures that pop up when least expected.
Charity: St. Francis of Assisi Church
Everything except furniture and large appliances

Left: Harrington Bros. Moving & Storage, San Francisco.

~~~~~ *Ocean* ~~~~~

OCEAN AVENUE THRIFT

1619 Ocean Ave. (between Faxon and Capitol), San Francisco 94112, (415) 239-8766. Tues–Sat 10 am–4 pm. Cash.

Trashaholics and thrift shop addicts watch out! If you're a junk shop junkie who gets high on the hunt, you'll find *Ocean Avenue Thrift* irresistible. Just let me dig through one more box, you'll beg. I only want to check out what's in the back corner, you'll whine. Starting with the 25¢ box and $1 rack on the sidewalk, this is a store bursting with bargains and surprises. Toys, children's clothes, collectibles, jewelry, books, magazines, picture frames…they've got it all at fabulous bargain prices. Three or four times a year they receive a shipment of big clothing for big men (including dress shirts, dress trousers, and work pants) from a local merchant. Although prices are already low, manager Ann-Mari Gettys is always open to a little bargaining.
Charity: San Francisco Waldorf School
Everything but furniture and large appliances

~~~ **Pacific Heights** ~~~

BOTTOM DRAWER THRIFT SHOP

2810 Pierce St. (at Green), San Francisco 94123, (415) 921-9195 (for pickup only). Tues, Thurs, Sat

10 am–3 pm, closed June–August and Dec. 15–Jan 2. Cash, local checks.

Once a convent where the Sisters of Benefits lived and performed their good works, this site now watches the ladies of St. Vincent de Paul Church Auxiliary perform their good works, which consist of running a first-class neighborhood thrift store. Neat, clean, and organized, there is a room for everything—women's dresses in one room, sportswear in another, books and linens in the hall, a room for kid's clothes and toys, a room for men's wear, a parlor full of furniture and housewares, and a kitchen full of—guess what?—kitchenware! The bathroom, bedecked with pillows and pictures, has been turned into a most charming dressing room. Quality is medium to high, prices (determined by a "rather vague system") are low to lower: men's suits go for $10, jackets are $5–$7, ties are $1, women's skirts run $3–$4, sweaters go for $5, and extra fine items are priced slightly higher (a brand-new black velvet Eileen West dress was $25).

Charity: St. Vincent de Paul school sports program
Everything except large appliances and large pieces of furniture

NEXT-TO-NEW SHOP
2226 Fillmore Street, San Francisco 94115, (415) 567-1627. Mon 1 pm–4 pm, Tues–Sat 10 am–4 pm. Cash, checks.

Among the many fine stores on Fillmore is the most profitable Junior League thrift shop in the country, *Next-To-New*. The window displays offer a good indication of the thought and care that goes into making this large one-room store a pleasant place to shop. Recently the window featured a "get in shape" theme—a variety of exercise equipment was displayed, including an exercise bike for $65, a rowing machine for $98.50, exercise videos for $8.50, weights for $18.50, sweats for $15.50, and an Oakland "A's" bag for $4.50. Carpeted, brightly lit, and well-organized, *Next-To-New* has a nook for books and records, a children's corner, cases and shelves of jewelry, and racks of men's, women's and children's clothing. Good quality clothing is your best bet here. "We keep only the best," says manager Lita Smith,"the rest goes to the Salvation Army and St. Vincent de Paul. We send 85% to the dry cleaners and we have a washer and dryer here in the store so every garment is clean." Considering the condition and quality of the clothing, prices are very reasonable: men's suits run $38–$42, sports coats $18–$20, dress shirts are $8.50, women's dresses cost $12–$125, skirts are $12.50, and sweaters are $12.50 also. Special half-off sales are held the week after Christmas, the week before Easter, and the last week of July. League members are required to work in the store as well as donate merchandise, which accounts for both the high quality of the stock and the youth and friendliness of the volunteers. *Charity: Community projects, which may involve the homeless, AIDS, substance abuse and adolescent pregnancy, and cultural enrichment for children without access to the arts* **Everything except large appliances**

REPEAT PERFORMANCE

2223 Fillmore St., San Francisco 94115, (415) 563-3123. Mon, Wed, Thurs, Sat 10 am–4 pm; Tues and Fri 10 am–6:30 pm. Cash, checks, MC/VISA.

It's not unusual to see a chauffeur-driven limousine pull up in front of *Repeat Performance* and a wealthy donor emerge to deliver an armful of designer gowns. The symphony has a cadre of devoted donors, and the merchandise in this store reflects their taste, affluence, and generosity. For up-to-date, high-style, designer-label fashions, *Repeat Performance* is hard to beat. New merchandise is constantly being added, and only the best is kept for the shop. Every two months merchandise is marked down to half price and whatever doesn't sell in four days is donated to the Salvation Army. The recently redecorated one-room shop is bright, clean, and well organized; men's, women's, and children's clothing is arranged by category and size. More expensive designer items are displayed in "The Boutique Corner," a rack behind

the counter. Gowns, furs, bridal gowns, and vintage fashions are stored in the back. Prices, determined by nine pricing volunteers (each with her own categories), are at the high end. "We're selling wants, not needs," explained a savvy volunteer. In the men's department a velvet smoking jacket was going for $20, a Calvin Klein jacket from Saks Fifth Avenue cost $30, a navy cashmere jacket was $65, a Giorgio Armani suit cost $150, and dress shirts ran $4–$10. In the women's department you could find sweaters for $7.50–$60, a two-piece red silk Pierre Cardin dress for $47, a Joannie Char dress for $36, or a full-length ranch mink coat for $1650. Housewares, bric-a-brac, and collectibles are definitely pricey but, like the clothing, mostly first class.
Charity: San Francisco Symphony
Everything except furniture and large appliances

SCARLETT'S

2121 Fillmore St. (between California and Pierce), San Francisco 94115, (415) 346-3770. Mon–Sat 11 am–6 pm, Sun 1 pm–6 pm. Cash, checks, MC/VISA.

I was so dazzled by the hundreds of hat boxes ($6–$50) and the wall of hats that I didn't even notice the extraordinary parade of fashion right before my eyes. The amount of merchandise crammed into this long, narrow store is staggering. From 1800's vintage pieces to contemporary designers, everywhere you look something catches your eye and cries out "Buy me!" Owner Patty Tolbert stocks at least 2000 different items: 90% women's dresses, suits, shoes and accessories, 10% men's wear. You can spend $1 or $1000; you can buy or rent anything in the store (with the exception of the fragile vintage gowns). Whether it's a beige satin Adele Simpson for $12 or a 1920's chiffon tea gown for $60, whatever you choose you will look smashing, glamorous, and completely original.

Consignment: Mon–Fri 2:30 pm–5 pm, Sun 2:30 pm–5 pm, 50/50 split, 90-day contract (note: only 10% of Scarlett's merchandise is consigned)

Men's and women's vintage clothing

SECONDS-TO-GO

2252 Fillmore St., San Francisco 94115, (415) 563-7806. Mon 10 am–4 pm, Tues–Sat 10 am–5 pm. Cash, checks.

The first impression upon walking into the long, narrow, one-room *Seconds-To-Go* is one of crowded confusion. An old drugstore rack spills over with magazines next to a hodgepodge of pictures, walkers, and whatever. Unpressed clothing is crowded on circular racks down the middle of the store, and a long rack of women's dresses runs half the length of the side wall. Shelves of household goods include a basket of high-priced lace fragments. A small alcove offers a good selection of children's books, toys,

and baby clothes. Hardback books go for $1, paperbacks for 50¢, and an interesting collection of old sheet music was priced at $3 per sheet. Collectibles, jewelry, objets d'art, and items of special interest are kept in the locked cases by the cash register. The chances of coming across something unusual for a fair price are pretty good. A friend who picked up a dainty petit-point mirror case (with mirror) and a matching manicure case (without implements) for $1 each at the half-off sale still regrets the petit-point evening bag for $12 she passed up. While *Seconds-To-Go* might not be worth a special trip, it's certainly worthwhile to stop in while you're on Fillmore.

Charity: Schools of the Sacred Heart scholarship funds

Everything except furniture and large appliances

THE STREET SHOP

2011 Divisadero St. (between California and Sacramento), San Francisco 94115, (415) 931-4382. Tues–Fri 10 am–4:45 pm, Sat 10 am–4 pm. Closed the month of August. Cash, checks, layaway.

"The world is invaded with junk," according to one staff person, but you won't find any at *The Street Shop*. The crème de la crème of thrift stores, *The Street Shop* specializes in quality, with an emphasis on designer clothes for women. Everything here—antiques, jewelry, and fresh, clean, stylish clothing—is meticulously displayed in a boutique-like setting; the

knowledgeable staff, trained in French haute couture, are happy to serve as fashion consultants. Support from Pacific Heights residents (both as shoppers and donors) keeps this one a winner. Prices are good, the half-price rack is better, and best of all are the half-off-everything sale in January and the sidewalk sale in June.
Charity: Mental Health Association of San Francisco
Women's clothing, antiques, collectibles, housewares

VICTORIAN HOUSE THRIFT SHOP
2318 Fillmore St., San Francisco 94115, (415) 923-3237. Mon 11 am–4 pm, Tues–Sat 10 am–5 pm. Cash, checks.

Victorian House...if the name leads you to expect laces, linens, and other treasures from a bygone era, you will not be disappointed. Elegant windows draw you inside, where you immediately encounter a glass case chock-full of silver, crystal, china, jewelry, and better collectibles. Cubbies, shelves, and cases of housewares and more collectibles line the long dark room. A dedicated shopper will turn up an occasional great buy in the crowded racks of women's clothes. The shoe selection features many fine names—Ferragamo, Evans—for $10–$20. You may find it impossible to resist the allure of a large cabinet with many small drawers, each labeled with contents— eyeglasses, gloves, slips, scarves, hats, nightgowns...chances are you will find something you never knew you wanted. Two small rooms in the very back offer women's sportswear and everyday household goods—small appliances, dishes, pots and pans—all at good prices.

Don't leave without checking out the downstairs (the staircase is located through a door to the left as you enter), where you will find furniture, an excellent men's department (sartorially splendid Willie Brown donates his suits to this very shop), a good selection of sports equipment (tennis rackets and golf clubs), electronic equipment (televisions, cameras, tape recorders), books and records, and vintage linens. *Victorian House* lives up to its promise of treasures...and if the prices seem a little high, wait for the half-off sales held regularly every two months.
Charity: Pacific Presbyterian Medical Center
Everything except large appliances

VINTAGE BOUTIQUE
2116 Fillmore St. (at California), San Francisco 94115, (415) 929-7748. Mon–Sat 11 am–7 pm, Sun 11 am–6 pm. Cash, checks, MC/VISA.

If a black ceiling, metal floor, mirrored walls, and loud music is your *ne plus ultra*, you'll find happiness shopping in *Vintage Boutique*. They stock fashions from the 1930's through the 1970's and are keen on anything with a cowboy theme—boots, Levis, gabardine shirts, suede, leather, and fine old wooenl blankets. Quality is high, prices are mid-range to high: dresses run $35–$90, jeans are $30, blankets cost $69–$100. The staff is friendly and the atmosphere is electric.

Men's and women's vintage clothing

∾ Pacific Heights/Lower ∾

BARGAIN MART

1823 Divisadero St. (between Pine and Bush), San Francisco 94115, (415) 921-7380. Mon–Sat 10 am–4:45 pm. Cash, checks, layaway, MC/VISA.

This large cavernous store (once used for coal storage) now sells everything under the sun, including furniture, clothing, housewares, antiques, collectibles...you name it. Quality varies, as do prices. Clothing lies at the low (very low) end of the price range and collectibles sit on the high side, while furniture fits somewhere in the middle. With so much to look over, you're bound to find something you like, want, or need. Don't miss the two small side rooms filled with furniture, books, and lots of miscellanea.

Charity: National Council of Jewish Women, which supports School Volunteers, the Center for Independent Living, WICS, et. al.

Everything

BEAR-LY NEW THRIFT SHOP

1752 Fillmore St. (between Post and Sutter), San Francisco 94115,

(415) 921-2789. Mon–Sat 10 am–5 pm. Cash, checks.

Set well back from the street, the stately Victorian housing the *Bear-ly New Shop* boasts a courtyard bordered by a wrought-iron fence. But the one-room shop is, frankly, a mess. A pushcart and a few racks full of clothes that have seen much better days represent the few sale items. "We don't really have special sales," a charming, gray-haired volunteer informed me, "because our regular prices are so low." And indeed, they are. No principle of organization was visible to my critical eye, but out of the chaos you are certainly apt to find a marvelous treasure and a great bargain. One visit turned up an 82-piece set of lovely old American dishes (serving pieces intact) for a mere $50, an ugly but sturdy upholstered armchair for $10, and a basket full of high-fashion hand-made Barbie doll outfits, complete with shoes and accessories, for $2.50 each.

Charity: University of California Medical Center in San Francisco

Clothing, household items, books

CROSSROADS TRADING CO.

1901 Fillmore St. (at Bush), San Francisco 94115, (415) 775-8885. Mon–Sat 11 am–7 pm, Sun 12 am–6 pm. Cash, checks, MC/ VISA.

Two years ago you could purchase Soloflex exercise machines to expand your muscles; today you can buy used clothing and expand your wardrobe. Definitely for the young at heart, the upbeat decor and heavy metal music get you in the mood to shop. Although they specialize in contemporary sportswear (they like good labels like Banana Republic and Ralph Lauren), *Crossroads* has a little bit of everythng: 1920's–1940's vintage are mixed in with contemporary clothes. You can spend anywhere from $1 to $200, although the average price is about $10.50. *Crossroads* buys, trades, and sells new and used clothing. If you see something you like, you can pay cash for it or you can bring in some of your nice clothes and receive 55% of the selling price in trade. Great for guys and gals who like a revolving wardrobe.

Consignment: Buys outright, 40% customer/60% store in cash, 55% customer/45% store in trade
Men's and women's vintage and contemporary clothing

DEPARTURES FROM THE PAST
2028 Fillmore St. (at Pine), San Francisco 94115, (415) 885-3377. Mon–Sat 11 am–7 pm, Sun 12 am–6 pm. Cash, checks, MC/ VISA.

The travel theme is delightfully documented at *Departures* with owner Stephen "Spit" Spigolon's personal collection of travel paraphernalia, which includes vintage suitcases, posters, and scarves. If your fashion fantasy includes a trip back in time, I suggest you make a journey to *Departures*, where you can rent or buy vintage formal wear and costumes. Stocking clothing from the 1920's through the 1960's with an emphasis on the 1950's and 1960's, the store features a wall of new crinolines ($10 to rent, $25–$30 to buy), poodle skirts, European pajamas ($5), and vintage tuxedos ($55 to rent, $40–$105 to buy). Vintage day dresses go for $7–$20 and evening dresses for $20–$30. Buy five scarves at $1 each and get one free.
Men's and women's vintage clothing

GOODWILL
1742 Fillmore St. (between Post and Sutter), San Francisco 94115, (415) 441-2159. Mon–Wed 10 am– 6 pm, Thurs and Fri 10 am–7 pm, Sat 10 am–6 pm. Cash, checks, MC/VISA.

I once counted 39 people shopping at the Fillmore Street *Goodwill* on a Friday afternoon. Don't tell anyone, but many San Francisco fashion plates get their goodies at this *Goodwill*. A beautiful store inside and out, when it comes to clothing, you can't beat it for price, quality, quantity, and merchandising pizzazz. Women's dresses are $5.75–$7.95, kid's clothes are $1.95–$3.95, men's suits go for $24.95, dress shirts cost $3.95, slacks are $5.95. You can also pick up reconditioned mattresses and box springs, small appliances, and new items (Palmolive and Zest soap three bars for $1, baby powder for $1.30, Fruit of the Loom shorts for $2). Antiques and

collectibles are scarce unless you get there in the morning and wait outside with the dealers for the store to open on the days when new shipments arrive (three times a week).
Charity: Goodwill
Everything except large appliances

THIRD HAND STORE
1839 Divisadero St. (between Pine and Bush), San Francisco 94115, (415) 567-7332. Mon–Sat 12 am–6 pm. Cash, checks, MC/ VISA.
In September of 1967 Charles and Jean Stewart opened the first vintage clothing store in California. Although many have since followed their example, the *Third Hand Store* still ranks among the best. Carrying Victorian through 1950's fashions for men and women, they have the finest selection of antique wedding gowns in the city, all priced $80– $500. This store should definitely be the first stop for any bride who wants a one-of-a-kind gown. For murder mystery parties or weddings, you will be pleased to note that full rental service is available: men's formal wear costs $45 for 48 hours. Their collection of vintage ethnic clothing and jewelry is also excellent. When Jean and Charles are off tango dancing in Argentina (as they are wont to do), manager Suzanne Ramsey can help you find the perfect outfit.
Men's and women's vintage clothing

~~~~~ **Presidio** ~~~~~

PRESIDIO THRIFT SHOP
Bldg. 204, the Presidio, San Francisco 94129, (415) 922-3384. Tues–Thurs 10 am–2 pm, first Sats 9 am–1 pm. Cash, checks.
A soldier's life is a peripatetic one. If the Army says go, then go you must, often leaving your belongings behind. The *Presidio Thrift Shop* gives army personnel a chance to make a little money off these goods and the general public a chance to pick up household items, clothing, furniture, and an occasional exotic artifact or collectible from some far-off land, all at reasonable prices. Of the least interest is clothing, except for the army uniforms, which can be purchased only by persons with valid military identification. Collectibles and esoteric artifacts are the most interesting, with abandoned house plants a close second. I just missed a gorgeous orchid plant, but Jobyna did manage to snag a wooden poker-chip holder, complete with chips, for $7. *The Creative Cottage* next door features a selection of handcrafted items ranging from quilts to quince jams—great for gifts.
Consignment: Only open to military personnel
Charity: Proceeds support various charities.
Everything

~~~~~~~~~~~

Right: Leftovers Thrift Shop, Walnut Creek.

~~~ Presidio Heights ~~~

GOOD BYES

3464 Sacramento St. (at Laurel), San Francisco 94118, (415) 346-6388. Mon–Sat 10 am–6 pm, Sun 11 am–5 pm. Cash, checks, MC/VISA.

Good Byes is a class act. Sole proprietor Margaret Hensley, who cut her merchandising teeth in Texas as a men'swear buyer, opened her first consignment store in 1975 in Dallas. After relocating to California, she opened *Good Byes* in August 1991. Decorated with antiques, props, and glorious pine pieces, *Good Byes* looks like a Polo shop and stocks first-quality pre-owned garments and new samples from sales reps and manufacturers. Hensley, who insists that sticking to just designers is snooty and puts people off, says she'll sell anything that was good originally. Labels like Southwick, Ralph Lauren, Daniel Hecter, Armani, Valentino, Bijan, I Magnin, Nordstrom, and Brooks Brothers seem to predominate the men's wear section and Ann Taylor, Albert Nipon, and Ungaro keep cropping up among the ladies' fashions. Hensley originally intended to carry only men's clothing, but was convinced to stock women's wear as well. *Good Byes* is without a doubt the classiest men's consignment store in San Francisco. Recommended highly for men who want to look like a million bucks without spending it—you can spend $150 instead and walk out in a new suit, complete with shirt and tie.
Consignment: Wed–Fri 10 am–6 pm, 50/50 split
Men's and women's clothing and accessories

TOWN SCHOOL CLOTHES CLOSET

3325 Sacramento St. (between Laurel and Presidio), San Francisco 94118, (415) 929-8019. Mon–Fri 9 am–5 pm, Sat 10 am–5 pm. Cash, checks, MC/VISA.

Surrounded by exclusive, upscale boutiques on trendy Sacramento Street, *Town School Clothes Closet* fits right in with its neighbors. A decidedly upscale thrift store with first-class merchandise (designer labels are the rule rather than the exception), *Town School Clothes Closet* is the place to go for upper-end jewelry, bric-a-brac, housewares, and clothing for men, women, and children. Because things tend to be a bit pricey, smart shoppers wait for the half-off sales held every three months.
Charity: The Town School
Everything except large appliances

~~~ Richmond/Central ~~~

ABBE'S

1420 Clement St., 1431 Clement St. (between 15th and 16th), San Francisco 94118, (415) 751-4567. Tues–Sat 11 am–5 pm. Cash, checks, MC/VISA.

Everyone said we had to go to *Abbe's*, so go to *Abbe's* we did. And let me tell you, the place was jumping. Crowds of shoppers were sifting through the racks, selecting armfuls of garments, and standing in line for a dressing room to try them on. You can't beat Abbe's for quantity. The original store boasts three rooms filled with racks so tightly packed with women's clothing it's hard to see what's there. If you're the kind of shopper who needs to see everything out there before making a decision, Abbe's is for you. They stock sizes 4–16; prices are reasonable. Look for the date on the tag, prices are reduced 20% each month for four months. Sorry guys, but Abbe's men's store is no more. The smaller Abbe's across the street from the big Abbe's now features bargain buys—everything in the store is $40 or less.

Consignment: Tues–Sat 11 am–4 pm, 50/50 split
Women's clothing and accessories

HEATHER'S BOUTIQUE
2249 Clement St. (between 23rd and 24th), San Francisco 94121, (415) 751-5511. Tues–Sat 11 am–5 pm. Cash, checks, MC/VISA.

Discriminating women who understand investment dressing will be pleased to discover Heather's Boutique, where they can fill their closets with designer clothing without taking out a bank loan. This attractive store, colored in pink and rose and featuring better quality and designer clothing sizes 4–24, has a fanatically loyal following of well-dressed women.

One customer shops only at Chanel and Heather's. While you will find some casual and cruise-wear, Heather's concentrates on sophisticated work outfits and elegant dress clothes. Labels like Adolfo, Escada, Givenchy, Valentino, Chanel, Sonia Rykiel, Jean Muir, Lilli Ruben, and Donna Karan appear on the designer racks with regularity. Prices start at 1/3–1/2 of the original cost and are reduced by 50% the last month of the consignment period and an extra 10% the last week.

Consignment: Tues–Sat 11 am–3 pm and by appointment, 50/50 split, 90-day contract
Women's clothing

KIMBERLY'S CONSIGNMENT SHOP
3020 Clement St. (between 31st and 32nd), San Francisco 94121, (415) 752-2223. Tues–Sat 11 am–5 pm. Cash, checks, MC/VISA.

Since 1966, Kimberly's has been dressing San Franciscans in contemporary high-end designer clothing for 1/4 of the original price. Owners Rita Gomez and Toni Petersen, a mother and daughter team, keep the big white store stocked with a lot of women's apparel, some men's clothing, and a case full of antiques, jewelry, and fancy bric-a-brac. They prefer designer labels because that's what sells. Look for names like St. John, Calvin Klein, Gianfranco Ferre, Raul Blanco, Ellen Tracy, and Anne Klein in the women's wear; Ralph Lauren, Giorgio Armani, and

Neiman-Marcus appear in the men's section. If you go to Millbrae you might check out their new store at 220 Broadway.

Consignment: Tues–Sat 11 am–3:30 pm, 40% consignor/60% store; 90-day contract for women's apparel and bric-a-brac, contract of six months for men's apparel

Antiques; men's and women's clothing

NINALLA CONSIGNMENTS

3771 Clement St. (at 32nd), San Francisco 94121, (415) 666-3227. Mon–Sat 11 am–6 pm. Cash, checks, MC/VISA.

Alla Minevich and her friend Nina took over a retail boutique two years ago and converted it to *Ninalla Consignments*. The only way you would know that the merchandise changed from new to used is by looking at the prices. The store is gorgeous, the clothes divine, and the look and feel of an upscale boutique remain. *Ninalla* features better quality and designer clothing (no more than two years old) as well as new San Francisco designers' samples. The woman who dresses in high style with dramatic flair will find that *Ninalla*'s was made for her. The shoes are spectacular. Ninalla also carries handmade lacquer boxes from Russia.

Consignment: Mon–Sat 11 am–6 pm, 50/50 split

Women's clothing

REGINA

5845 Geary Blvd. (between 22nd and 23rd), San Francisco 94121, (415) 386-8577. Mon–Sat 11 am–7 pm. Cash, checks.

Some women would never wear jeans; their style is too original, too exotic for anything so ordinary. Every garment they possess is a piece of wearable art that sparkles with sequins and rhinestones, or glows with the shimmer of velvet or leather. If you prefer fancy and flamboyant to frumpy and functional, *Regina* is the perfect place for you to deaccession your old and acquire something new (to you). *Regina* also carries Paleckh (handmade lacquer boxes from Russia), stacking dolls, and beautiful Russian scarves. Brush up on your Russian for an interesting conversation with owner Regina Khod.

Consignment: Mon–Sat 11 am–7 pm, 50/50 split

Women's clothing

～～ Richmond/Inner ～～

BUSVAN FOR BARGAINS

244 Clement St. (between Vallejo and Green), San Francisco 94118, (415) 752-5353, and 900 Battery (near Broadway), San Francisco 94111, (415) 981-1405. Mon–Sat 9:30 am–6 pm, Sun 12 am–6 pm. Cash, checks, MC/VISA.

Be sure to wear your walking shoes when you go hunting for bargains at *Busvan*. The store is enormous: over 40,000 square feet of furniture and housewares. (We only checked out the Clement Street store, but I hear the Battery warehouse is even bigger.) 75% of the merchandise is new furniture just like you'd find at Macy's or Emporium, all at discounted prices. The mezzanine features antiques and almost-antiques at antique-store prices. For the real bargains, check out the basement. I found the secondhand stuff down there unappealing and overpriced, but you could pick up some great deals on damaged new furniture selling for peanuts.

Furniture and housewares

MAX'S CLOTHING STORE

583 6th Ave. (at Balboa), San Francisco 94118, (415) 387-4073. Mon–Sat 12 am–6 pm. Cash.

I found George Krimsky and a friend playing chess in the back of this little tiny store in a residential neighborhood. Max, I learned, had recently died at the age of 92 and his good friend George had taken over *Max's Clothing Store*, which sells new and used suits, sports coats, trousers, and shirts. *Max's* merchandise is geared toward the sedate rather than flashy dresser. Suits sell for $110–$150, trousers for $10–$40, sports coats for $30–$90. Among the leisure suits you will find such labels as Christian Dior, Bill Blass, and Pierre Cardin. George, a jeweler by training, can also fix your watch or sell you a new one.

Men's clothing

∼∼∼ Russian Hill ∼∼∼

CRIS

2056 Polk St. (at Broadway), San Francisco 94109, (415) 474-1191. Mon–Sat 12 am–6:30 pm. Cash, checks, MC/VISA.

Women with more style than shekels should beat a path to Cris Zander's small consignment shop with high-tech decor. Anyone can put some pizzazz in their fashion profile with a little help from Cris, who likes to combine a t-shirt from The Limited with slacks from Donna Karan for that I'm-so-chic-I-can-wear-anything look. Combining contemporary consignment clothing with new samples, ends-of-lines, and new jewelry by local artists, Cris offers a consistently high-style look for wannabe jet-setters. Sizes run 4–14, and prices are extremely low, considering the high quality.

Consignment: Mon–Sat 12 am–6 pm, 50/50 split

Women's clothing, some men's clothing

∼∼∼ South of Market ∼∼∼

GOODWILL

241 10th St. (between Howard and Folsom), San Francisco 94103, (415) 252-1677. Mon–Sat 10 am–6 pm. Cash, checks, MC/ VISA/DISCOVER.

Brick walls and exposed wood beams make this the best-looking *Goodwill* in the city. Although it's not as well organized as some of the more upscale stores, and the color coordination tends to fall apart, you can't beat it for good buys on collectibles, furniture, and clothing.

Charity: Goodwill
Everything except large appliances

~~~ **The Sunset** ~~~

BABY BOOM
1601 Irving (at 17th), San Francisco 94122, (415) 564-2666. Mon–Sat 10 am–6 pm, Sun 12 am–5 pm. Cash, checks, MC/VISA/AM EX.

You can buy, sell, or rent almost anything you need for kids ages newborn–eight at *Baby Boom*. 70% of the furniture is new, while 75% of the kid's clothes are used. You have to ask to see the maternity clothes, which are kept in a small store around the corner. Mothers-to-be will find a good selection of business suits with good labels like Japanese Weekend, and Mother-hood, as well as a few casual outfits. Stock turns over every two and a half weeks. Prices are a little high for resale, but the guaranteed buyback policy evens it all out. If you're lucky, Christine McNamara, sales clerk cum stand-up comic, will assist you and keep you in stitches.

Consignment: Buys outright for cash or trade and guarantees to buyback (with restrictions)
Maternity clothing; children's clothing, furniture, and equipment

MARY'S ATTIC
2031 Irving St. (between 21st and 22nd), San Francisco 94122, (415) 665-2950. Mon–Sat 10 am–6 pm, Sun 10 am–4 pm. Cash, MC/VISA.

A small store, neat as a pin and run by a friendly Spanish-speaking staff, *Mary's Attic* carries the usual thrift store fare—clothes, housewares, and bric-a-brac, with a few unusual items like four tires for $59.99, a swing-o-matic for $13.99, and Mexican party favors for 99¢.

Charity: Ciudad De Los Ninos
Everything but furniture and large appliances

SMALL CHANGE
1234 Ninth Ave. (between Lincoln and Irving), San Francisco, (415) 566-1234. Mon–Sat 11 am–5 pm, Sun 12 am–4 pm. Cash, checks, MC/VISA/DISCOVER.

Small Change is an appealing store carrying clothing, books, and toys for small fry ages newborn–14. Half of the merchandise is new and half is used.

Consignment: Mon–Sat 11 am–5 pm, 50/50 split, 90-day contract
Children's clothing

~~~ **Upper Market** ~~~

WORN OUT WEST
582 Castro St. (between 18th and 19th), San Francisco 94114, (415)

~~~~~~~~~~

Right: Glen Stroud at Worn Out West, San Francisco.

431-6020. Mon, Tues, Sat, 11:30 am–6 pm; Wed–Fri 11 am–7 pm; Sun 12 am–5:30 pm. Cash, MC/ VISA.

Worn Out West may not be everyone's cup of tea. But for men who are into leather—jackets, pants, chaps, accessories—this is it! A gorgeous upscale store catering mainly to the gay market, Worn Out West has the best selection of used leather anywhere. You can save a bundle too; jackets go for $65–$350, and they carry designer labels like Montana. This is not a vintage shop; nothing is more than 10 years old. In addition to the extensive selection of leather, cowboy, and uniform "dress up" garments, they stock high-end wear-to-work suits and the largest selection of Levi's 501s in the Bay Area. Owners Joe Caggiano and Rob Bovlier will help you put together an eye-catching outfit for Leather Pride Week—or their in-house designer can custom make it for you.

Consignment: Mon–Sat 12 am–5 pm, Sun 1 pm–5 pm; 60% consignor/40% store if sells in first month, 50/50 split if sells in second month, 40% consignor/ 60% store if sells in third month; also buys outright
Men's clothing

∿ Van Ness/Civic Center ∿

AMERICAN RAG COMPAGNIE
1305 Van Ness Ave. (at Sutter), San Francisco 94109, (415) 474-

5214. Mon–Wed 10 am–9 pm, Thurs–Sat 10 am–10:30 pm, Sun 12 am–6 pm. Cash, checks, MC/ VISA/AM EX.

Wow! What a store! What a concept! Located in a former auto showroom, American Rag gives new meaning to the word vintage. Featuring 40% authentic fashions from the 1940's, 1950's, and 1960's, and 60% new reproductions of period garments, this enormous, gorgeous, even-parents-will-love-it store makes vintage shopping respectable. Of course you pay a little more for all this glitter and respectability—Levi's 501's can run you $39 and baseball jackets are $94 and up, not to mention the $300 new cowboy shirts (old can be had for $20). If you think of shopping at American Rag as entertainment, it's worth it. Not all prices are sky-high; many of the used garments are reasonably priced, in light of their excellent condition. Just look for the the tag that tells you, "This garment is recycled. The fashion intended is its antiquity and uniqueness.... Secondhand."
Men's and women's clothing

THE OTHER SHOP
112-A Gough St. (near Oak), San Francisco 94102, (415) 621-1590. Mon–Sun 12 am–6 pm. Cash, checks, MC/VISA/AM EX.

Packed full of goodies reflecting the taste of eight different dealers, this eclectic collective offers a little bit of everything, from turn-of-the century to yesterday. Collectors can pick up some pricey precious gems, yet prices are still affordable for people just starting to furnish their first apartment. Prices are flexible, and your success in bargaining on any particular item depends upon who is minding the store. The deliberately cramped look makes for an exciting shopping experience.

Furniture, collectibles, vintage clothing

SALVATION ARMY

1185 Sutter St. (between Larkin and Polk), San Francisco 94109, (415) 771-3818. Mon–Sat 9 am–5 pm, Thurs 9 am–7 pm. Cash, checks, MC/VISA.

The smaller of the two *Salvation Army* stores in the city seems to specialize in furniture. While their prices are not the lowest in town, they are still reasonable and the selection of antique, semi-antique, and contemporary furniture offers something for every taste—a glass-topped wrought-iron table for $65, a five-piece dining set for $295, an antique fire screen for $50. As always, the prices on Army clothing are hard to beat. You'll findsome jewelry in a locked case. Small antiques and collectibles are nowhere to be seen (check the store on Valencia Street in the Mission instead).

Charity: Salvation Army
Everything

~~~ **Visitation Valley** ~~~

GENEVA SWAP MARKET

Geneva Drive-In, 607 Carter, San Francisco 94110, (415) 587-0515. Sat and Sun 7 am–4 pm. Purchase method varies by dealer.

The admission prices jump from 50¢ on Saturday to 75¢ on Sunday. If you want to sell, your price jumps from $10 on Saturday to $15 on Sunday.

Everything

SAVERS

2840 Geneva Ave. (2 blocks east of the Cow Palace), San Francisco 94014, (415) 468-0646. Mon–Wed 9 am–7 pm, Thurs and Fri 9 am–9 pm, Sat and Sun 10 am–6 pm. Cash, checks, MC/VISA.

Although well-lit and sensibly organized, this gigantic *Savers* is not as attractive as some other *Savers*. There is certainly no dearth of merchandise, especially clothes and housewares. I found prices too high for the quality of the goods— $13 for tea pots without tops? Come on! For higher quality and lower prices give me *Goodwill* or *Salvation Army* any day. They do offer a 20% discount to seniors every day and everyone on Sunday.

Charity: Privately owned, supports the Peninsula Association for Retarded Children and Adults
Everything

SAN FRANCISCO	Appliances/large	Bridal	Clothing/children	Clothing/men	Clothing/women	Collectibles	Furnishings/children	Furniture	Housewares	Maternity	Tools, etc.	Toys	Vintage	Page number
BALBOA TERRACE														
St. Francis Store			X	X	X	X	X		X		X	X		101
BAYVIEW														
Goodwill		X	X	X	X	X	X	X	X	X	X	X		101
DOWNTOWN														
Community Hospice	X	X	X	X	X	X	X	X	X	X	X	X	X	101
Goodwill		X	X	X	X	X	X	X	X	X	X	X		102
Love Project			X	X	X	X		X	X		X	X		102
Rafael House		X	X	X	X	X	X	X	X		X	X		102
EXCELSIOR														
DeMello's Furniture								X						102
HAIGHT/ASHBURY														
Aardvark's Odd Ark				X	X								X	103
Buffalo Exchange				X	X								X	103
Held Over				X	X								X	103
La Rosa				X	X								**X**	105
New Government				X	X								X	105
St. Vincent de Paul		X	X	X	X	X	X	X	X	X	X	X	X	105
Spellbound				X	X								X	106
Sugartit			X	X	X								X	106
Wasteland			X	X	X			X					X	106
HAYES VALLEY														
Countess Olizar					X								**X**	107
Jinx				X	X	X							X	107
Sharp Brothers	X					X	X	X	X		X			108
Velvet Pelvis				X	X	X		X					X	108
LAKESHORE														
Lake Merced Market	X	X	X	X	X	X	X	X	X	X	X	X	X	109
MISSION/INNER														
Aron Furniture	X							X						109
Community Thrift		X	X	X	X	X	X	X	X	X	X	X	X	109
Clothes Contact				X	X								X	109
Cottrell's						X		**X**	X					110
Felino's Vintage				X	X			X					**X**	110

SAN FRANCISCO	Appliances/large	Bridal	Clothing/children	Clothing/men	Clothing/women	Collectibles	Furnishings/children	Furniture	Housewares	Maternity	Tools, etc.	Toys	Vintage	Page number
Goodwill		X	X	X	X	X	X	X	X	X	X	X		110
Harrington Bros.						X		X	X					112
Hocus Pocus						X		X						112
Jim's Used Furniture						X		X						112
Kernan's Moving								X						112
No Name Collect.						X		X						113
Pink Paraffin			X	X	X	X		X	X				X	113
Purple Heart	X	X	X	X	X	X	X	X	X	X	X	X		113
Salvation Army	X	X	X	X	X	X	X	X	X	X	X	X		114
Thrift Town		X	X	X	X	X	X	X	X	X	X	X		114
Upstairs, Downstairs						X		X						114
NOB HILL														
Attic Shop	X		X	X	X	X	X	X	X	X	X	X		115
Buffalo Exchange				X	X								X	115
Cathedral Shop	X		X	X	X	X	X	X	X	X	X	X		115
NOE VALLEY														
Always and Forever				X	X								X	115
Chamaeleon				X	X								X	116
Mary's Exchange					X									116
Natural Resources			X				X			X				116
One More Time				X	X								X	117
Peek-A-Bootique			X				X					X		117
NORTH BEACH														
Old Vogue				X	X								X	117
St. Francis Shop			X	X	X	X	X	X	X		X	X		119
OCEAN														
Ocean Ave. Thrift			X	X	X	X	X		X			X	X	119
PACIFIC HEIGHTS														
Bottom Drawer			X	X	X	X	X	X			X	X		119
Next-to-New Shop			X	X	X	X	X	X	X	X	X	X		120
Repeat Performance			X	X	X	X	X		X			X		121
Scarlett's				X	X								X	121
Seconds-to-Go			X	X	X	X	X		X			X		122
Street Shop					X	X			X					122

SAN FRANCISCO	Appliances/large	Bridal	Clothing/children	Clothing/men	Clothing/women	Collectibles	Furnishings/children	Furniture	Housewares	Maternity	Tools, etc.	Toys	Vintage	Page number
Victorian House			X	X	X	X	X	X	X		X	X	X	123
Vintage Boutique				X	X								X	123
PACIFIC HGHTS./LWR.														
Bargain Mart	X		X	X	X	X	X	X	X		X	X	X	124
Bear-ly New			X	X	X	X			X			X		124
Crossroads				X	X								X	124
Departures				X	X								X	125
Goodwill	X		X	X	X	X	X	X	X	X	X	X		125
Third Hand Store	**X**			X	X								X	126
PRESIDIO														
Presidio Thrift	X		X	X	X	X	X	X	X	X	X	X		126
PRESIDIO HEIGHTS														
Good Byes			**X**	X										128
Town School			X	X	X	X	X	X	X			X		128
RICHMOND/CENTRAL														
Abbe's					**X**									128
Heather's Boutique					X									129
Kimberly's Shop				X	X	X								129
Ninalla					X									130
Regina					X									130
RICHMOND/INNER														
Busvan for Bargains								X	X					130
Max's Clothing				X										131
RUSSIAN HILL														
Cris				X	X									131
SOUTH OF MARKET														
Goodwill		X	X	X	X	X	X	X	X	X	X	X		131
SUNSET														
Baby Boom			X				X			X		X		132
Mary's Attic			X	X	X	X		X			X	X		132
Small Change			X									X		132
UPPER MARKET														
Worn Out West				X										132

SAN FRANCISCO	Appliances/large	Bridal	Clothing/children	Clothing/men	Clothing/women	Collectibles	Furnishings/children	Furniture	Housewares	Maternity	Tools, etc.	Toys	Vintage	Page number
VAN NESS/CVC. CNTR.														
American Rag				X	X								X	134
Other Shop				X	X	X		X	X				X	134
Salvation Army	X	X	X	X	X	X	X	X	X	X	X	X		135
VISITATION VALLEY														
Geneva Market	X	X	X	X	X	X	X	X	X	X	X	X	X	135
Savers	X	X	X	X	X	X	X	X	X	X	X	X		135

~~~~~ **Belmont** ~~~~~

GINNY'S GARMENT EXCHANGE & BOUTIQUE

951 Old Country Road (next to Wendy's), Belmont 94002, (415) 594-4848. Tues–Sat 10:30 am–5:30 pm. Cash, checks, MC/VISA/ DISCOVER.

Located in Landmark Center, this smallish clean, bright store bills itself as "Decidedly Upscale Resale." The white walls, checkered floor, cheval mirror, and wicker settee give it the feel of an upscale specialty shop. Some of the service, however, is decidedly cool. "Good labels" predominate over designer labels, everything is immaculate and well organized, and the up-to-date styles are moderately priced: an Ann Klein silk sarong skirt for $25, a Scott McClintock velvet blazer for $23, a St. John's knit outfit for $75.
Consignment: Tues–Sat 10:30 am–4:30 pm, 50/50 split
Women's clothing

SALVATION ARMY

650 El Camino Real, Belmont 94002, (415) 591-5499. Mon–Sat 9 am–5:30 pm. Cash, MC/VISA with a minimum of $20.

From the outside, this large, bright one-room store complete with a weather vane-topped steeple looks as if it might have been an Ethan Alan showroom in a former life. Inside, the store is divided down the middle, with one half devoted to racks and racks of clothing and the other half to furniture, appliances, housewares, etc. At this store you have the *Salvation Army* at its best: clean, well-organized, enormous variety in merchandise and quality, and above all good prices.

A determined shopper can find just about any imaginable article of clothing. We saw a stylish Adrienne Vittadini for $4.50 right next to an aged, worn Sears Roebuck irregular for $3.50. Brand new Jessica McClintock wedding gowns were $25. Finding the perfect piece of furniture may take a bit more patience, but we did find on one visit a darling good-as-new white wicker chair for $39.50 and a handsome leather armchair (as is—a little wear on one arm) marked down to $39.50. The good selection of wood desks (including a charming secretary), dressers, and end tables all looked and smelled as if someone had gone crazy with a can of white spray paint.
Charity: Salvation Army
Everything

THIS'N'THAT SHOP

Good Shepherd Episcopal Church, 1336 5th Avenue (one block west of El Camino Real),

Belmont 94002, (415) 591-6166.
Wed and Fri 10:30 am–1:30 pm,
second and fourth Sats 10 am–1
pm. Cash, MC/VISA.

Located in a former Sunday school basement classroom, This 'n' That Shop has been holding a "perpetual rummage sale" since 1960. Although its hours of business are limited, this is one thrift shop you won't want to miss (look for the big red and yellow banner and sandwich boards.) Prices are so low you might even feel the urge to bargain up. "Our prices are so low we don't make a lot of money," one volunteer confided, "but we turn our merchandise over so fast the shop always looks nice." (The "we lose money on every sale, but we make it up in volume" philosophy.)

The shop, two windowless rooms joined by a narrow hallway, features clothing and bric-a-brac in the front room and household goods, toys, books, and the sales rack in the back. With a few exceptions, clothing is of fair to good quality, but exceptionally well priced. The greatest bargains and treasures are to be found among the knickknacks and collectibles. When the shop is the beneficiary of an estate, the "God Squad" (as the volunteers call themselves) try to get the books and art works appraised and sell them for fair value. But we did hear two tales of under-pricing: a Roseville plate that sold for two dollars was later found to be valued at $300. Recently, a steady customer reported that he had sold a string of ivory beads to an antique store owner for $120 after paying $2 for them at This 'n' That.

Charity: Projects of Episcopal Church Women, including special needs of the Good Shepherd Church as well as cash donations to Salvation Army, Christmas Bureau, Women's Shelter, and Samaritan House

Everything except furniture and large appliances

~~~~ Burlingame ~~~~

AMERICAN CANCER SOCIETY DISCOVERY SHOP

1410 Broadway, Burlingame
94010, (415) 343-9100. Mon–Sat
10 am–4 pm. Cash, checks, MC/
VISA.

Following the usual Discovery Shop model of a clean, well-organized, pleasant place, the Burlingame store offers the thoughtful addition of wheelchair-accessible racks and shelves. Marge Humphrey, who has managed the Burlingame shop for six years, explained the store is so nice because "we only keep the best." The Salvation Army comes twice a week to pick up the rejects. It also helps to be located next door to Victoria's Closet, where would-be consignors are encouraged to donate unsold merchandise to the Discovery Shop. Clothing prices are reasonable, although designer items can get a little pricey—we saw a Donna Karan beaded dress for $225. The shop is constantly rotating merchandise. After two months on the floor everything is marked down 50%, and after another 30 days it goes to the $1 rack in the back of the store. *Charity: American Cancer Society* **Everything except large appliances**

CIRCLES
121 Park Road, Burlingame 94010, (415) 347-6162. Tues–Sat 10 am–5 pm. Cash, checks, MC/ VISA.

Three generations are behind this new upscale consignment shop, which opened in November 1991. With a background in retailing, daughter Michelle Newman-Light brings the merchandising expertise that gives *Circles* the air of an exclusive specialty boutique. (Mother Sora Lei Newman provided the financial brains and backing, and a baby granddaughter visits occasionally.) Occupying the entire top floor (over a beauty shop) of a restored 1906 Victorian, four ample rooms each feature a different specialty: leather and accessories, evening gowns and designer wear, sports separates, and day wear.

While the prices at first glance may seem high, we're talking genuine designer labels...haute couture. If you care about that sort of thing, *Circles* will dress you in designer clothing for about a third of the original cost. Or if you just want to build a wardrobe of high quality, up-to-date fashions without taking out a bank loan, you can do that, too. A San Francisco executive recently came away with

twelve pieces for under $600. (Escada and Missoni names were on the labels.) For a few special clients, *Circles* offers a personal wardrobe consultant service to weed mistakes out of your closets and coordinate your wardrobe. *Consignment: Tues and Thurs 10:30 am–4 pm, or by appointment; 50/50 split* **Women's clothing, jewelry, accessories**

MISS JODI'S
1419 Burlingame Ave., Fox Mall, 2nd floor, Burlingame 94010, (415) 343-0520. Mon–Sat 10 am–5 pm. Cash, checks, layaway.

Diana Borrelli opened *Miss Jodi's* in July 1991 and by January 1992 had already outgrown her original small store and moved to a larger space across the hall. The new store is still small and crowded, filled with a jumbled assortment of pre-owned women's clothes (no pants or shoes), hats, and accessories; new evening dresses on consignment from a local bridal salon; and close-out nail polish from the beauty salon next door. *Miss Jodi's* also takes handmade boutique items on consignment for the holiday shopping season.

If your taste runs more to flash and glitz (moderately priced) than sedate classic styles, *Miss Jodi's* might be just the place for you. *Miss Jodi's* does offer the advantage of a tailor shop across the hall, and custom tailoring may be negotiated in the price of the garment.

*Consignment: By appointment,
50/50 split, 60-day contract*
**Boutique items, women's
clothing**

PRIMROSE HOUSE OF VALUES
*307 Primrose Road, Burlingame
94010, (415) 343-1920. Mon–Sat
10 am–4 pm. Cash, checks.*

As the name suggests, this darling
thrift shop resembles nothing more
than a quaint English cottage, right
down to the lace-curtained windows in the back. The volunteers
who run the store are so friendly
you almost expect them to offer
you a cup of tea. Although good
buys abound on the crowded racks
of men's, women's, and children's
clothing, the best buys are to be
found in the cases, counters, and
shelves of household goods, bric-a-
brac, and collectibles. Everyday
housewares and small appliances
are dirt cheap. *Primrose House*
pricers seem to know their collectibles and antiques, and price
them according to what the market
will bear. Still, many collectibles
slip by and end up as unbelievable
bargains. A friend picked up a
1920's overnight bag in perfect
condition for $3 and a beautiful
ceramic plate, also in perfect
condition, for 75¢.

Seasonal new merchandise
donated by local merchants is
saved for special holiday displays.
A January visit turned up an entire
counter of Valentine's Day items,
from cards to lace garters, for a
fraction of their original price. And
if your name is Wanda or Brad (or

almost anything else) you could
pick up a personalized key ring for
$2. Twice a year *Primhouse House*
holds a half-off sale on selected
merchandise. But with their good
prices (paperbacks are six for $1),
you don't have to wait.
*Charity: Catholic Charities, which
supports non-denominational
senior services*
**Everything except furniture
and large appliances**

VICTORIA'S CLOSET
*1452 Broadway, Burlingame
94010, (415) 344-1665. Mon–Sat
10 am–5:30 pm, Sun 12 am–5 pm.
Cash, checks, MC/VISA.*

Conveniently located right next
door to the Cancer Society's
Discovery Shop, Victoria's 3000
square-foot closet—formerly a
television repair shop, appliance
store, and upholstery shop—is any
clothes lover's idea of heaven. Tall,
stunning Rosalee Chapman, the
owner (there is no Victoria), who's
always elegantly dressed (one
assumes from her own store),
makes you feel right at home. "We
have something for everyone," she
says, "we don't just do designer.
We are label conscious—no Sears,
JC Penney, or Mervyns—but we
like to have a lot of things so people
can buy a pair of jeans and a flannel
shirt for $5 or a designer dress for
$1000. When you walk in this store
you should be able to walk out with
something you love that fits your
budget."

Despite its size and the huge
volume of merchandise, the

sensible layout and gracious accoutrements keep *Victoria's Closet* from overwhelming. The center of the store boasts a long counter filled with an amazing assortment of costume jewelry—from vintage to funky to modern. Charming paintings and fashion prints adorn the walls, and an occasional knickknack, like a crystal decanter or a piece of antique silver, contribute to the elegant atmosphere. All items are marked down after 30 days, so there is always a good selection of sale merchandise. In addition, there are two major sales a year when 90% of all merchandise is reduced. Sign up on the sale mailing list.
Consignment: Tues–Fri 10 am–4:30 pm, 50/50 split
Women's clothing, jewelry, a few collectibles

El Granada
~~~ (Half Moon Bay) ~~~

THE ALTERNATIVE THRIFT SHOP
522 Plaza Alhambra, El Granada 94018, (415) 726-9911. Mon–Sun 11 am–5 pm (call first to be sure). Cash, checks.

A million miles from nowhere, this small, funky one-room thrift shop is worth the trip, if only for the gorgeous scenic drive. The appeal is not so much the used merchandise—clothes are definitely downscale but cheap, knickknacks are apt to be more interesting—but more the ambience provided by the crusty owner Cindy Judkins.

We liked the looks of the place, from the shabby oriental carpet on the floor to the sardonic sign above the counter reading "Psychiatric Help 5¢–$100." A born-and-bred recycler, Cindy also sells braided rugs for $45–$60. Not to be missed is Cindy's own collection of "hardtimes jewelry" and objets d'art—one-of-a-kind works she assembles from forgotten pieces, some uniquely beautiful and some plain strange. Pins run $15–$35.
Everything except large appliances

~~~ Los Altos ~~~

AMERICAN CANCER SOCIETY DISCOVERY SHOP
142 Main Street, Los Altos 94022, (415) 949-0505. Mon–Sat 10 am–4 pm. Cash, checks, MC/VISA/DISCOVER.

Los Altos' one and only thrift store, this pretty little shop follows the *Discovery Shop* pattern with blue awnings, blue carpet, and upscale merchandise tastefully displayed. Unfortunately, on our visit there was a noticeable lack of merchandise.
Charity: American Cancer Society
Everything except furniture and large appliances

~~~ Menlo Park ~~~

AFTERWARDS
1137 El Camino Real, Menlo Park 94025, (415) 324-2377. Mon–Sat

10 am–6 pm, Thurs 10 am–8 pm.
Cash, checks, MC/VISA.

"A Discovery You Don't Have to Be Wealthy to Enjoy," headlined the *San Francisco Chronicle* society column. "Don't tell anyone, but a lot of the Atherton/Woodside rich and famous crowd have discovered Katie and Bob Hanson's ultra fancy consignment store, *Afterwards*, in Menlo Park—and they've been going there to buy," columnist Pat Steger informed her readers. When a resale shop makes the *Chronicle*'s society column, you can bet it's pretty special. The owners of this truly upscale consignment boutique cut their merchandising teeth as managers of Palo Alto's *Polo* store, and it shows. "We wanted to replicate the *Polo* store at a better price point," explained Hanson. The atmosphere—enhanced by for-real antiques—is more posh than Ralph Lauren. An old Brunswick pool table holds men's trousers, hats are displayed on pool sticks, new silk ties are spread out on an antique pine piece, and classical music plays softly in the background.

High quality men's, women's, and children's pre-worn clothing sells for 25%–30% of the original price. New merchandise—they carry a lot of sales reps' samples—goes for 50% of retail. Although designer labels abound—we saw a Caroline Herrera dress for $699—*Afterwards* also stocks classics from Macy's and Nordstrom. On a typical day, a man from the nearby Veteran's Hospital purchased a pair of chino trousers for $8 and a steady customer bought a Hermes blazer for $500. *Afterwards* offers tailoring and consulting service: the Hansons will come to your home and help you realize the strengths and weaknesses of your current wardrobe. As a matter of policy, *Afterwards* donates 5% of its pre-tax profits to charity.
Consignment: By appointment; pre-worn items 40% consignor/ 60% store, new items 50/50 split
Antiques; clothing for men, women, and children

AMERICAN CANCER SOCIETY DISCOVERY SHOP
746 Santa Cruz Ave., Menlo Park 94025, (415) 325-8939. Mon–Sat 10 am–4 pm. Cash, checks, MC/ VISA.

A typical Cancer Society *Discovery Shop*, this one follows the pattern of clean, bright, well-organized thrift shops with generally high-quality used merchandise and good prices. Of note are the shop windows, which are even more beautifully decorated than usual. Apparently beneficiaries of the Jessica McClintock generosity, here we found new wedding gowns for $80–$140 and bridesmaids' dresses for $30–$45.
Charity: American Cancer Society
Everything except large appliances

MERRY-GO-ROUND
713 Santa Clara Ave., Ste. 12 (upstairs), Menlo Park 94025, (415) 325-1225. Mon–Fri 10 am–

5:30 pm, Sat 10 am–5 pm. Cash, checks, layaway, MC/VISA.

Mrs. Miller, the stately formidable proprietor of *Merry-Go-Round*, has been in business since April 15, 1966. Located up some stairs and down a hall, the shop still bears traces of its original incarnation as a bridal salon. Somewhat schizophrenic in its decor, the first of the store's two good-sized rooms is all feminine elegance, with pink and white striped wallpaper, pink wall to wall carpeting, pleasant dressing rooms, and highest quality garments tastefully displayed. A majority of the gowns, dresses, suits, and furs bear the best designer labels—Joanie Char, Anne Klein, Jaeger, Albert Nipon, Valentino, Raul Blanco, St. John, Ferragamo, Louis Feraud, Geoffrey Beene—with an occasional Victoria's Secret thrown in for variety's sake. While the $100, $200, and $300 price tags seem high to the average thrift shopper, they are actually bargains considering what these garments cost originally. The second room, sans carpet and wallpaper, has a more utilitarian atmosphere, with great quantities of sportswear crowded on the many racks. Quality, though, is still high and prices good.
Consignment: By appointment, 40% consignor/60% store
Women's clothing

Left: Eden Tanovitz and Loretta DePorceri, owner of Countess Olizar, San Francisco.

NEW LIFE BOUTIQUE
879 Santa Cruz Ave., Menlo Park 94025, (415) 325-3333. Tues–Fri 11 am–5 pm, Sat 12 am–4 pm. Cash, checks, MC/VISA.

Located behind the health food store, this small (600 square feet) shop is crammed to the rafters with women's clothing, jewelry, and accessories. Maternity clothes are stored in the back—ask for them. Known for twenty years as *Glad Rags*, the shop became *New Life Boutique* when current owner Carol Domingo took over. *New Life* specializes in gowns—great for proms and glitzy nights out. Sizes run 4–24 with a noteworthy selection of larger sizes (often hard to find in consignment stores). Despite overcrowding, quality is good and prices are reasonable. Things should be even better when planned expansion takes place. Parking in rear.
Consignment: By appointment, 50/50 split
Women's and children's clothing, maternity clothing

Mountain View

GOODWILL
855 E. El Camino Real, Mountain View 94040, (415) 969-3382. Mon–Thurs 9 am–7 pm, Fri 9 am–8 pm, Sat 9 am–6 pm, Sun 11 am–6 pm. Cash, checks, MC/VISA.

Housed in a two-room warehouse-like structure, the Mountain View *Goodwill* is less upscale and larger

than most of its sister stores. What it lacks in cleanliness, elegance, and merchandising pizzazz it makes up for in quantity and variety of goods for sale. The furniture selection is unusually large for *Goodwill*.
Charity: Goodwill
Everything except large appliances

THRIFT MART
92 W. El Camino Real, Mountain View 94040, (415) 961-2616. Mon–Sat 9 am–6:45 pm. Cash, checks, MC/VISA.

A large, well-organized store with lots of everything, *Thrift Mart* uses ongoing sales to live up to its self-bestowed moniker, "The Discount Thrift Store." Park in the lot, pick up a shopping cart, and peruse the aisles of clothing arranged by color (mostly low end: Sears, J C Penney), racks of pictures, shelves of household goods, and quantities of furniture. In general, quality is medium to low; prices are low to very low. An occasional surprise will keep you interested. For example, one visit turned up a freestanding wood-burning stove for $500 and a four-piece white bedroom set, including a four-poster bed, for $200. A glass case teaming with dolls bears a sign warning, "Barbie and collectable dolls not included on discount days."
Charity: Privately owned, associated with Adult Independence Development Center of Santa Clara County
Everything

OPPORTUNITY SHOP
740 Villa, Mountain View 94041, (415) 968-6876. Mon–Fri 10 am–5 pm, Sat 11 am–4 pm. Cash, checks.

The jumbled window of miscellanea and the rack of $3 dresses outside the store give you a hint of what you will find within. A medium sized one-room store gives the impression of clutter without actually containing a great deal of merchandise. Clothing, accessories, and household goods make up a large part of the inventory. In general, quality is fair to medium; prices are reasonable to cheap. On the plus side, the volunteer staff is friendly, new arrivals are featured on a separate rack, and if you do uncover something wonderful (of course this is a possibility), it won't cost you an arm and a leg.
Charity: ORT (Organization for Rehabilitation and Training)
Everything except furniture and large appliances

~~~~~ Pacifica ~~~~~

DIANA'S ENCORE BOUTIQUE
2500 Francisco Blvd., Pacifica 94044, (415) 738-0558. Tues–Sat 12:30 am–5:30 pm. Cash, checks.

Warm, friendly Diana makes shopping in this small, crowded consignment store a pleasure. Catering to the mature woman (most of her clientele is over 25), *Diana's* is well stocked with high quality larger sizes (16–52), and very small sizes (2 and 4). Quality

is good and prices are reasonable: dresses run $25–$130, blouses cost $7–$30, suits are $30–$70. Don't miss the jewelry selection—some are on consignment and some are fanciful handmade pieces Diana purchases directly from the jeweler. Check out the $5 and $10 racks. Maternity clothing is kept in the dressing room.
Consignment: Tues and Wed and by appointment, 40% consignor/ 60% store
Women's clothing and accessories

THE KID'S ROOM
115 Manor Drive, Pacifica 94044, (415) 355-5009. Mon–Fri 10 am–6 pm, Sat 10 am–5 pm. Cash, checks.

You won't mind the clutter and mess in this *Kid's Room* when you see the great buys in new and used kid's clothes (sizes newborn–16). Owner Michael Alford, the earth-mother type and a mother of four, has made it her mission to ease the stress of modern parenting. She not only has some of the best prices around, but she also runs a clearinghouse for kids. If you need a baby-sitter, housekeeper, or car pool, she can refer you to the right person. She also keeps a wish list for baby furniture and the like. Everything is for sale here, and better yet, most things can be rented—cribs, strollers, snow suits, even tuxedos—all for $1 dollar a day! Anyone who has ever shelled out $50 to a formal-wear store for a ring bearer's outfit will find that

price hard to believe. Kids will love the 25¢ basket of toys, and parents will love the September and January 50¢ sales.
Consignment: 40% consignor/ 60% store
Maternity clothing; toys; children's clothing and furniture

~~~~~ **Palo Alto** ~~~~~

THE BARGAIN BOX
318 Cambridge Ave, Palo Alto 94306, (415) 326-0458. Mon–Sat 10 am–4 pm. Cash, checks, MC/ VISA.

A striped awning and flower-filled window boxes lend a jaunty air to this good-sized thrift shop. The pleasant front room features women's clothing, all well-orga-nized and offered at good prices. Several smaller back rooms hold a less well-organized "Children's Corner;" a great book section tended weekly by a librarian volunteer; a small music room which sells large and small instru-ments (including three organs); the "Bazaar" that features housewares and costumes; and a section devoted to collectibles, jewelry, and higher-priced items. The large furniture section in back has a good selection at medium prices—an upholstered chair for $125, a five-piece dining room set for $950, sofas for $150.

This all-volunteer store has been in business since 1956—helping people in the community find affordable merchandise; putting on fashion shows for clubs, churches, and professional organizations; packing and removing leftover household items from estates and leaving the premises "broom clean;" and arranging neighborhood donation drives.

Charity: Children's Health Council Consignment: Accepts furniture and objets d'art on consignment, 60% consignor/40% store
Everything except large appliances

GOODWILL

4085 El Camino Real (at West Meadow), Palo Alto 94306, (415) 494-1416. Mon–Thurs 9 am–7 pm, Fri 9 am–8 pm, Sat 9 am–6 pm, Sun 11 am–6 pm. Cash, checks, MC/VISA.

In 1991 readers of the Palo Alto weekly newspaper voted this *Goodwill* the best thrift shop in Palo Alto. Admitted *Goodwill* aficionados that we are, we have to agree. Santa Clara boasts the finest *Goodwill* stores in the Bay Area, and this one is the queen of the county. Newly built, the store is clean, well lit, and organized into departments—men's wear, women's wear, household goods, shoes, etc.—which are in turn organized by color. Floor and window displays rival Macy's best, men and women have their own dressing rooms, and prices are very reasonable.

Like all *Goodwills*, the best buys and the best selection are to be found in clothing and household goods—furniture is more limited and collectibles are more expensive.

Charity: Goodwill
Everything except large appliances

MARKET OF THE FLEA

545 Emerson Street, Palo Alto 94301, (415) 325-0116. Mon–Sat 11 am–3 pm. Cash, checks.

From the outside *Market of the Flea*, located in downtown Palo Alto, looks just like its antique-store neighbors. Desirable, high priced antiques and collectibles fill the windows. Inside, treasures are everywhere—china, glassware, old typewriters, ancient sewing machines, pictures, books, games, puzzles, unique pieces of small furniture—all selling at top dollar (but still less than next door). Relegated to the back of the store is a disorderly array of not-particularly-stylish-nor-fresh clothing and rather mundane household goods. Loyal shoppers who look forward to the *Market of the Flea*'s annual antique sale will be disappointed to learn than no sale is planned for 1992.

Charity: Community Association for the Retarded
Everything except large appliances and large pieces of furniture

REPEAT PERFORMANCE

2323 Birch Street, Palo Alto 94306, (415) 322-3657. Mon 11 am–4 pm. Tues–Sat 10 am–5 pm. Cash, MC/VISA.

This small non-profit consignment shop is packed to the gills with merchandise, mostly high quality, up-to-date women's clothing selling at 1/2 to 1/3 of the original retail price. Women whose jobs require corporate dressing will appreciate the superb selection of suits (almost all good labels, with a smattering of exclusive designers) priced $30–$70. The merchandise turns over quickly in this crowded shop due to regular markdowns: 10% after 30 days, 20% after 60 days, and everything half off after 90 days. Be sure to check the half-off rack in the very back for great bargains.

Consignment: By appointment, 40% consignor/60% store
Charity: Family Service Association of the Mid-Peninsula
Women's and children's clothing and accessories

SECOND SEASON RESALE SHOP
380 Cambridge, Palo Alto 94306, (415) 323-6827. Mon–Fri 10 am–4 pm. Cash, checks, MC/VISA.

Two large, airy rooms are cheerful, bright, exceptionally clean, and well organized. The first is devoted to women's clothing, housewares, and knickknacks. The red carpeted back room houses books, shoes, men's clothing, accessories, and magazines. Every effort has been made to make shopping a pleasant experience, the prices are terrific, and the volunteers are helpful and friendly. The only drawback we encountered on our visit was the scarcity of merchandise.

Charity: The Morgan Center, which benefits developmentally disabled children and adults
Housewares, collectibles, men's and women's clothing

TURNABOUT SHOP
2335 El Camino Real (between California and Cambridge), Palo Alto 94306, (415) 321-9853. Tues–Fri 11 am–4 pm, Sat 11 am–3 pm. Cash, checks, MC/VISA.

Established in 1947, the *Turnabout Shop* now occupies its own store, built just for them, complete with blue awnings and stylishly decorated windows. The men's department in the front is attractively laid out with an impressive selection of suits, sports wear, and masculine-type accessories (portable bars, sporting equipment, etc....) From high-style to downright dowdy, the women's clothing here represents one of the most eclectic gatherings we've seen...all styles, all sizes (there's a particularly impressive selection of larger sizes 14–20), all prices, and a range of labels, including Ralph Lauren and L. L. Bean. Furs are stored in the locked cupboard in the back of the store, and don't overlook the furniture, jewelry, and household items. The *Turnabout Shop* has a layaway plan and will pick up and deliver large purchases for a price. Don't forget to sign the mailing list for the sales.

Charity: Senior projects, including two residences and day care for the frail and elderly
Everything except large appliances

~~~ Redwood City ~~~

THE DISCOVERY SHOP OF THE JUNIOR LEAGUE OF PALO ALTO
2432 Broadway (across from CalTrain station and SamTrans bus stop), Redwood City 94063, (415) 363-2238. Mon–Sat 10:30 am–4 pm. Cash, checks.

Redwood City's only upscale thrift shop, the Junior League's well-maintained store is day to *Thrift City's* night. Furniture is set up in attractive vignettes with tables set for dining, sofas and chairs arranged in conversational groups, and coffee tables accessorized. Everything is clean and quality is high (with prices to match). *Discovery Shop* donors must shop frequently at Nordstrom, I Magnin, and Saks Fifth Avenue, since they have so many choice items to give away. Ladies, take your pick from the best designer labels (a Caroline Herrera dress for $125 or a St. John knit for $65) as well as popular ready-to-wear designer lines like Liz Claiborne and Albert Nipon (try them on in the pretty dressing rooms). Don't forget something for the kids from the back of the store. Men will find the quality of their clothes high but the selection smaller (sports jackets run $20–$45).

The crème de la crème, located on the mezzanine, includes furs, evening and bridal gowns, lingerie, and truly rarefied items like a six-panel cormandel screen priced at $1250 (retail value $2000). All other treasures—collectibles, antiques, china, silver, crystal, and such—are marked "The Treasuree" and priced sky high. Everyday household items are of similar high quality and high priced. (Don't miss the large selection of books and magazines for 50¢.) Thrift shoppers with champagne tastes and beer budgets should wait for BARGAIN DAY, when you can fill a brown grocery bag for only $1. Look for the flyer announcing this great sale, held twice a year.

Charity: Junior League community projects and services
Everything but large appliances

ST. VINCENT DE PAUL
831 Main Street, Redwood City 94063, (415) 369-5898. Mon–Sat 9 am–5 pm. Cash, checks, MC/ VISA.

Like many *St. Vincent de Paul* stores we visited, this one is full of treasures for the hardy, confirmed thrift shopper. If you park in the Walnut Street parking lot next to *Thrift City* you can enter through the back of this long, crowded store and get the full impact of utter chaos. The front entrance on Main Street—between two antique shops—gives a slightly more sedate impression with its department store windows and good-hearted attempts at display. The cases in front are full of collectibles,

~~~~~~~~~~~~~~~~~~~

Right: Felino's Vintage Clothing, San Francisco.

antiques, furs, and assorted curiosities…almost all reasonable to dirt cheap. Clothing (also dirt cheap) tends to be concentrated in the front room. Don't forget to look in the many drawers for children's clothes, 50¢–$1.50, and sewing patterns for 10¢. Furniture is everywhere. It varies from real steals to reasonable: a seven-piece art deco bedroom set for $600, a seven-piece dining room set for $250, or a good desk for $25 as the real prize. We saw a beautiful down-filled Victorian love seat upholstered in powder blue velvet with a matching chair for $75 and $45, respectively. Treasures like these arrive in the morning and are sold by noon, so frequent visits are necessary to catch the best buys. For $20 St. *Vincent* will deliver your large purchases to your home.
Charity: St. Vincent de Paul
Everything

SALVATION ARMY
600 Veterans Blvd., Redwood City 94063, (415) 368-7527. Mon–Sat 9:30 am–5:30 pm, Thurs 9:30 am–8 pm. Cash, MC/VISA.

Park in the ample lot of this tan California-style stucco building with a red tile roof. Large, clean, and well-organized (like most *Salvation Army* stores), this one is also exceptionally neat—the stacks of place mats, napkins, and what-have-you are kept in the strictest order. Electronics, books, and records each have their own alcoves. There is lots of every-thing—furniture, large appliances,

and clothes (although there's nowhere to try anything on). Prices on everything are good to great, with an additional 15% discount for seniors.
Charity: Salvation Army
Everything

SAVERS
875 Main Street, Redwood City 94063, (415) 364-5545. Mon–Wed 9 am–7 pm, Thurs and Fri 9 am–9 pm, Sat and Sun 9 am–6 pm. Cash, checks.

Billed as "The Thrift Department Store" (one of six in the Bay Area and 50 in the western U.S. and Canada), this *Savers* claims to recycle 20,000 items each week. Quantity is their strong suit. The ground floor of this large two-story mart presents an extensive inventory of new and used clothing (all well-organized by color and size) for men, women, and children. Prices and quality are generally low to medium, although persistence will turn up great buys (a Norma Kamali blouse for $4.99). We found housewares, also on the ground floor, low in quality. The second floor offers an uninspiring selection of furniture and appliances and a somewhat better array of linens and books. *Savers* offers two advantages: one-stop shopping for the whole family, and a seven-day exchange policy!
Charity: Privately owned, sup-ports organizations to help the developmentally disabled
Everything but large appliances

THRIFT CITY

852 Walnut Street, Redwood City 94063, (415) 367-0646. Mon–Fri 9 am–7 pm, Sat 10 am–7 pm, Sun 10 am–6 pm. Cash, checks, MC/ VISA.

The warehouse theme of the corrugated steel-walled exterior is carried out inside by the vast expanse of cement floors, high ceilings, and dim lighting. Although dreary, *Thrift City* is remarkably clean and shows a definite attempt at organization. Collectibles, strategically placed in the front of the store, may provide some pleasant surprises (an accordion in its case for $300), but no bargains. Furniture offers no surprises other than high prices; large and small appliances are more reasonably priced. Clothing abounds, mostly moderately priced items (low to medium quality) for men, women, and children, but there are a few classy items here and there. Among the men's suits priced $15– $20 we found a British-made tweed for $40. New (but shopworn) bridal gowns were $50. The plastic bags filled with miscellaneous items can be worth a gamble—they're only $1.99. We picked up one containing a dozen vintage advertising cook booklets—a nice find for lovers of ephemera.

Charity: Privately owned, supports Veterans Rehabilitation Center
Everything

~~~~ San Bruno ~~~~

FAMILY FASHION FAIR AND RESALE SHOP

364 El Camino Real, San Bruno 94066, (415) 589-7755. Mon–Fri 10 am–4 pm, Sat 10:30 am–3:30 pm. Cash.

Toys, fireplace implements, ice skates, and other miscellanea fill the window of this crowded and disorganized shop. You'll have to sift through a lot of junk to find the jewels (like never-been-worn Arnold Palmer golf shoes for $10 or handmade Italian ceramic boxes for $3). Sears, Mervyns, and labels of that ilk predominate in the clothing selection, but prices are lower than quality, with men's suits priced $10 and sports coats priced $3–$5. Some of the women's clothes are so out of style you could wear them for Halloween. But you gotta love a place that sells hand-crocheted bookmarks three for a quarter.
Everything except furniture and large appliances

KIDS CLOSET

591 San Mateo Ave., San Bruno 94066, (415) 589-6400. Mon–Fri 10 am–5 pm, Sat 10 am–4 pm. Cash, checks.

For the fastidious thrift shopper, *Kids Closet* is your best possibility in San Bruno. Owner Pattie Lindberg keeps the roomy store stocked with kids' (newborn–14 for boys, newborn to women's sizes for girls), women's, and maternity clothes, plus baby equipment and furniture, all in good condition and selling for 1/2 to 1/3 of their retail price. Thrifty shoppers wait for the half-off sales held twice a year in February and August. If you don't think you're getting a great deal, then check out the prices for new goods in the children's store across the street.

Consignment: By appointment, 40% consignor/60% store for clothing, 50/50 split for furniture and baby equipment

Children's clothing, furniture, and equipment; women's clothing; maternity clothing

OPPORTUNITY SHOP

437 San Mateo, San Bruno 94066, (415) 871-7170. Mon–Sat 10:30 am–3:30 pm. Cash.

The decorated windows—one was filled with a ski theme, and the other with Valentine's Day—let you know they make an effort. The blue carpeted front room featuring women's clothes, jewelry, and knickknacks is neat and organized. The back room housing the dressing rooms, a limited selection of men's and children's clothes, and more women's clothing, is less presentable. Prices are higher than they should be given the overall quality of the merchandise. An occasional good label does pop up now and then, and the book selection is quite good.

Everything except furniture and large appliances

SALVATION ARMY

300 Camino Real (at Crystal Springs Road), San Bruno 94066,
(415) 583-3589. Mon, Tues, Thurs, Sat 9 am–5 pm; Wed and Fri 9 am–8 pm. Cash, MC/VISA.

For thrift shopping in San Bruno, the *Salvation Army* is your best bet. The furniture selection on our visit included some unusual antiques as well as contemporary pieces in good condition, all at good prices. The books and records corner had an enormous selection of records (large for 75¢, small for 10¢). Clothing, your typical *Salvation Army* fare, was all half off.

Charity: Salvation Army

Everything

~~~~~ **San Carlos** ~~~~~

COLLEEN'S CLOTHES COTTAGE

903 Laurel Street (on the corner of Laurel and Arroyo), San Carlos 94070, (415) 593-5915. Mon–Sun 10 am–5 pm. Cash, checks, MC/VISA.

After it opened in 1982, *Colleen's Clothes Cottage* expanded to take over the former video store on the corner. Colleen, the ebullient red-haired proprietor, prides herself on having something for everyone: costumes, vintage clothing, square dance outfits...."I don't cater to one age group. An eighty-year-old lady can get a cardigan, girls can save on working clothes, and I have designer for someone who wants that. I wouldn't be in business if I had to depend on designer clothes," said Colleen. The store is packed to the gills with clothing in a broad range of quality and prices.

Colleen is also selling her own collection of costume jewelry—four large showcases full. A lot is vintage, with an exceptionally good selection of hard-to-find clip earrings.

Costumes are big business. The Halloween crowd, community theater groups, high school drama teachers, and murder mystery party guests take advantage of the large costume inventory available year-round. ("It's cheaper than renting.") Thrifty brides have been known to outfit the wedding party from the costume rack. (Many of the so-called costumes look suspiciously like bridesmaids' gowns, or is it that many bridesmaids' outfits look like costumes?)

Consignment: Mon–Fri 11 am–4 pm, 40% consignor/60% store, 105-day contract
Costumes, women's clothing, jewelry

FAMILY TREE

1589 Laurel Street (at Central), San Carlos 94070, (415) 592-6150. Tues–Sat 10 am–4 pm. Cash, checks.

Your first impression of *Family Tree* might be that you have stepped into an upscale gift shop. Cloth-draped tables hold artistic arrangements of china and glassware; mirror-topped tables reflect polished silver dishes; glass cases display jewelry, collectibles, and an interesting collection of knick-knacks. Merchandise is first class; prices are high. The back of the store offers a mundane inventory of low-priced women's clothing. *Family Tree* is a pleasant place to shop when you're willing to spend a little more for that special item—a wedding gift, perhaps. The last Thursday of each month is Daisy Day, when most items are half off.

Charity: Family Service Agency of San Mateo County, which supports children's programs as well as senior services
Everything except furniture and large appliances

THE PERFECT ROSE

657 Laurel Street, San Carlos 94070, (415) 593-7455. Mon–Sat 10 am–5 pm. Cash, checks, MC/VISA.

Named for the Dorothy Parker poem, this elegant consignment boutique carries out the rose theme with rose colored carpet, rose patterned wallpaper, and the scent of roses. Ulla Pironi, the Swedish owner cum novelist and poet, opened *The Perfect Rose* seven years ago in Belmont and moved five years ago to the current location. Her clothing (half consignment, half new) for the sophisticated woman is of the highest quality selling for 1/3 to 1/2 of the retail price (a Joan Little handknit suit for $45, a $400 Jaeger suit for $100, a Liz Claiborne wool dress for $40). Merchandise is well organized and tastefully displayed—each dress is protected by a plastic cover. The store also carries tasteful new and vintage costume jewelry and accessories. On principle, furs are not accepted.

Unsold merchandise is donated to *Rafael House* in San Francisco. *Consignment: Mon–Thurs by appointment, 50/50 split, 90-day contract*
Women's clothing, jewelry, accessories

THRIFT CENTER
1060 El Camino Real, San Carlos 94070, (415) 593-1082. Mon–Sat 9 am–7 pm. Cash, MC/VISA with a minimum of $25.

The sheer quantity of merchandise contained in this enormous 8000-square-foot store is its greatest calling card. A lack of organization and a lot of dirt make this a place not for the faint-hearted. But if low prices and a large selection excite you, it may be just your cup of tea. They really do have an amazing assortment of items for sale—doors, sinks, vacuum cleaners, barbeques, headboards, bicycles, and clothing (including an entire rack of military uniforms and a good selection of costumes). I defy you to name a small appliance they don't carry. You're guaranteed to find the unexpected here...a complete croquet set of mallets, balls, wickets, and stands for $10.99, a metal cat carrier for $5.99, an Aprica stroller for $20.99.

Everything is priced to sell. Clothing, always especially cheap, is reduced 50% on Tuesdays 9 am–

Left: Alésha Neville at Community Thrift Shop, San Francisco.

12 am and 30% on Saturdays. Only collectibles and "antiques" are in the mid to high range, although some goodies do slip by. Park in the lot behind the store and enter through the back. You can buy freshly popped popcorn for 50¢ at the sales counter.
Charity: Privately owned, supports Cerebral Palsy Association
Everything

~~~ **City of San Mateo** ~~~

BARGAIN BOUTIQUE
31 North B Street, San Mateo 94401, (415) 344-4208. Tues–Sat 10 am–4 pm. Cash.

This clean, light, well-organized shop specializes in women's clothing and also has a small selection of children's clothes and a few knickknacks. Better, more expensive garments are displayed on a rack behind the counter: a Paris dress for $90, a never-been-worn designer gown for $225 (the owner gained too much weight). All the merchandise is in good condition and moderately priced. We found an exceptionally good selection of sweaters on our winter visit. There are no regular sales, but all unsold garments take a stint on the $5 rack before being shipped to Oakland!
Charity: Children's Home Society of California
Consignment: Tues–Fri 10 am–3 pm, 50/50 split, 90-day contract
Women's and children's clothing, some bric-a-brac

BIBBIDY BOBBIDY BO-TIQUE

*4222 Olympic Blvd., San Mateo
94403, (415) 341-6577. Mon and
Sat 10:30 am–5 pm, Tues–Fri
10:30 am–6 pm. Cash, checks.*

Carrying new and gently used
children's clothing (sizes 0–6X),
furniture, and equipment, this
delightful shop owes its charm as
much to the warmth and wit of the
mother, daughter, and granddaughter proprietors as it does to its
whimsical decor. It's clean, bright,
and very well organized; you will be
delighted with the displays of high
quality merchandise at great prices.
The new arrivals rack is replenished
twice a week. Don't miss the shelf
of new books—publishers'
samples—always on hand. Added
pluses are the children's play area,
and a small library of child-rearing
books available for customers' use.
Buys: By appointment
**Children's clothing, toys,
equipment, and books**

NESBITT RESALE

*128 North B Street, San Mateo
94401, (415) 342-1237. Tues–Sat
10 am–6 pm. Cash, checks, MC/
VISA.*

This funky little for-profit junk shop
offers a small inventory of furniture
and household goods at better-
than-thrift-store prices. Most pieces
are run of the mill, but a few
interesting/unusual/beautiful items
at bargain prices make it worth a
quick visit when you're thrift
shopping on B street.
**Furniture, household goods,
collectibles**

PICK OF THE LITTER THRIFT SHOP

*1801 South Grant (across from
the Dunfrey Hotel), San Mateo
94402, (415) 345-1024. Mon–Sat
10 am–4:30 pm (standard time),
10 am–5 pm (daylight savings
time). Cash, checks.*

Staffed by dedicated, friendly
volunteers, *Pick of the Litter* is one
of our picks. "We have the best
prices and the cleanliest store,"
claimed one charming volunteer,
with good reason. Despite the
store's enormous size (6000 square
feet), merchandise is so well
organized you can easily find what
you want. In addition to the
expected large selection of clothes,
small appliances, and housewares,
Pick of the Litter has a good
offering of furniture for the home (a
two-piece sectional sofa for $40, a
day bed for $40) and old but
serviceable office furniture—desks
for $45, chairs for $35, four-drawer
files for $34. Not-so-usual offerings
included a rack of wet suits for $15
each, a large selection of computers ("you name your price"), new
sports trophies, and pet items (they
go fast). In the truly unusual
category, we found two "not-for-
real-fires" fireplaces for $45 each,
complete with imitation electric
logs ($10). Not to be missed is the
exceptionally well-organized books
and records section lovingly tended
by dedicated volunteer Mark Sabini.
Pick of the Litter has one blowout
half-off-everything sale each year.
Check the chalk board on your left
as you enter from the back parking

lot for daily "In Store Specials." On our visit the board read "pink tags $1, sweaters $1, purple tags half off, all Harlequin and Silhouette Romances $1."

Charity: Peninsula Humane Society

Everything except large appliances

RAGS & RICHES

715 South B Street, San Mateo 94401, (415) 348-3590. Mon–Sat 10 am–4 pm. Cash, checks.

Windows designed by the visual merchandise class of the College of San Mateo are perhaps the highlight of this midsize shop. The merchandise is well organized, with the first of the two rooms devoted to women's clothing, jewelry, and a special section for teens. New arrivals and vintage are featured on the front racks. The adjoining room offers furniture (a large upholstered chair for $20), small appliances (including a not-so-small home mangle for $35), children's clothing, and the sales racks (we saw a great pink cotton Liz Claiborne on the $2 rack and a half-off rack full of the real bargains).

Charity: Notre Dame High School Scholarship fund

Everything except large appliances

ST. VINCENT DE PAUL

113 South B Street, San Mateo 94401, (415) 247-5101. Mon–Sat 9 am–5 pm. Cash, checks, MC/ VISA.

The San Mateo *St. Vincent De Paul* sports a window full of delectable collectibles at moderate prices. Inside, one good-sized room offers just about anything you could want—refrigerators for $65, two ancient upright pianos for $100 each, lawn mowers, and the usual crowded racks of clothing for men, women, and children, all better than reasonably priced: men's suits for $20, women's dresses for $10–$15 (we saw a Silk Vogue Alley, a high-style Karen Alexander, and a smart outfit from Saks Fifth Avenue, all in that range). A second room holds furniture—upholstered chairs for $20, a wooden desk for $50, sofas marked $120 and $150, a dresser for $100. Sterilized mattresses are stored in the single dressing room. One visit turned up a score of hand-made wooden windmills for $20 (for the folk art lover) and a large box of brand-new pink satin toe shoes. (At the low price of $2 we would have bought a pair, just for prancing around in, if they had come larger than size 4.) Although the store's pricing seems some-what erratic and organization is not a strong point, a persistent forager is bound to come up with at least one treasure per visit. We watched one prosperous-looking matron walk off with two beautiful antique wooden picture frames, glass intact, for $1 each. *St. Vincent* will pick up your donation, and they will also deliver your large purchase for a $20 charge.

Charity: St. Vincent de Paul

Everything

2ND GO-ROUND

151 W. 25th Avenue, San Mateo 94403, (415) 341-4530. Mon–Sat 11 am–5:30 pm. Cash, checks, MC/VISA.

A fairly large store crammed to the rafters with merchandise, *2nd Go-Round* can dress the entire family, from newborn to mom and dad, in quality used clothing. Specializing in clothing, toys, and books for kids, *2nd Go Round* also carries a good selection of better quality women's wear and maternity clothes and a few select men's items ("only the best designers"), all priced at one third of their retail cost. You can also find new merchandise—some on consignment from stores going out of business. Owner Judy Shrier (who sports a lapel full of intriguing rhinestone pins) claims to stock the largest selection of Guess jeans in the area. The great buy in the winter season is the huge selection of ski outfits (she sold 400 ski bibs at $20 each in 1991). The dress-up section is stocked with costumes (lots of tutus) all year round. Shrier's husband sells new and used Macintosh computers in the back of the store.

Consignment: By appointment, 40% consignor/60% store
Women's and children's clothing, toys, accessories, computers

SHAWN'S YOU NAME IT SHOP

710 South B Street, San Mateo 94401, (415) 347-2217. Mon–Sat 12 am–5:30 pm. Cash, checks, MC/VISA.

Recently relocated from its original Belmont location, *Shawn's You Name It Shop* lives up to its name. You name it, they have it: used furniture, collectibles, toys, dishes, books, antiques, curiosities… almost all at fabulous bargain prices. Bigger than it looks, *Shawn's* is a collective of antique and collectibles dealers, each with a mini shop offering delights and surprises. From comic books to Navajo pottery to art deco furniture, there's something for everyone (even a smattering of vintage clothing), all at remarkably low prices. Although almost everything seemed well priced to begin with, individual dealers offer additional discounts of up to 20%. We saw some real steals on furniture, including a five-piece art deco bedroom set for $400 and a pair of unique kidney-shaped mirrored end tables for $40 each.

Furniture, collectibles, antiques, books

THRIFT SHOP EPISCOPAL CHURCH OF SAINT MATTHEW

Baldwin Ave at N. El Camino Real, San Mateo 94401, (415) 344-0921. Thurs–Sat 10 am–2 pm, closed in the summer. Cash, checks.

Located in the basement of the impressive grey stone Episcopal church, this successful thrift shop has been in business for over 33 years. Closed for the summer and open only three days a week the rest of the year, this popular shop still earns $57,000 a year. Devoted customers come from as far as Placerville and Marin County to check out the high-quality bargains.

Don't be misled by the two very elegant pieces of furniture, permanent fixtures of the shop, containing valuable (and expensive) antiques, which create the impression of a high-priced boutique. Prices get more reasonable and the atmosphere more thrift-shoppish as you progress deeper into the shop. With the exception of the antiques (a Limoges creamer and sugar bowl set for $45, an 1840's cruet set for $95), prices are good and the selection of interesting household items, books, and toys is very good. Although the furniture selection is limited on any given day, regular shoppers speak in glowing terms of their truly great buys. Overall, clothing is high quality and very inexpensive (a Laura Ashley dress for $5, a Nordstrom dress for $9, shirts for $1.50, wool coats for $6). Don't forget to check for goodies—gloves, handkerchieves and the like—in the drawers of the antique breakfront. Manager Chris Figone recommends the annual blowout sale held every June before the shop closes for the summer. The store and the adjacent music room are filled with merchandise at prices "so cheap it's incredible." Call for exact dates.

Charity: Various projects of the League for Services, including a women's shelter, a half-way house, and a hospice
Everything but large appliances

TURN-STYLE SHOP
60 North B Street (between Baldwin and Tilton), San Mateo 94401, (415) 342-2367. Mon and Tues 10 am–4 pm, Thurs–Sat 10 am–4 pm. Cash.

Located right across the street from *Bargain Boutique*, this upscale thrift shop is one of our favorites in San Mateo. Newly redecorated with pale blue carpet, blue counters, striped wallpaper, and color-coordinated swag, the shop has the feel of an exclusive dress shop from the 1940's. The single good sized room is divided into areas: better women's clothing in the front (great buys—a three-piece Krizia suit for $20), less expensive women's clothing by the dressing rooms (even better buys—we saw a vintage 1960 camel's-hair coat from Ransahoffs for $8 and several 1960's mini dresses for even less). A fanciful train announces "The Little Children's Corner" filled with toys and clothing (most items priced $2–$3). Another area is devoted to men's clothing (a basket of never-been-worn Ralph Lauren silk suspenders for $7 each), and still another area offers small appliances and household goods (a battery-operated fingernail dryer was a steal at $2).

Charity: Assistance League of San Mateo County, which provides a shopping service for seniors, a visiting service, and the Peninsula Braille Transcribers Guild
Everything except furniture and large appliances

⁓ South San Francisco ⁓

GOODWILL
225 Kenwood Way (at El Camino and Spruce), South San Francisco 94080, (415) 737-9827. Mon–Sat 10 am–6 pm, Sun 11 am–6 pm. Cash, checks, MC/VISA.

Located in a former deli in the Brentwood shopping center, this *Goodwill* is a pleasant place to shop, as *Goodwill* always is. Although not one of the top-of-the-line stores, this one is still chock-full of good clothing buys.
Charity: Goodwill
Everything except large appliances

ST. VINCENT DE PAUL
344 Grand Ave at Linden, South San Francisco 94080, (415) 589-8445. Mon–Sat 9 am–5 pm. Cash, checks, MC/VISA.

The store window lets you know what to expect: it's dusty, dirty, and chock-full of miscellaneous items apparently placed there without rhyme or reason. A hand-lettered sign reads "$1 Sale—Blouses, skirts, sweaters, pants, shirts, coats, dresses—each piece, suits—each piece," and another states "New Wedding Gowns $65, Veils $25, Bridesmaids $30." This shop is definitely not for the squeamish…it's dank, dark, disorganized, and so crowded with merchandise there's scarcely room to walk. The main floor consists of a warren of small rooms featuring (from front to back) household items, small appliances, knick-knacks, collectibles, clothing, linens, and large appliances. Books and records are in a windowless attic and furniture is kept in the basement.

For the fastidious it's a definite miss, but for the confirmed bargain hunting thrift shopper it's a must. Everything is dirt cheap! Much of it is something you wouldn't want even for free: cracked plates, chipped glassware, clothing so out of style it just misses vintage status by months. But among the junk are real jewels. A fashion-conscious friend picked out a handsome outfit of white wool trousers and a stylish dress shirt (total $2), and another friend found a french mug for 50¢ to match her dishes. In the basement we saw an attractive honey colored velvet sofa for $50, a hardwood chair with Queen Anne legs for $5, a bentwood rocker like new except for the bull's eye drawn in crayon on the back, and for lovers of country decor, a large ceramic lamp painted with an American Eagle that with a new shade would look right at home in your living room. If you can't afford even *St. Vincent*'s good prices, the helpful staff will direct you to the office, where you will receive a voucher which can be exchanged for store merchandise.
Charity: St. Vincent de Paul
Everything

SAN MATEO COUNTY	Appliances/large	Bridal	Clothing/children	Clothing/men	Clothing/women	Collectibles	Furnishings/children	Furniture	Housewares	Maternity	Tools, etc.	Toys	Vintage	Page number
BELMONT														
Ginny's Exchange					X									140
Salvation Army	X	X	X	X	X	X	X	X	X	X	X	X		140
This'n'That Shop			X	X	X	X	X		X			X	X	140
BURLINGAME														
Discovery Shop		X	X	X	X	X	X	X	X	X		X		141
Circles					X									142
Miss Jodi's					X	X								142
Primrose House			X	X	X	X	X		X				X	143
Victoria's Closet					X	X								143
EL GRANADA														
Alternative Shop				X	X	X	X	X	X	X				144
LOS ALTOS														
Discovery Shop			X	X	X	X	X		X			X		144
MENLO PARK														
Afterwards			X	X	X	X								144
Discovery Shop		X	X	X	X	X	X	X	X			X		145
Merry-Go-Round					X									145
New Life Boutique			X		X					X				147
MOUNTAIN VIEW														
Goodwill			X	X	X	X	X	X	X	X	X	X	X	147
Thrift Mart	X	X	X	X	X	X	X	X	X	X	X	X		148
Opportunity Shop			X	X	X	X	X		X				X	148
PACIFICA														
Diana's Boutique					X					X				148
Kid's Room			X				X			X		X		149
PALO ALTO														
Bargain Box			X	X	X	X	X	X	X			X	X	149
Goodwill		X	X	X	X	X	X	X	X	X	X	X	X	150
Market of the Flea			X	X	X	X	X	X	X			X		150
Repeat Performance			X		X									150
Second Season				X	X	X			X				X	151
Turnabout Shop			X	X	X	X			X					151

SAN MATEO COUNTY

	Appliances/large	Bridal	Clothing/children	Clothing/men	Clothing/women	Collectibles	Furnishings/children	Furniture	Housewares	Maternity	Tools, etc.	Toys	Vintage	Page number
REDWOOD CITY														
Jr. League Shop		X	X	X	X	X	X	X	X	X		X		152
St. Vincent de Paul	X	X	X	X	X	X	X	X	X	X	X	X		152
Salvation Army	X	X	X	X	X	X	X	X	X	X	X	X		154
Savers		X	X	X	X	X	X	X	X	X	X	X		154
Thrift City	X	X	X	X	X	X	X	X	X	X	X	X		155
SAN BRUNO														
Family Fashion		X	X	X	X	X		X	X	X		X		155
Kid's Closet		X		X		X								155
Opportunity Shop		X	X	X	X	X	X	X	X	X	X	X		156
Salvation Army	X	X	X	X	X	X	X	X	X	X	X	X		156
SAN CARLOS														
Colleen's Cottage					X									156
Family Tree		X	X	X	X	X		X				X		157
Perfect Rose					**X**									157
Thrift Center	X	X	X	X	X	X	X	X	X	X	X	X		159
SAN MATEO, CITY														
Bargain Boutique		X			X	X								159
Bibbidy Bo-tique		X			X				X			X		160
Nesbitt Resale						X			X	X				160
Pick of the Litter		X	X	X	X	X	X	X	X	X	**X**	X		160
Rags & Riches			X	X	X	X	X	X		X		X	X	161
St. Vincent de Paul	X	X	X	X	X	X	X	X	X	X	X	X		161
2nd Go-Round			X	X	X		X			X		X		162
Shawn's Shop						X		X					X	162
Episcopal Shop			X	X	X	X	X	X				X	X	162
Turn-Style Shop			X	X	X	X	X		X			X	X	163
SO. SAN FRANCISCO														
Goodwill	X	X	X	X	X	X	X	X	X	X	X	X		164
St. Vincent de Paul	X	X	X	X	X	X	X	X	X	X	X	X		164

~~~~~ **Campbell** ~~~~~

CORINTHIAN THRIFT SHOP
1405 Hacienda, Campbell 95008, (408) 866-7502. Tues–Sat 10 am–4 pm, Thurs 10 am–7 pm. Cash, checks.

If you're looking for low-quality, low-priced household goods you might want to try this shop. Drinking glasses, cups, saucers, and plates are all in the 25¢–50¢ category. Clothes, too, are inexpensive: men's jeans for $1, shirts and trousers for $2.50, suits for $20–$30. (The day we visited, most clothing was half off the marked prices.) An alcove features women's clothing, most of it out of style and medium to low quality, but some of it old enough to be considered vintage. A locked case holds some appealing collectibles while a sign advises, "Items in glass case are never included in sales." You do get a free magazine with every purchase.
Charity: Senior Citizens of Corinthian House
Everything except large appliances

TICKLED PINK
342 E. Campbell Ave., Campbell 95008, (408) 378-4333. Mon 12 am–6 pm, Tues–Sat 10:30 am–6 pm. Cash, checks, MC/VISA.

If your love for vintage does not include a desire to own it, you can rent from *Tickled Pink*, located in the historic building that once housed Campbell's first volunteer fire department. *Tickled Pink* has clothing from the 1920's through relatively contemporary times for men and women to rent or buy. From the men's department you can rent a tuxedo or gangster suit or purchase classic Pendleton shirts, cowboy boots, Levis jeans, and jackets. Women will find an eclectic selection from the 1920's through the 1960's for rent as well as contemporary clothing for sale. With 25 years of theater experience, owner Angele Bagley can put her knowledge of costume to work to help you put together the perfect outfit.
Vintage clothing for men and women, costume rentals

~~~~~ **Cupertino** ~~~~~

DE ANZA COLLEGE FLEA MARKET
21250 Stevens Creek Blvd., Cupertino 95014, (408) 864-8414. First Sats 8 am–4 pm, second Sat in June. Purchase method varies by dealer.

Your entrance fee is absolutely nothing at this flea market. The seller's fee is $14 for a single booth and $30 for a double.
Everything

THE KID'S CLOTHESLINE

10191 S. De Anza, Cupertino 95014, (408) 865-0292. Mon–Sat 10 am–6 pm. Cash, checks, MC/ VISA.

Customers have been known to ask "Why are these clothes so inexpensive?" Indeed, price is the only indication that *Kid's Clothesline* is a resale store. This place is without a doubt the most beautiful children's resale store in the Bay Area. The 2500 square-foot shop, newly redecorated with a mauve carpet and rainbow graphics on the walls, boasts high-tech fixtures, two bathrooms, a changing table, and an on-site laundry where everything is rewashed, disinfected, mended, and ironed before you see it. Quality is high and prices are low, with most items (sizes newborn–14) under $5. The few exceptions include coats and high-end dressy dresses—an $80 Nicole for $28–and a line of beautiful handmade christening outfits for $40.

Kid's Clothesline was started by owner Katrena Wong, mother of two daughters 16 years apart, after shopping for new clothes for her second child. "I thought I could help other people just like me who are in shock. We try to make people feel resale doesn't need to be dark, dirty, and dingy." She succeeds.

Buys: Buys outright by appointment
Children's clothing, accessories, and equipment

～～～ Los Gatos ～～～

ELEANOR'S DISCOUNT FASHIONS

720 University Ave. (between Lark and Blossom Hill), Los Gatos 95030, (408) 395-3955. Sun–Wed 10 am–6 pm, Thurs and Fri 10 am–9 pm. Cash, checks, MC/ VISA.

Once a gravel and cement business, this sprawling complex of 19th-century wooden structures now houses *Eleanor's Discount Fashions*. For the past 26 years, Eleanor has lived and raised her family here in one of the buildings and filled the others with an assortment of women's clothes, the sheer quantity of which boggles the mind…and 400–800 new items are added every week! If Eleanor doesn't have it, you don't need it (unless you're a first-time bride in search of a formal white gown). Dresses, suits, sportswear, cocktail and formal wear, lingerie, shoes, coats, purses, jewelry, furs, from petite to extra large, cheap to dear, good labels to designers—Eleanor has it all. The buildings are a bit funky, but the staff is friendly and helpful and the selection can't be beat.

Consignment: Thurs–Sat 10 am–5 pm, 40% consignor/60% store
Women's clothing

HAPPY DRAGON THRIFT

245 West Main, Los Gatos 95030, (408) 354-4072. Mon–Sat 10 am–4 pm. Cash.

Founded in 1958, *Happy Dragon Thrift* has been doing business in its present converted feed store location for the past 25 years. 125 active volunteers wash, sort, clean, organize, price, and keep the store in pristine condition. The majority of merchandise for sale is clothing cheap enough to make any dragon happy (men's suits for $5–$6, trousers for $1.25–$1.50). Among the mundane you will be sure to find something extraordinary—a vintage wedding gown, new hand-knit baby sweaters for $10, a beaded evening bag, or fine antique linens. (One volunteer delights in washing, ironing, and removing stains from linens.) Antiques and collectibles (priced slightly higher than other merchandise), as well as women's shoes and purses, are displayed in the glass front cases. A frequent customer recently complained to the volunteers, "You ladies have become smarter, now you are taking things to be ap-praised." As a rule, however, items are sold well below their appraised price—a $65 guitar went for $20. You can pick up a free magazine on your way out.

Charity: Eastfield Ming Quong, a mental health center for emotion-ally troubled children

Everything except large appliances and large pieces of furniture

~~~~~ **Milpitas** ~~~~~

CHILDREN'S HEARTLAND RESALE BOUTIQUE
379 Jacklin Road, (in Foothill Square next to Nob Hill Foods), Milpitas 95035, (408) 942-8855. Tues–Sat 10 am–5 pm. Cash, checks, MC/VISA/DISCOVER/AM EX.

Lace curtains in the window and latticework inside set the tone for this clean, well-organized children's resale shop. You can tell children are a high priority with the owner and friendly staff; a toy room is set up just for them and kids' videos are playing. (Be forewarned, however, that unattended children will be sold.) Price and quality are very good (sleepers for $1.79, blanket sleepers for $2.99), and sizes run newborn–10. If you don't see what you want, sign up on the wish list at the desk.

Children's clothing, toys, equipment and furniture (except cribs)

SAVERS
60 Dempsey Rd., Milpitas 95035, (408) 263-8338. Mon–Wed 9 am–7 pm, Thurs and Fri 9 am–9 pm, Sat and Sun 10 am–6 pm. Cash, checks, MC/VISA.

The best organized, cleanest, brightest *Savers* around has done everything possible to make shopping easy and pleasant. Pick up a shopping cart as you enter this former supermarket and follow the many signs to real bargains. From their huge inventory you should be able to find something for every-one, from baby clothes in the 49¢–99¢ range to great dress-up costumes. Muzak plays, clean bathrooms are available upstairs, and there are even chairs to relax in while waiting your turn in the dressing rooms. Regular shoppers should check out the new merchandise racks. Everyone should look for the green tag indicating a special shipment. On the down side, the furniture selection is small and many collectible items are overpriced.

Charity: Privately owned, affiliated with HOPE Rehabilitation Services

Everything except large appliances

~~~~ **Morgan Hill** ~~~~

MITZIE'S CONSIGNMENT FASHIONS

325 W. Main Ave. (corner of Main and Hale), Morgan Hill 95037, (408) 779-0808. Mon–Fri 10 am–6 pm, Thurs 10 am–7:30 pm, Sat 10 am–5 pm. Cash, checks, MC/ VISA/DISCOVER.

Mitzie's has something for everyone—men, women, teens, and kids will find good quality clothing in good condition for good prices. Women will appreciate the wide range of sizes (up to size 26), quality (good to designer), styles, and prices (from a $1.60 item on the bargain rack to a $300 suit previously owned by Priscilla Presley). Besides selling Shaklee products in a small back room, Mitzie also carries movie stars' clothing from *A Star is Worn* consignment shop in Los Angeles. If you are star struck and the right

size you could, for only $149, be the proud owner of a pair of Maude Frizon shoes worn by Jacylyn Smith in a recent film.

Consignment: By appointment, 40% consignor/60% store

Clothing for men, women, and children

~~~~ **San Jose** ~~~~

AMERICAN CANCER SOCIETY DISCOVERY SHOP

1451-A Foxworthy Ave., San Jose 95118, (408) 265-5535. Mon–Sat 10 am–4 pm. Cash, checks, MC/ VISA.

The blue awning is missing, but everything else about the San Jose store is definitely up to *Discovery Shop* high standards. Upscale by anyone's standards, the former bicycle shop has been transformed into a dream of a resale boutique with large, beautiful wheelchair-accessible dressing rooms, blue wall to wall carpeting, and up-to-date store fixtures. On our visit a week after their grand opening (they had just moved from Lincoln Ave.), helpful volunteers lamented that all the best merchandise had been sold. The leftovers were certainly nothing to sneeze at: dozens of pairs of Ann Taylor shoes (worn once in a fashion show) for $20, new high-style casual jackets for kids and adults for $25, and barely worn designer labels. If they can keep this up, this is a definite must for thrifty fashion-conscious women and children.

Charity: American Cancer Society
Everything except large appliances

CAPITOL FLEA MARKET
Capitol Drive-In, 3630 Hillcap Ave., San Jose 95136, (408) 225-5800. Thurs 7 am–5:30 pm, Sat and Sun 6 am–5:30 pm. Purchase method varies by dealer.
If you want to walk in, it will cost you $1. If you bring your car, it will cost you $2/car.
Everything

GOODWILL
1579 Meridian Ave., San Jose 95125, (408) 266-7151. Mon–Thurs 9 am–7 pm, Fri 9 am–8 pm, Sat 9 am–6 pm, Sun 11 am–6 pm. Cash, checks, MC/VISA.
The Willowglen *Goodwill* is another feather in the *Goodwill* cap. The kid's section, set up like an upscale children's shop, sets this *Goodwill* apart from its sister stores. And where did they get all those new Dan Post cowboy boots for men ($39.99)?
Charity: Goodwill
Everything except large appliances

GOODWILL
1125 Saratoga Sunnyvale Rd., San Jose 95118, (408) 252-3193. Mon–Thurs 9 am–7 pm, Fri 9 am–8 pm, Sun 11 am–6 pm. Cash, checks, MC/VISA.
Another beautiful *Goodwill*—this one doesn't charge tax.
Everything except large appliances

GOODWILL AS IS
1080 N. Seventh, San Jose 95112, (408) 998-5774. Mon–Sat 10 am–5 pm. Cash.
The sign on the door reads "Wholesale only," but no one stopped us from entering the vast warehouse of *Goodwill As Is.* Inside, we found what seemed to be acres of barrels filled with clothing and another acre or two of furniture and assorted items too large for barrels. Shoppers ranged from the crazed (a young man sifting through barrels at breakneck speed in search of neckties, flinging unwanted articles of clothing hither, thither and yon) to the compulsive (a white-gloved matron carefully selecting and neatly folding sweaters). Merchandise that doesn't sell at *Goodwill* stores and items that are rejected beforehand end up here to be sold at greatly reduced prices. Most merchandise is sold wholesale by the barrel (clothing is $120/barrel, shoes go for a mere $50/barrel, and miscellaneous items are also $50/barrel), but we were told we could purchase individual items of clothing for $1 each and other articles at prices given by the manager. Believe it or not, we saw some pretty nifty items—including a 1940's print tablecloth we had been coveting. We recommend *Goodwill As Is* only for the truly adventurous and dedicated thrift shopper.
Charity: Goodwill
Everything

THE RUBBER DUCKY

1080 Saratoga Ave. (in Maple Leaf Plaza), San Jose 95129, (408) 246-3238. Mon–Sat 10 am–6 pm. Cash, checks, MC/VISA.

A small size shop with a big inventory, racks at the *Rubber Ducky* are so packed it's difficult to get to the clothes you want. Parents with older children will be pleased to find a limited selection of used Nintendo and Genesis games for sale, $20 and $30 respectively. The owner's enterprising 12-year-old son sells baseball cards by the pack.

Children's clothing, some women's clothing

ST. VINCENT DE PAUL

2040 S. Seventh, San Jose 95112, (408) 993-9500. Mon–Sun 10 am– 6:30 pm. Cash, checks, MC/VISA.

If you like *St. Vincent de Paul* thrift stores, here is one to knock your sox off. Park in the lot next to the Emergency Center, walk up the ramp into the huge (10,000 square feet) corrugated steel warehouse, deposit the kids in the striped tent in the middle of the store where they can play Atari games, watch cartoons or ride a mini merry-go-round for free, and start shopping.

St. Vincent fans that we are, we must admit that some of the stores are less than clean—but this one is immaculate. No effort has been

Left: Worn Out West, San Francisco.

spared to make shopping here a pleasure. Ten paid staff members and numerous volunteers are helpful and friendly. In addition to the usual merchandise you expect to find at *St. Vincent*—low priced run-of-the-mill clothing and lackluster housewares—are items you won't find anywhere else. For instance, hundreds of solid wood doors from an old hotel (complete with brass room numbers) for $75 each, an entire case full of eyeglass frames (top name brands from a defunct optical store) for $15 each, and 8000 new pairs of women's shoes (some top name brands, all in boxes) selling for $4.95 a pair. Antiques displayed in charming vignettes are, according to the manager, the best buy. We've never seen so many pieces of genuine antique (over 100 years old) or almost-antique furniture in a thrift store. Prices are high, but the manager vows, "We're willing to work with you." And they will deliver. Appliances are well priced and guaranteed to be in working order. October 1 is the date to look for vintage clothing, which is saved up all year for Halloween (we did spot a fabulous 1940's wedding gown in perfect condition for $4.50 in mid-January.)

Charity: St. Vincent de Paul
Everything

SALVATION ARMY

4140 Monterey Rd. (in the Seven Trees shopping center), San Jose 95125, (408) 578-1288. Mon–Sat 9:30 am–5:30 pm. Cash, MC/VISA.

This big, bright *Salvation Army* has furniture in the front, clothing and housewares in the back. Set tables and pictures on the walls lend this store a more upscale air than some sister stores. Both prices and quality are reasonable—sofas go for $45–$70, and jeans (rows of them) are a good buy at $4.60–$9.60. The ubiquitous new Jessica McClintock wedding gowns run in the $150 range, but alas, there are no dressing rooms in which to try them on.

Charity: Salvation Army
Everything

SAN JOSE FLEA MARKET
12000 Berryessa Rd., San Jose 95133, (408) 453-1110. Wed–Sun dawn to dusk. Purchase method varies by dealer.

Admission to this five-day event is free. The seller's price starts at $15 for Wednesday, moves to $10 each for Thursday and Friday, and jumps to $25 on Saturday and Sunday.

Everything

SARA'S CONSIGNMENT FASHIONS
448 N. San Pedro, San Jose 95220, (408) 298-1100. Mon–Sat 11 am–5:30 pm. Cash, checks.

"Enter with a happy heart" reads the sign over the door of *Sara's*, the Cadillac of used clothing boutiques. Located in the oldest standing saloon in San Jose, next door to the Military Medal Museum and Research Center, a trip to *Sara's* is more fun than stepping behind the looking glass. Sara calls the decor

arty disarray; we call it wonderful and magical."It's my nature to fill all the corners," says Sara, and fill them she does—the four rooms are gussied up with shirred fabric, lace, antiques, teddy bears, bric-a-brac, hats, jewelry, net and roses, and loaded with affordable new and nearly-new fashions on consignment from dress shops, defunct bridal salons, and the area's smartest women. Sara has something for everyone at prices everyone can afford. From new bridal (a Neiman Marcus exclusive, originally $2350, was $1400 and going down) to vintage to business suits from Gumps (originally $450, marked down to $75) to sportswear, all selling at 1/3 or less of their original retail price. "People get hooked on this store and can't go to Macy's," said Sara. Go often to check out the markdowns. Even if you don't live in the San Jose area a visit to *Sara's* is worth the trip.

Consignment: By appointment, 50/50 split, 90-day contract
Women's clothing, vintage clothing, antiques, collectibles

SAVERS
222 Business Circle (corner of Stephens Creek and Bascom), San Jose 95128, (408) 287-0591. Mon–Wed 9 am–7 pm, Sat and Sun 10 am–6 pm. Cash, checks, MC/VISA/DISCOVER.

Typical *Savers*—huge, organized, good signage, well-lit, and pleasant. Good buys on ladies' costumes:

lots of 1950's and 1960's vintage for $7.99–$12.99. We fell in love with a Swan Lake tutu for $7.99. If you like surprises, always intriguing at *Savers* are the plastic bags filled with assorted goodies—priced at $1.49 and $1.99 a bag.
Charity: Privately owned, affiliated with Hope for the Retarded
Everything except large appliances

THRIFT BOX

1362 Lincoln Ave. (corner of Minnesota, across from Posey Garden), San Jose 95125, (408) 294-4490. Mon–Sat 10 am–4 pm. Cash.

Established in 1947, the *Thrift Box* has been in its present location for ten years. The former theater was recently redecorated with new linoleum and blue carpeting, roomy mirrored dressing rooms for women, and a rustic wooden one for men. A washing machine and dryer in back ensure that all clothes are fresh and clean. Clothing, organized by type and size, is reasonably priced (women's suits $7–$20), with good labels well represented. Books are plentiful and organized by categories. Don't miss the fine selection of coffee-table books in the locked case. By far the best deal are the greeting cards for every occasion, which fill several racks and are scattered in baskets everywhere
Charity: Lucile Salter Packard Children's Hospital at Stanford
Everything but furniture and large appliances

THRIFT CENTER

916 Story Rd., San Jose 95122, (408) 297-3061. Mon–Sat 9 am–7 pm. Cash, checks, MC/VISA.

One of six in the Bay Area, this *Thrift Center* bills itself as "a unique thrift store." It's not. What it is is big, organized, and well stocked with everything from beds to bicycles. Among the clothing you'll find more Sears than Ralph Lauren. The prices are right with daily sales, and we liked the sign that figures out 30% and 50% discounts for you.
Charity: Privately owned, supports United Cerebral Palsy
Everything except large appliances

THRIFT CITY

1795 Alum Rock Ave. (at Eastgate), San Jose 95116, (408) 259-7683. Mon–Sat 9 am–6 pm, Sun 10 am–5 pm. Cash, checks, MC/VISA.

Big, dark, and dirty, with low ceilings and a cement floor, we found this *Thrift City* ugly and depressing, with only low, low prices to recommend it. Old and new clothing organized by size and color was for the most part soiled, out-of-date, and low in quality, but prices are even lower (t-shirts 25¢– 75¢, dress shirts 99¢, men's sports coats $1.99–$6.99). The new and used furniture in the second room is in keeping with the clothing— cheap and ugly (sofas $39–$69).
Everything except large appliances

THE TRADING POST

1589 Meridian Ave. (at the corner of Hamilton and Meridian), San Jose 95125, (408) 267-6900. Tues–Sat 11 am–6 pm.

Long gowns and bridal wear in a lovely old armoire catch your eye as you enter. Unfortunately, dark wood paneling and an ugly green shag rug make this long and narrow shop seem more crowded than it already is. You'll find a good variety of medium-priced labels—Lanz, Chaus, and Jennifer Moore, with a scattering of Liz Claiborne, Scott McClintock, and Talbott—in sizes 2–24, selling for half their original retail cost. Everything was an additional 10% off the day we visited. Check out the 2/$10 sale rack.

Consignment: By appointment
Women's clothing and accessories

TRISHA'S TREASURES

3691 Union Ave (behind Race St. fish market), San Jose 95124, (408) 371-1863. Mon–Sat 10 am–6 pm, Sun 11 am–6 pm. Cash, checks.

First impression: this place is a dump! Second impression: this place is a dump but we love it! Privately owned *Trisha's Treasures*, formerly *Mr. Picky's*, proclaims itself to be "a higher form of secondhand store." The higher form they are referring to, we assume, has nothing to do with cleanliness, order, or bright lights. (Maybe it has something to do with the Elvis-on-velvet decor of the dressing room.) In any case, we found the loquacious saleswoman a delight and had to believe her when she claimed she had the cheapest prices in town for antiques. Dealers buy from them, she insisted, and with their low prices we could see why. On our visit we found a host of armoires (all under $300), a hand-painted table and four chairs for $349, and an art deco vanity for $149. Trisha buys, sells, trades, accepts consignments, delivers free of charge in the area, and throws periodic blowout parties for customers and friends.

Furniture, clothes, antiques, collectibles, jewelry, books, and records

~~~ Santa Clara, City of ~~~

GOODWILL

2800 El Camino Real (at Keily Road), Santa Clara 95051, (408) 247-2800. Mon–Thurs 9 am–7 pm, Fri 9 am–8 pm, Sat 9 am–6 pm, Sun 11 am–6 pm. Cash, checks, MC/VISA.

Another nice but not spectacular *Goodwill.*
Charity: Goodwill
Everything but large appliances

SALVATION ARMY

1494 Halford Ave. (near El Camino Real and Lawrence Expressway), Santa Clara 95051, (408) 249-1715. Mon–Sat 9:30 am–4:45 pm. Cash, MC/VISA.

Smaller than other sister stores, the

Santa Clara *Salvation Army* lacks the pristine, neat-as-a-pin quality you sometimes find. Merchandise is half furniture and household goods, half clothing. New Jessica McClintock wedding gowns were selling for $149. There's a senior discount of 15% off original prices every Tuesday
Charity: Salvation Army
Everything

~~~~~ Saratoga ~~~~~

ECHO SHOP OF ST. ANDREWS CHURCH
14477 Big Basin Way, Saratoga 95070, (408) 867-3995. Tues–Fri 10 am–4 pm, Sat 10 am–3 pm. Cash, local checks.

Right on the main street of downtown Saratoga sits a pretty white house with green shutters and a manicured lawn. Guess what's inside? A first-rate thrift shop run by the Episcopal Church Women of Saint Andrews, with four rooms of clothing, toys, books, knickknacks, and collectibles. Frequently recipients of estate donations, the volunteers have "very good things" appraised to know how to price them. The church women are critical of the things they put out for sale, so the quality is high. Clothing is seasonal; costumes are saved for Halloween and dressy outfits for the holiday season. A rack of vintage clothing is a permanent fixture, and a good selection of St. Andrews school uniforms is always on hand. Twice a year—in late

September and mid-March—the store closes to totally clear out for the next season. During the week before closing, everything in the shop is half off, with the last day designated "Treasure Bag Day," when you can fill a shopping bay for $3.50.
Charity: Community outreach projects of Saint Andrews Parish
Everything except furniture and large appliances

THE SECOND ACT
12882 S. Saratoga-Sunnyvale Rd., Saratoga 95070, (408) 741-4995. Mon–Sat 10:30 am–5 pm, Sun 1 pm–5 pm. Cash, checks, MC/VISA.

A lot of consignment stores claim to be upscale resale, but this one really is—4600 square feet devoted to first-rate antiques and furniture, highest quality new and previously owned women's clothing, and a small selection of new children's clothing. To say (as the owner did) that they try to be particular about what they take is an understatement. Selection is as extensive as quality is high; you will find everything from shoes to furs to evening gowns (no wedding gowns) in every size (including many large sizes), all high style with good to designer labels. Prices are very fair given the quality of the merchandise, with some real bargains in the high-end designer garments, like a Jaeger dress (originally $1000) for $149.50 and a Caroline Herrera (originally $690) for $175. Devotees of local designer William Flower will be happy to know that *Second Act* is his outlet in the Bay Area. Mothers who want to dress their children like royalty will be ecstatic when they see the gorgeous (but not cheap) new children's wear. *Consignment: By appointment, for antiques 60% consignor/40% store, for clothing 50/50 split* **Antiques, furniture, clothing for women and children**

~~~~~ Sunnyvale ~~~~~

GOODWILL
151 E. Washington, Sunnyvale 94086, (408) 736-8558. Mon–Thurs 9 am–7 pm, Fri 9 am–8 pm, Sat 9 am–6 pm, Sun 11 am–6 pm. Cash, checks, MC/VISA.

Kitty-corner to Macy's, this *Goodwill* looks every bit as upscale as that venerable retail establishment. The window displays, designed with true artistry, are the best we've seen and the floor displays inside are first-rate. Neat, clean, and well-organized, the merchandise is the best *Goodwill* has to offer. Every effort has been made to make the store inviting and enjoyable. We were especially taken with the children's department, where footlockers full of toys and enchanting displays turn bargain hunting into an adventure. *Charity: Goodwill* **Everything except large appliances**

NEARLY NEW SHOP
225 E. Maude, Sunnyvale 94086, (408) 732-6202. Tues–Sat 10 am–3 pm. Cash.

In 1990 the *Nearly New Shop* moved from Palo Alto to its gorgeous new location, a bright, spacious (4000 square feet) former drugstore decorated in trendy tones of rose and celadon. The friendly volunteers take great pride in their shop, confident that they have the most reasonable prices on the peninsula. Men's, women's, and children's clothing is first quality for low, low prices—men's like-new dress shirts for $3, wool suits for $7–$10, women's blouses for $2–$5, suits for $15–$25, dresses for $7–$10. Housewares, knickknacks, and collectibles abound—you are sure to find something wonderful without half trying. You won't want to miss the Christmas Boutique, held from mid-November through December 20, with 25,000 items for sale (used treasures collected throughout the year and boutique items handmade by the volunteers). *Charity: PEO (Philanthropic Educational Organization) Home for Women in San Jose* **Clothing, collectibles, housewares, toys**

THE UPSTAIRS GALLERY
182 S. Murphy Ave., Sunnyvale 94086, (408) 992-0277. Wed–Fri 11 am–6 pm, Sat 11 am–5 pm. Cash, checks.

Brenda Klocko's *Upstairs Gallery*, tucked away on the second floor of a landmark building on historic

Murphy Avenue, combines upscale consignment with a hodgepodge of original works by local artists. Consignment apparel, geared toward the working woman who doesn't want to waste time or money, is high quality for reasonable prices. While shopping for your work wardrobe you can check out the arts and crafts (which include Amish quilts and anthracite coal jewelry and figurines), peruse the two huge scrapbooks filled with historical photos of Sunnyvale, or relax with a cup of coffee and enjoy the soothing atmosphere

Consignment: By appointment, 50/50 split

Women's clothing, arts and crafts

SANTA CLARA COUNTY	Appliances/large	Bridal	Clothing/children	Clothing/men	Clothing/women	Collectibles	Furnishings/children	Furniture	Housewares	Maternity	Tools, etc.	Toys	Vintage	Page number
CAMPBELL														
Corinthian Thrift			X	X	X	X	X	X	X		X	X		167
Tickled Pink			X	X									X	167
CUPERTINO														
Deanza Market	X	X	X	X	X	X	X	X	X	X	X	X	X	167
Kid's Clothesline			X				X					X		168
LOS GATOS														
Eleanor's Fashions					X									168
Happy Dragon Thrift		X	X	X	X	X	X	X	X	X	X	X		168
MILPITAS														
Children's Heartland			X				X					X		169
Savers		X	X	X	X	X	X	X	X	X	X	X		169
MORGAN HILL														
Mitzie's Fashions			X	X	X					X				170
SAN JOSE														
Discovery Shop			X	X	X	X	X	X	X			X		170
Capitol Flea Market	X	X	X	X	X	X	X	X	X	X	X	X	X	171
Goodwill (Meridian)			X	X	X	X	X	X	X	X	X	X		171
Goodwill (Saratoga)		X	X	X	X	X	X	X	X	X	X	X		171
Goodwill As Is	X	X	X	X	X	X	X	X	X	X	X	X		171
Rubber Ducky			X		X		X						X	173
St. Vincent de Paul	X	X	X	X	X	X	X	X	X	X	X	X		173
Salvation Army	X	X	X	X	X	X	X	X	X	X	X	X		173
San Jose Flea Market		X	X	X	X	X	X	X	X	X	X	X		174
Sara's Consignment			X		**X**	X							X	174
Savers	X	X	X	X	X	X	X	X	X	X	X	X		174
Thrift Box			X	X	X	X	X		X			X	X	175
Thrift Center	X	X	X	X	X	X	X	X	X	X	X	X		175
Thrift City	X	X	X	X	X	X	X	X	X	X	X	X		175
Trading Post					X									176
Trisha's Treasures			X	X	X	X			X					176
SANTA CLARA, CITY														
Goodwill	X	X	X	X	X	X	X	X	X	X	X	X		176
Salvation Army	X	X	X	X	X	X	X	X	X	X	X	X		176

SANTA CLARA COUNTY	Appliances/large	Bridal	Clothing/children	Clothing/men	Clothing/women	Collectibles	Furnishings/children	Furniture	Housewares	Maternity	Tools, etc.	Toys	Vintage	Page number
SARATOGA														
Echo Shop			X	X	X	X	X		X	X	X	X	X	177
Second Act			X		X	X		X						177
SUNNYVALE														
Goodwill	X	X	X	X	X	X	X	X	X	X	X	X		178
Nearly New Shop			X	X	X	X			X				X	178
Upstairs Gallery					X	X								178

INDEX

About the Author

Charlene Akers has worked as a museum development director, corporation controller, and free-lance writer. She currently lives in Oakland with her husband, son, and dog.